"I am in a healthier place now. Thank you for writing this book. This book has helped me work through things years of therapy never could."

— BOOK CLUB PARTICIPANT

"As a mandated reporter, this book gave me the knowledge to recognize red flags during counseling sessions and for those things I am required to report. It is going to be a valuable tool to help women discern between healthy and unhealthy behavior earlier in relationships."

— PASTOR AND STATE MANDATED REPORTER

"Thank you so much for writing this book! I appreciate the way you used very simple terms rather than get bogged down in more legalistic terms and definitions."

— SEXUAL ABUSE SURVIVOR, ADVOCATE, AND SPEAKER

"This book will be a resource of prevention and hope for many."

— DOMESTIC ABUSE SURVIVOR AND ADVOCATE

"You have entered a brave new realm to share your story so others might recognize the similarities and potential challenges. It provides insights from a brutally honest platform, so others may not have to experience the same treatment, and further might feel encouraged and empowered to positions of strength. I am honored to have had this unique preview. Thank you.

— Early Reader

Changing the story of
interpersonal abuse

...but
that's
not Me

ERIKA SHALENE HULL &
DR. CHERYL LEJEWELL JACKSON

Write to info@redthreadbooks.com if you are interested in publishing with Red Thread Publishing. Learn more about publications or foreign rights acquisitions of our catalog of books: www.redthreadbooks.com.

Paperback ISBN : 978-1-955683-35-7

Ebook ISBN : 978-1-955683-36-4

Cover Design: Sierra Melcher

Erika Shalene Hull's Author Photo © Zeus Vi Deity

Dr. Cheryl LeJewell Jackson's Author Photo @ Ailin Mirabal

CONTENTS

*To all of the women, men, and children suffering
at the hands of an abuser.*

To the women who came before us and the women who will come after us.

To the mothers trying to raise strong women and respectful men.

*To the mothers, fathers, friends, and family supporting women through
their abuse journey: may you know you're not alone.*

BOOK LEGEND

Pendulum swinging - Used when we discuss a range of abuse. We often highlight that there are extremes, but there are also many examples that fall in between. We want people to recognize the in between as easily as the extremes.

Light bulb - An "ah-ha" moment recognizing abusive behaviors. Whether they picked it up because it's what they've known or if they took on the tendencies of their abusers, or even as a trauma response, many of us display abuse behaviors even after leaving it.

The flag - These are red flags that as you are reading, you may want to pay attention to in a relationship or signs someone else may be in an abusive situation.

Coffee cup - After a particularly tough section, we encourage you, the reader, to take a break and a deep breath. We acknowledge this is hard, and you may need to pause from time to time.

Puzzle pieces - Puzzle pieces indicate clues, insights, or tips that are particularly tactical or actionable. You may see one or a pile, but one-by-one, they help the reader begin to put the picture together (or see the picture more clearly).

PART ONE
FOUNDATION FOR
ABUSE

Our Intent

Cheryl

Meeting at a conference in October of 2019, we began a journey that ended in a very different place than either of us expected. When Erika approached me at my author table, I was instantly intrigued by her courage and passion. I was drawn to her story, knowing it was one that must be told. As we began to peel back the layers, I felt my own past on display. Our stories collided, and we knew we were onto something much bigger than ourselves.

We were not just telling her story or mine, but all of ours.

In addition to our experiences, we shared the reality that neither of us had the voice, the words, or the language to describe our experiences. And because we didn't have the words, we weren't able to associate those experiences with abuse. We looked for images and stories that matched our own, and came up one black eye and a bloody lip short. Even when the images did match the experiences, it somehow didn't point to us. We were strong, independent, smart women raised in happy, Christian homes. There was no way we were in abusive relationships.

Despite the evidence placed before us, we still argued, "... but that's not me."

We continued, thinking we could somehow earn better treatment or the love we longed for. Years later, we both still struggle with blaming ourselves and reliving the past. The sad part is, we are only two women in a sea of women struggling with these thoughts. **The time has come to fight back, to give women the words to describe their experiences, and to stop perpetuating the cycle of abuse.**

... But That's Not Me combines illuminating facts with a compelling story-line which includes the voices and experiences of multiple different women. Our hope is that this book will touch the lives of victims around the globe, giving them the voice they lost somewhere along the way.

Erika

Cheryl and I experienced very different situations, yet our stories were eerily similar. We both married fairly young. I started a family early in marriage and quickly began juggling motherhood and a career. She dove into a high-level career, delaying the start of a family.

Both of us were the primary providers for our families from early on. Where I slowly lost all economic control at the hands of an abusive husband, she was saddled with all economic responsibility.

I experienced significant physical abuse in my relationships, while her's never reached that point. I left one abuser and walked right into another that was ultimately far worse than the first. After she left her relationship, she spent five years bouncing from one abusive situation to another: from abusive partners, friends, and jobs.

In both cases, the abusive relationships ended many years ago, but I am still subjected to almost daily contact by my abuser, despite moving into a new strong, healthy relationship. Not only due to physical proximity to my abuser but also because I bore children by him. With no shared children, property, or assets, she left the relationship and moved 800 miles away, never having contact again after the divorce was final.

Despite these differences, we were struck by how similar our experiences actually were, from the types of abuse, to the cyclical pattern of our abusers' behavior, to how long the divorce process took. Even in completely different circumstances and living in states with completely different laws, the separation and divorce process dragged out around two years. This is not uncommon based on the experiences of other women..

Initially, we wanted to differentiate our stories so you could follow along our respective journeys. There were more than a handful of times, though, that we literally had to ask one another whose story it was. There was so much validation in knowing that we weren't alone.

That's when we realized that we weren't writing our *stories*, we were writing our *story*, and maybe we are writing your story too.

We aren't trying to bring attention to ourselves or invite pity. It takes a great deal of courage and vulnerability to share stories of abuse, and revisiting these experiences can be extremely retriggering if not outright retraumatizing. But after much deliberation and self-examination to clarify our own motives, we realized that if our stories could help other women recognize and escape that same pattern of abuse in their own lives, we could not stay silent.

We are certainly not writing this book to bash our abusers. This book isn't about them at all, and it really isn't even about us. Our goal is to highlight the victim's experience, to shed light on something that is rarely discussed in the open, but runs rampant behind closed doors. We hope to begin changing the perception of abuse for abusers, victims, and allies by increasing our collective knowledge and awareness of abuse. Our purpose is to help you see things differently and therefore change your reality.

As an abuser, you can recognize your behaviors for what they are and stop the cycle. As a victim, you will have a vocabulary and validation for what you are experiencing. Regardless of where you are in your relationship, recognizing your experiences as abuse can help you raise your standards, set better boundaries, and determine what you are or are not willing to live with.

YOU have the power to change it. As women, moms, co-workers, friends, and especially as men willing to step up and confront the realities of abuse, we must be better allies. We must stop perpetuating the cycle of abuse by normalizing, justifying, and blaming the victim. **We must start changing the story.** We must open the line of communication, talking to our daughters, girlfriends, co-workers, and sons.

It's not easy. Change takes conscious and continuous effort. Whether you are in an abusive relationship, supporting someone who is, or just learning more, you need this information. We all need this information. Knowledge leads to awareness, which leads to recognition. This book is less about leaving bad relationships and more about changing the story; stopping abuse before it becomes a habit, before it goes too far.

Once you read this information and hear these stories, you can't un-know them. Once you have the information, it becomes your responsibility to act on it.

May you find the courage to act.

With our love and encouragement,

Erika and Cheryl

I Don't Belong Here

The morning is dark and cold. I don't know if the sun is covered by the clouds or if it's a beautiful day. All I feel is darkness. Like looking at a bright window through closed eyes. There is light, but I'm not quite sure where it's coming from, or if I'm really seeing it at all. The clock on my dash reads 9:58 AM as I pull into one of two empty parking spots right in front of the front door.

The building can't be more than 800 square feet. If I had a choice, I never would have chosen this place. But I don't have a choice. After being denied by every attorney's office in town, this was the only one I could find with an opening and that didn't charge for an initial appointment. With no money or access to money, I'm limited in options.

I'm scared. Petrified would be a better word. I have no idea how to do this. I consider for a moment just putting the car in reverse and getting out of here. But it took an act of congress just to get here today. Finding someone to watch the kids, creating a cover story for using the family car, and even lining up an emergency *alibi, this is my only chance. If I can't get out of the car right now, I never will.*

I put the car in park and walked the four, maybe six steps to the front door. For a dilapidated building, the door is actually very welcoming. As I grab hold of the handle, my hands shaking, I begin to feel the strength returning to my body.

I can do this!

With a burst of confidence, I push open the door and step through.

Across the tiny room, the receptionist is on the phone. "Sure, let me look. What was the name again?" As my foot hits the threshold, I hear the one name that could make my blood run cold.

He found me.

No matter how hard I tried, how far I drove, or how long I had planned, he still managed to put himself two feet from me.

For the first time, I realize there truly is no escape. I don't know exactly what I need, but I know I need help. Whether I am in shock or frozen in fear, I can't speak. I feel the blood rush away from my face; my hands and feet become too heavy to move.

I came here with a purpose. At this point, I just need someone to take over. I knew this would be hard, but right now, it feels impossible.

The receptionist asks if I am okay and if I need help. My mouth forms the words, but nothing comes out. I want to scream, but instead simply mouth the words, "It's him. He knows I'm here. He knows," over and over again.

I am ushered to a seat and a paper cup of water is placed softly beside me. Although she moves quickly, I hardly notice any movement at all. It's all in blurry slow motion. As quickly as my world is caving in around me, somehow, it feels like a slow fade.

But something has shifted. For the first time, I am not the only one seeing it. At last, it has come out of the secret corners of our home and is on full display for others to see. For years, I wondered if I was crazy or just bitter. I tried changing my attitude, seeing things differently, and being a "better person." I thought there was something wrong with me, that perhaps I really was just making all of this up. For the first time, someone else is seeing what I see. I feel a strange mixture of fear, embarrassment, and relief. A doorway to freedom has been cracked open, even if only an inch. The mere thought sends panic racing through my body once again.

If I leave right now, maybe I can still smooth it over...

No, that wouldn't work.

I could make a run for it!

Oh yeah? With what money?

My kids are still there. Oh God, what am I going to do?

The attorney calls me into her office and asks me to tell her what is going on. The receptionist had already spoken to her, but she needs me to provide some background information. I don't get very far before she kindly stops me and says, "I have heard enough. You need to file a civil protection order."

I don't even know what a civil protection order is, much less how to get one. She goes into detail about what that means and what getting one entails, but I'm not fully grasping what she's telling me. She leaves for a moment to consult with her partner. As I sit in the small, quiet office, I feel like I am going to pass out.

How am I going to do this?

When the attorney comes back, I know something is wrong. Her expressionless demeanor now shows signs of concern as she informs me that she cannot represent me since my husband had previously called to inquire about making an appointment with another attorney in the practice. She promises to do as much for me as she can and begins walking me through how to do the paperwork myself.

If I have to do this alone, I'm not sure I can.

With the patience of a kindergarten teacher, the attorney walks me through each step. The overwhelmed look must have been written all over my face and across my entire body. As easy as she makes it sound, I'm not sure I am strong enough to follow through.

I don't want to hurt him; I just want out.

Reading my hesitation, the attorney stops and says, "Sweetie, you need to file for a civil protection order, or you won't be alive after this weekend."

———

I arrive at the crisis center a little after 2pm. I am ushered into a small office in the front room. For the safety of myself and everyone else at the facility, I am asked a series of questions to ensure I wasn't being followed.

Is my car traceable? I wondered. It was hard to shake the thought.

Once she was certain I wasn't being actively followed, she began going down a second list of questions:

"Have you been...?"

"Has he ever...?"

To my surprise, I find myself answering "yes" to every question.

I mean, I know I'm sitting in a place for battered and abused women, but that's just a technicality. I don't really belong here. I mean, I'm not abused. Like, not really abused. I'm unhappy and scared, and sometimes afraid for my children, but I don't belong here.

Do I?

THE MOVE

It is a beautiful spring morning, not unlike many mornings in this house through the years, though in reality I've lived here for 10 years now. I remember when we showed up as the happy family smiling for the camera as we slapped "sold" across the real estate sign in the front yard. This house was the fresh start I started to believe was so desperately needed. A new town, a new home, a new life. He made it all sound amazing.

How could I be so naive?

I still ask myself that question. The truth is, I don't know.

Looking back, it's always so clear. In the moment, though? Now that's where we struggle to see.

Outside of these walls, no one even knew. These walls are the only ones who saw everything; they knew the truth. They hold secrets even I have tried to forget. When I look at them, I remember.

Leaving is bitter-sweet. This home is the last significant piece of my past, a past I am so ready to walk away from, yet know I never truly will. It is a part of me now. The person I was before is forever altered. As much as I would like to get her back, she is different; she will always be different.

The light from the bare windows highlights the faint shadow where the drywall was once broken by a TV remote.

Those beautiful vacuum lines in the carpet, a sign of a clean home. In the light, I can see a section that was missed or just disrupted, I'm not sure which. I feel the tightening in my stomach and the urge to pull the vacuum back out to make them perfect, even though it has already been loaded and locked in the moving van. Deep down, I know it's okay, but my body won't let me forget.

I check the kitchen drawers one last time. The drawer drags a little and catches like it often did. That time my hand caught the edge after he knocked the cream out of my hand.

The shower. The bedroom. The hall. They all hold memories that sometimes still feel like current events.

I turn to look back one final time. I sat right there in that corner as he hauled his belongings out, one after another just a few years ago.

Miraculously, the lady from the crisis center was able to persuade the judge to take my case the very day that I visited the attorney, despite the fact that every single person in the courthouse was in training that day, except for the one judge who agreed to see me. I am still not sure how she made that happen.

He is served at 10PM, twelve hours after my initial visit with the attorney. I am emotionally and physically exhausted, but the day is not over. I watch from the corner as he moves essentials out of our home, this home, with hate in his eyes, threatening my life with his every breath whenever no one else is in earshot. I know he means it, too.

Through the window, I can see him laughing as he talks with one of the officers in the yard. To them, I am just a bitter, angry wife taking her husband for everything he's worth. They've been to the house before, after a neighbor had called for help and even when my own daughter called. They didn't believe me then; they won't believe me now.

Why would they? Abusers don't live in expensive houses, in beautiful neighborhoods, with nice cars parked in the driveway, do they? Abused women have bruises and bloody lips, don't they? Abusers are not attractive and charming and funny, are they? They aren't from respected professions, like doctors or lawyers, military or teachers, are they?

I'm a strong, confident, educated woman from a decent family. I know what an abused woman looks like, and that's not me.

Is it?

The reality is, there is no identifiable "type of woman" who finds herself in abusive situations.. It can happen to anyone, at any time, and it's not a reflection of anything beyond the universality of that experience.

How does this happen? Why couldn't I just get away? How did I get here?

I still ask myself these questions. Looking back, I am beginning to put the pieces together. It is starting to make sense; I can see the picture beginning to take shape.

Maybe this resonates with you, or you can see it in someone you know. Perhaps a friend, co-worker, daughter, niece, or granddaughter is in an abusive relationship that they can't see. Perhaps you can't even see it but know something is just a little off. Maybe you don't see yourself in my story at all. I don't know that I would have either. But maybe you can see it in someone else. Be an ally. Don't give up on them, especially after they have gotten out.: they will need you more than ever.

The Set-Up

My childhood was standard. Raised by parents who faithfully served in our community, loved their children, and loved each other.

I was raised in a community of people who followed a particular doctrine, not unlike any other intentional community where people surround themselves with others who have similar beliefs or goals. As such, I was somewhat guarded and cut off from the rest of the world. I was raised to be a leader, reaching people for my community, while caring for their hearts. My parents were an example of a caring, respectful, and traditional biblically aligned marriage.

My father was the head of the household and led his family with authority and conviction. He was the ultimate decision-maker and also the ultimate point of accountability. Biblical submission of the woman was part of my upbringing, but it was based on both people being loving, respectful, and born-again Christians. It was the example and foundation of expectations in my own future relationships, though I did not fully understand all aspects of the agreement, what that meant or what actually went into that kind of relationship. To me, it just looked like it came naturally. Although I was part of a unique community including deep biblical study, I had a very normal childhood. I participated in group sports, attended public school, took ballet lessons, and occasionally was allowed to hang out with friends. My parents rented a house in a typical neighborhood, and they managed to stay 100% debt free.

At 19, commissioned by an organization, I set out on my own in a world I didn't know. I was so sheltered from the realities of the world growing up that I struggled to relate to the people and things around me. I was naive to life outside of my home and community. Like many children growing up in conservative families, whether raised by strict religious beliefs or geographically removed from the realities of life, I was in the world but not of the world. The world was a new, exciting, yet scary place, and I struggled to navigate it. My eyes were opened to people and ideas outside of my tiny corner of the world. I began making friends with people who believed differently than I did. I began to see other perspectives and a variety of lives. Within a few months' time after turning 20 and completing an entire 6 month mission, I was working as a live-in nanny and housekeeper in the home of local leadership and working a "secular" job to pay the difference of the cost of my room and board. I had started asking questions, challenging some of the upbringing and teachings, and speaking up about things that had happened to me. The short of it was I was accused of being dishonest, confused by the world, not obeying the teachings, accusing men of things "goldy men would never do" and the best was, "If that really happened to you, we would have known." Under the guidance of the leadership of the organization, after an 8 hour "meeting" with the local leadership, two additional people and my parents on speaker phone. I was given less than 24 hours to leave, deemed "mark and avoid" which included no contact with my family and everyone I knew, forced to leave the community I had known my entire life. In less than 24 hours I was homeless and completely alone, living in a Ford Astro minivan, stuffed to the brim with whatever I could fit from my bedroom, with absolutely nowhere to live or idea how to navigate. I was lost and struggling to find my place in a world I didn't know, completely cut off from my family and the life I once knew.

As far as I can remember, I wanted to be a wife and mom. As far as I knew, that's just what you did. While searching for my place, I stumbled into a relationship that would forever change the course of my life. Finally, I would have all of those things I was groomed to want: a husband, a family, a home. I quickly fell head over heels for a man and a life I had always dreamed about. I was so caught up in the fairytale, I didn't stop to consider if this man was really ready for marriage. I just grabbed hold with both arms and was committed to making my dream work.

Many of us grow up believing this is just what you do. In reality, not everyone is made for or ready for marriage and children. Grow up, get married, have a family. There aren't any other options. Even though that's what I was groomed to believe, I truly wanted it more than anything and lost myself chasing that dream. I knew everything wasn't great, but I thought it wasn't anything we couldn't work out. He loved me and I loved him; surely, we could make it work. When I became pregnant, there was no longer a debate as to whether or not we would get married. We were married, started a family, and the dream was on the verge of coming true.

It wasn't long before I realized my fairytale wasn't as happy as it looked in movies. As I grew up and into the responsibilities of motherhood, he sunk deeper into his childish tendencies. Although I thought of my parents as an amazing couple and role models of spiritual commitment, I began to realize that they weren't as forthcoming about a lot of things that I should have been taught as a teenager in preparation for my own relationships.

I didn't understand the realities of marriage; I only saw the good. I never saw my parents fight. I didn't know what to do when things got messy because I didn't even realize things could get messy. I was trying to build a marriage with someone who didn't have the same physical, mental, or spiritual maturity as I did, but I was unprepared because I didn't realize that was a possibility when looking for future mates. I didn't realize this was something you had to work for. I just thought people grew together, like my parents did, without any real effort. Since I understood marriage was something everyone wanted, I thought it should be easy or come naturally. It sounds so naive now, but how do we know these things if a beautiful, perfect marriage is all we see? It is critical to see the arguments, the struggles, and the growth together. Parents may think they are protecting their children from these realities, but they are actually setting them up for failure in their own relationships.

I later spoke to my mom about being angry and frustrated. She shared that she was once so mad at my dad that she didn't speak to him for two whole days. I had no idea. She never let on that she was ever angry or frustrated in her marriage. Maybe she thought she was protecting me from looking negatively at my father, but it just served to shelter me, making me feel like I was the only one who ever got angry with my partner. As if I was the only one struggling in their marriage.

When parents don't share their struggles with their children or even show them how to have a healthy argument, children struggle to develop an accurate picture of what marriage can, or perhaps "should" look like.

I continued to put on a brave face and try to "work it out" because I thought I was the one doing something wrong. It may not have initially changed anything, but understanding how authentic marriages work would have been an important lesson going into my marriage.

I heard friends and co-workers talk about their husbands and marriages. Many of them were miserable. These women were older than me, married for longer, and had great careers. They were successful in so many areas, yet still had lousy marriages. Their husbands didn't sound any better than mine. If they couldn't get good husbands and have good marriages, why did I think I was any different? Why should I deserve a good marriage? I was beginning to think my parents' marriage was an unattainable anomaly, and having terrible marriages was starting to sound normal. Suddenly, mine didn't seem so strange. Even worse, it sounded like that was something I would just have to live with if I wanted my dream of having a family.

For almost 13 years, I tried living up to an example, a standard, with someone who was never on the same level as the example I had growing up. I put my heart into a marriage that had already fallen apart, making compromises I never should have made in an attempt to make my marriage work. Divorce wasn't even in my vocabulary. I stayed because that's just what you did.

I was working with an outdated definition of love. I wasn't clear on what love was and was even less clear on what love was not. Every day, I would sweep up the crumbs and form them into what others would recognize as a happy marriage. I put on a face that smiled when others asked how things were going and kissed in front of the camera. To the outside world, we were a happy couple and model family. I had a beautiful home, my children were well-behaved, and my career was taking off. Inside those walls, my husband couldn't keep a job, leaving me to play the dual role of homemaker and breadwinner. I was walking on eggshells around him, yet having to remain strong for my kids. Being in a relationship with someone who doesn't act like a partner is an incredibly lonely feeling.

Determined to make it work, I let things slide for far too long, picking up the slack to keep the image I wanted so badly to see. I would wake up at three o'clock in the morning and not know where he was. When he did keep a job, it was to pay for alcohol and drugs, which began to take over more and more of his life. His desire for other women led to him bringing them home to share our bed. I believed if I walked the line just right, we could avoid an argument and almost feel "normal."

When I did bring it up, he would disconnect, leaving for long periods of time. There would be people at our house at all hours of the day or night doing drugs while our children slept down the hall. As our family grew, I grew up. He, on the other hand, was still trapped at the age of 19. I thought we would just naturally grow together. Instead, we grew farther and farther apart. I was ill-prepared to deal with this new world because I grew up in such a bubble. I didn't even know these things existed, that this was a possibility; how could I have ever prepared for this? It was even a running joke. He would say, "Girl, you have so much book knowledge, but you are common sense dumb." It was true; I had no street knowledge. He had a ton of it, but lacked responsibility.

I seriously thought about leaving once. My career was growing, and I knew if I really focused, I could save enough money to start a new life with my children. It would take some time to line some things up and make a clean break. Before I could save up enough to leave, I suddenly lost my full time career. My husband was deep into his addictions at this point and used my retirement savings to fund it. As the primary breadwinner and the only consistent income, we were wiped out. I sat on my bathroom floor as the little blue line appeared on the pregnancy test and watched my chances of leaving slip farther and farther away. At that point, I recommitted to making it work. I clung to the hope and prayed that one day he would change just enough to make it a little more bearable. That's all I needed. I really believed I could handle it from there.

Things went from bad to worse. He began stealing money from me for drugs or other luxuries we didn't need. I was pregnant and unable to buy food or clothes for our other two children. His anger was getting worse, and he was lashing out more often.

When our son was an infant, he was yelling so much that my baby was hiding under the table, terrified. That was the turning point for me. I had finally hit the point where I couldn't take it anymore. I could no longer pretend to be a family with someone who was not acting like a partner.

When you still care for someone but don't love them the same anymore, your mind can trick you into thinking that there is a chance. Sometimes caring gives you the false hope that things really can get better. It keeps you hanging on long past the point where you should have given up. I wish I had recognized the signs earlier; recognizing that I could care for him and still choose not to be with him.

Not long after, I divorced my husband and sought to start over. Being fresh out of an abusive relationship, I was determined to not make the same mistakes. I knew what I was looking for, and I would not settle for anything less.

It's funny how having a laser-focus on what you don't want can make you blind to so many other things. Walking out of one bad relationship actually set me up to walk right into another, one that was far worse than I ever could have imagined.

Defining The Language We Use

The U.S. Department of Justice "defines domestic violence as a pattern of abusive behavior in any relationship that is used by one partner to gain or maintain power and control over another intimate partner." [1] Despite this technical definition, the general population often still thinks about domestic violence in terms of physical assault that results in visible injuries, and it's not just people who have never experienced abuse who think this way. Even victims, including ourselves, are guilty of this way of thinking.

> *I remember times where I would fight back and say, "Why don't you just hit me, it would be so much easier." In my mind, I wasn't a battered woman until there was a physical sign.*

But this is just one type of abuse. It's so easy to think, "that's not me" when we hear stories of abused women. The more we deny it, the longer we cling to the hope that our relationship can be saved or we aren't so lost that we can't find our way back to the life we have been dreaming about since we were little girls. As long as we can't see ourselves in the statistics and headlines, then there is still hope. Sadly, it is this way of thinking that keeps many of us in abusive, hopeless relationships for far too long until all hope of escape really is gone.

The reality is, physical abuse is the tip of the iceberg. It often only shows itself after years of mental, financial, and verbal abuse have wreaked havoc. It is just part of a very large, deep web of mental pain and anguish. Still, we struggle to recognize the intensity and severity of the damage that abuse has caused.

Over the years, physical abuse has become less acceptable. We have given abusers a handbook for how to be more effective psychological abusers. We have made movies, documentaries, and entire television series about how to psychologically torment your victim and get away with it. Abusers have learned how to be more subtle so as to not get caught. They have taken notes and learned from the mistakes of others. They don't start hitting their victims in the face the first day. Rather, they reel them in with displays of love and affection. They gain the support of the victim's friends and family then slowly cut them off from their social network. They build them up, making them feel good, then tear down their sense of self-worth. When the victim has lost all sense of self, that's when they step it up. They have learned how to leave scars that won't heal, in places no one sees.

It is our goal in this book to shift the power back to the victims, helping them become psychological warriors in their own lives. We aim to give them the tools to stop, fight, and change the patterns of abuse, to show victims how to be their own superhero in the midst of being abused. You do *not* have to wait for your abuse to reach a certain point before you seek help. Not every unhealthy relationship reaches the point of domestic violence, nor does it have to. Whether or not the behaviors you are experiencing would be classically categorized as abuse doesn't matter. Even in non-abusive, unhealthy relationships, we encourage you to take your power back and regain the value you deserve.

At its core, domestic abuse is about control, whether psychological or physical. Abusers may engage in behaviors intended to limit their victims' freedom of movement or stop them from contacting other people such as friends or family. It may involve stopping victims from engaging in social activities, sports, school, or work. Abusers may control their victim's finances or threaten them to do what they want through force or manipulation.

Controlling behaviors can also look like the abuser doing things in plain view that they know the victim wouldn't want them doing, they know would hurt the victim, or the victim has specifically asked them not to do. This type of "in your face" behavior is not only disrespectful and derogatory, it also shows the level of control the abuser has in the relationship. It is as if they are saying, "I can do anything I want and you can't do anything about it."

Throughout this book, we will discuss a wide range of abusive behaviors. You may not experience all of these behaviors, or experience them to the same degree as described here. These are simply examples of real experiences from real women. It is not a blueprint or absolute. Your experience may look totally different. The intent here is to highlight the multiple types and faces of abuse in an effort to bring awareness to this pervasive disease plaguing our society as a whole.

Adamant that they are not in an abusive relationship, it is not uncommon for humans to argue or attempt to justify similar behaviors they experience. Although denial is a huge issue with victims not recognizing the abuse for what it is, there may certainly be instances where a partner will engage in any number of the behaviors we will discuss and would not be classified as an abuser. One reason is intent. Intent is a primary differentiator between slips, mistakes, personality characteristics, and other "justifications" for behaviors that would be considered abuse. It is often difficult for an outsider to determine whether a single instance is abuse or something else. Intent behind actions is important.

Everyone is abusive at one point or another. We say things that we shouldn't and lash out in times of stress. In a healthy relationship or with healthy individuals, it happens, we show remorse, and try not to do it again. The intent is not to wear down and hurt long term, even if we intend for it to sting in the moment. If they are still a loving and caring person, if there is no evil intent behind it to dominate,control and hurt, then it may be a situation worth fighting for. We, the authors of this book, are absolutely supporters of marriage and partnerships and don't encourage all marriages to come to an end. The reality is relationships take work, and some come to an end too soon. We live in a throw-away society where marriage is often considered disposable. That said, many women will indeed cling to terrible relationships and situations much longer than they should because of the idea that divorce is equal to failure.

The focus of this book is on helping women recognize when their relationship is destructive and dangerous due to domestic abuse. We are willing to risk women taking a second look at an otherwise potentially healthy relationship to encourage women in bad relationships to do the same. By doing so, even good, but damaged relationships may actually grow *stronger* as a result.

Consistency or prevalence of the behavior is often mistaken as a way to identify abuse. Just because someone hits you only once a year does not mean it isn't physical abuse. It is not a mistake or a flaw. He wasn't provoked and it wasn't an accident. It is abuse.

Same with any other form of abuse. Telling jokes at your expense, harassing, manipulating, name-calling, etc., is never okay. There is no safe or acceptable amount of cruel, harmful treatment. When an abusive behavior is inconsistent with a person's character, then it may be a sign that it was a slip and may be met with a little more grace. Even so, the behavior must be addressed and discussed. How they respond to this conversation is an important indicator of the true character of your partner and whether or not the behavior is likely to recur. As Maya Angelou wrote, "When someone shows you who they are, believe them the first time."

It is our hope that by outlining this information and shedding light on the realities of abuse, women will begin to recognize their partners' abusive behaviors sooner and take action to seek help, including getting out of the situation, before the abuse escalates to dangerous or even deadly levels.

All forms of domestic violence and the associated abusive behaviors can have devastating consequences on the victim. Though life-threatening, physical abuse puts the victim at the highest immediate risk, other forms of abuse can be even more devastating, saddling the victim with lifelong challenges.

The availability of information out there is fierce. The problem is not the amount of information, but the ability to recognize what is happening in the moments of the abuse. We get so wrapped up in the terminology and stereotypes that we often fail to see it for what it is. Perhaps by telling you our stories, the stories of two average, hard-working moms in middle-America, it will be more relatable to you. It would be a lot safer and more comfortable to keep these stories to ourselves, but when we look at the faces of our children, of our friends, and of women who are suffering in silence, we can't sit back and keep quiet any longer.

> *By telling our story, we hope to encourage you to believe in yourself and know that you are worthy and deserving of a loving, healthy relationship, and so much more.*

But first, we need to discuss some specific language we use throughout the book. The language we use to describe specific behaviors or abuse has significant implications. We have become accustomed to certain words, and they have lost their power. Others have been so misused, they are meaningless. We aren't speaking the same language when it comes to abusive behaviors and how they affect us, and we are therefore unable to fully understand or express the realities of our situations.

We will cover a few of the words here at the beginning to lay a foundation, but throughout the book, we will take the opportunity to discuss why we use a specific word over another when appropriate. Until we have accurate and common language to discuss our experiences, it will be difficult to connect in a meaningful way and make the difference we need to make. Our intention with this book is to give language to those things that were previously unspoken. For so long, we didn't have the words to describe and understand what we were going through. As a result, like so many other women, we didn't say anything.

The words abuse, confinement, isolation, coercion, manipulation, and divorce weren't even in my vocabulary. Sure, I had heard them before, but I lived in such a bubble, they never made their way across my mind, much less my lips. I had no words, no language to describe what was happening to me. Instead of putting words to it, I could only describe how I felt, which made me an "irrational, emotional woman." I started to believe that was true. I thought I was just unhappy but couldn't understand why. It wasn't until we started writing this book that I truly felt validated, heard, and understood for the very first time. I had language and words to describe what was happening to me, and felt, for the first time, that maybe I wasn't alone and I had actually experienced something worthy of the pain I was feeling.

Here are examples of terminology you will see used throughout this book.

Normal

Although we try to avoid it, you may catch us using the term "normal" (e.g., "in normal relationships..."). The word normal is often used to reflect the average or healthy relationship. When possible, we will substitute the word we actually mean instead of continuing this flawed thinking. Unfortunately, many relationships are not healthy. Many family settings are actually not very happy at all. We strive to be "normal," but that is indeed not what we want.

When I was a kid, I wanted a "normal" family. My parents were a little different (through the eyes of a teen) and owned a small business where we all chipped in after school, on holidays, and during weekends when needed. I thought it was weird that they often worked on Saturdays but attended every event my brothers and I ever had. The older I got, the more I realized that we actually had a pretty spectacular home life. I wanted to be "normal" like my friends, but they were often left alone on

Saturday night while their parents had a social life. Their parents worked 8-5 jobs and couldn't take off on Friday afternoon to accompany the band to every football game. They rarely ate dinner together and their parents didn't talk to them about life at the table. As it turns out, "normal" is not what I thought it was.

She vs He

Throughout our writing, we use the pronoun "she" to represent the victim and "he" to represent the abuser. We are not intending to bash men and recognize that many abusive relationships actually involve a female abuser and male victim. Although those relationships follow similar patterns, and male victims can certainly gain valuable insight by applying the information in this book to themselves, our focus is primarily on the female victim and male abuser because that is what we experienced. Our primary focus is on the women and the female victim, so our book is thus gendered that way. As mothers to boys, we recognize the value in having men appropriately represented in their own stories and hope to one day see that.

Types of Relationships

Furthermore, this book is primarily focused on abuse involving romantic or intimate partners. That said, many of these scenarios can apply to any other abusive relationship as well. We often find ourselves in abusive or toxic relationships with friends, co-workers, bosses, within our religious community or even jobs.

When I finally left my marriage, I had moved to a job that was killing me. As I was talking to my mom one day, she said, "you are just in another bad [read:abusive] relationship." That's when I realized I had walked right into another situation that resembled the marriage I had just left, only this time it was my job.

When we talk about "domestic abuse" that simply means abuse that is on your home ground. A domestic terrorist is simply a terrorist on their home ground. It doesn't have to be your house. It can be your place of work, school, etc. We encourage you to think of all of your relationships and consider whether or not it is healthy. You deserve to be treated well in all areas of your life, but especially in your romantic relationships.

Abuser

There are many words we could use for abuser: wrongdoer, victimizer, perpetrator, aggressor, criminal, offender, culprit. Rather than getting cute or creative, we opted to keep it simple. We don't care to mix it up at the risk of potentially downplaying the language, or perhaps inadvertently suggesting that one type of abuse is worse than another based on how we define the person engaging in the behaviors. Everything described here is real, painful abuse, so we will define the abuser as such throughout the book.

Label of abuser versus the *act* of being abusive or abusive *behaviors*

Someone does not have to be labeled as 'abuser' to engage in abusive behaviors, just like an abuser may engage in non-abusive behaviors (in addition to the abusive ones that earned the title). It is interesting to note that addicts and alcoholics are often referred to as 'abusers' as well. In this case, they are abusing their power, and thus abusing their victims.

Even when intent to cause pain is not the primary driver, the fact that power is indeed being abused also makes the term appropriate for our perpetrators. The focus of this book is on the behaviors themselves, in an attempt to increase awareness and recognition. For ease, we will refer to the person demonstrating the abusive behaviors as the 'abuser' throughout this book. If it helps you feel better about labeling the perpetrator, feel free to think of the level along the lines of 'abusing power' instead of having intent to control and abuse. Whatever it takes.

Victim

Similarly, there are a number of ways to discuss the victim of abuse. Unlike the previous discussion, changing the language around the word 'victim' is more about changing the mentality or thinking around the result of that abuse more than the person themselves. We aren't just defining the person experiencing abuse in the moment but also the person moving on afterwards. It is a much more complex and important discussion. Although both carry weight in terms of the impact of labeling, we are obviously more concerned about that impact to the victim rather than the abuser, thus the longer discussion.

More and more, we are beginning to see the term 'victim' being replaced with terms like survivor, thriver, overcomer, recipient, or sufferer. People, rightfully so, don't want to be labeled as a victim. The term carries a number of negative connotations including the implication that a victim was a helpless receiver of something negative and still carries around pain and suffering. It suggests weakness or a lack of control of their current situation. No one wants to be classified as a victim but rather a survivor, thriver or any other term that represents that they can through difficulty stronger than before.

We relate to this mentality of turning pain into strength, and support the use of other terminology when appropriate. Though we do not want to dwell on the stigma or reality that something negative happened, that *is* what this book is primarily about. It captures the essence of what one experiences throughout an abusive relationship. A victim is someone impacted by another; someone harmed, injured, or killed due to an accident or some else's actions. Two definitions of a victim that fit our purposes include someone whose personal rights have been violated by criminal, violent, or aggressive acts and someone who has viewed or been affected by a violent or traumatic incident. [2]

The abuse experienced by the victim and/or their family is not an accident but rather a violent and traumatic incident (usually more than one). The victim's rights have certainly been violated by criminal, violent, and/or aggressive acts, which are at the hands of their abuser. Victims truly are trapped in a cycle of defeat. Their abuser has broken them down and victimized them time after time, without their consent or ability to stop it. Although we love the idea of 'survivor', that doesn't always capture what we are specifically discussing here. We would love to use another term that captures the strength of our victims while not undermining the sheer horror and torture they experience, but we remain unable to find such a word to perfectly capture both ends of the spectrum. If you have a suggestion, please share it with us.

People often struggle with the idea of the 'victim mentality.' We are not promoting that victims carry the pain with them forever, blaming their past for their future, and using it as an excuse for everything that goes wrong. In fact, we are very much promoting the opposite. We are giving victims the tools to not only recognize these situations but to get out and regain what they lost along the way.

Agreement vs. Consent

Throughout this book, we use both of these terms: agreement and consent. We will repeat some of this to provide additional clarity, but this is such a significant discussion, we wanted to take a moment to talk about it here. On the surface, these two words may seem identical and are often used interchangeably. In fact, the only reason we are discussing it now is because during the writing of this book, we discovered a major difference in how we were using the words and the impact each of the words had on us. We really struggled to understand what we were *trying* to say and which word best represented that idea. For one of us, 'consent' was the softer term that carried a "yeah fine" tone to it while 'agree' represented a stronger action of being 100% all in. For the other, it was the complete opposite where agreement was given with the hopes of just moving on from a given topic or action.

It can feel minor or a bit like dragging the topic out to discuss the difference in these two terms, but the words we use, and the intention we attach to those words, really do matter. How we use them impacts how we feel and the actions we take. By definition it would seem that these two words are the same. As a matter of fact they are synonyms of each other. However, the basis of their meaning has a different emphasis.

In legal contracts the words have different applications. To agree to do something is a legal or contractual context that is generally used to assume an obligation. Consent differs in that it is an acknowledgement that the other person will do something and the subject will tolerate it. When the term agree is used, the action is performed by the person who agreed, when consent is used the action will be performed by the other person and will be tolerated by the first.[3] By this definition, if I agree to bring in the groceries, then *I am* going to bring in the groceries. If I offer my consent, I am consenting to *you* bringing in the groceries.

At the heart of this, no matter what word is in your chosen vocabulary it is important to understand that compliance does not count as consent or agreeing, though you may go through with the action and even verbally say "Okay." Throughout this book, we will talk about times when an action was taken or a decision made during times of stress. In cases where no true options exist, such as threats or abuse, compliance in and of itself does not equate to either consent or agreement. Psychologically, this can be distressing for victims because of the strong innate drive to experience alignment between thoughts and actions. Abusers often use previous compliance to influence a victim's further actions.

This is not an uncommon discussion and is often debated when it comes to the topics of consent, coercion and compliance. Some profess that humans are responsible for the choices they make and that alone is where the responsibility for the things that happen to us lies. However, most of the time the people debating this are imagining hypothetical scenarios in their minds, which cannot accurately capture how someone would behave in a particular situation. We like to believe that most people–including ourselves–would behave in bold, firm manners as ways to respond to offensive or inappropriate behavior but the fact remains that until you are faced with those circumstances you don't know how you will react.

What does all of this mean, and why does it matter? While you may have felt coerced into doing things you don't want to do, others tend to not recognize the coercive pressures you felt. Because they didn't directly feel the pressure, they didn't recognize the coercion for what it was. The result of this line of thinking is that we tend to view other people's actions as more free and autonomous than how they experience them in reality. The assumption is that they must have "wanted to go along with something on some level; otherwise they would just have said 'no,' or said 'no' more forcefully." [4]

Through the book we outline six categories of abuse. As you read through each one, we encourage you to set aside your existing notions of what abuse looks like or what qualifies as abuse in your mind. There may be pieces of information that you disagree with, but we ask that you continue reading with an open mind. It takes effort and strength to set aside your beliefs and be open to new ones. You may be able to read an entire chapter in one sitting, or you may need to pause and digest before moving on. For many of you, the stories and examples you read will shed light on what you are currently experiencing or even bring up memories you haven't wanted to think about in a long time. There may be moments where you have a realization that what you are experiencing is abuse. That is a lot to take in and process. If you need to pause, do that. This book is intended to be consumed at your own pace. The more you reflect on your experiences or the experiences of others you know, the more the information will become a part of you. When that happens, you will be better positioned to stand up for yourself or someone else when the opportunity arises.

The words and ideas in this book should create a mental shift in its readers. We want you to see things differently. When that happens, it lays the foundation for a mental shift from what abuse is 'supposed' to look like to what it really is. It's time to take our power back, and that begins by recognizing abusive behaviors for what they are and setting better boundaries for ourselves.

We are delighted that you have decided to come on this journey with us and grab hold of your own worthiness. Let's dive in.

HOW WE GOT HERE:
OPPRESSIVE SEXISM

*"The oldest injustice in human history is
the way we treat women."*

Cultural Influences

The culture around us plays a significant role in how we behave. A society's culture is a set of shared beliefs, language (including choice of words as well as the spoken or national language), customs, values, norms, mores, rules, tools, technologies, products, organizations, and institutions. The language we use and the behaviors we allow influence what we consider acceptable and unacceptable. In general, culture influences the way we view the world around us. We discussed earlier how the words we use to talk about abuse creates a culture of acceptance. Not only do the words influence the culture, but the culture then promotes the language we use to talk about it. It's a cycle that must consciously be changed, which is difficult because many of the things we say to each other are based on cultural beliefs that have been around for centuries. We don't always recognize them, but they have made their way into our language, behavior, laws, and thoughts regarding abuse.

Language is an influencer of and influenced by a culture of abuse, but it's not the only influencer. Unlike the rest of the book, where pronouns could easily be flipped to represent a male victim and female abuser, this section is specific to a culture of the female victim and male abuser. Although the spirit of these concepts may remain applicable, these particular cultural influences are not interchangeable.

Through our extensive research and experience we have identified six pervasive and widespread cultural conditions that allow and encourage men to abuse women:

- Misogyny Throughout History
- Male Privilege
- Women as Property /The History of Marriage
- Toxic Masculinity
- Lack of Boundaries
- Silence

Each of the above cultural conditions are essential to understand and gain a deeper perspective as we continue to acknowledge what we are up against as women, so we've written a supplemental ebook that goes into depth on each one. To learn more about this topic and further explore the cultural trends that have influenced the treatment of women throughout history and continue to drive the way women are viewed and treated still today, visit our website at www.butthatsnotme.com. Here you can download your copy of our ebook, and access other tools available to not only understand how we got here but also to begin changing the narrative.

The bottom line, though, is that it is against this cultural backdrop that all of the stories in this book take place. We remind you of this for two reasons. First, to help you contextualize the stories in this book as part of a cultural continuum, a pattern of abuse that stretches back as far as recorded history, rather than a few anomalous occurrences suffered by a few unlucky individuals. And second, to help you recognize any abuse you may have suffered or witnessed in your own life as part of that same larger pattern.

In other words: it's not just you. Or us. Or any of the women in this book. None of us are alone in this, because we live in a culture so steeped in oppressive sexism that it has become as invisible as it is insidious. It is, quite simply, life as we have always known it.

A New Mental Map

When beliefs, values, and systems are designed to support our existing mental maps, it is almost impossible to naturally change those maps. We must consciously begin the process of breaking down old maps and replacing them with new ones. It can be painful to recognize how your beliefs regarding someone can be so ingrained in stereotypes. Most people don't want to believe that.

This is a great time to pause and discuss where this idea of *normal* comes from. Throughout this book, we have attempted to use the term that we actually mean such as 'healthy' in place of 'normal.' However, we have reached the point where a deeper discussion of 'the norm' is required.

In its most basic definition, a norm is something that is usual, typical, or standard. It is commonly used in scientific research to test a hypothesis, comparing an experimental treatment to what would typically exist in the average population or control group. In medical studies, for example, researchers may administer an experimental drug to one sample and a placebo or sugar pill to the other. The group receiving the placebo is considered the "control group" because they did not receive the treatment. The idea is that the control group will represent the norm or what the "normal" experience will be without the treatment. The experimental group can then be compared to this norm to determine how *different* the effects will be with the treatment.

A critical piece of this puzzle is that the make-up of each sample must be representative of the population. When sampling, careful attention must be made to gather participants that represent various demographics including race, gender, age, socioeconomic status, health, number of children, marital status, etc. Without proper representation, we can't get a solid and accurate picture of how participants "on average" or "as a whole" will respond. Rather, we would get good information on how a small subset of people with very specific experiences would respond.

Similarly, as a society, we have come to use the term 'normal' to represent the most common or typical state of being. We develop this ideal based on how we view the people and experiences around us. We do this through stories, interactions, and generally experiencing life with others.

Most recently, social media and technology has become an integral part of developing our idea of what normal actually is. Regrettably, what we see, whether digitally or in the flesh, is not always an accurate representation of that person's lived experience. We are typically only exposed to a small subset of their lives, and often only the experiences they want us to see. In other words, we have an "unrepresentative sample" of experiences, a cherry-picked selection rather than a random sampling. Like a professor only picking her top students to fill out the end of year evaluation. It just isn't representative.

We develop ideals around what is normal. We create a picture in our heads, and we want to know that we fit in and how. It creates a sense of normalcy and allows us to know how to interact within that environment. Without a sense of community, experiencing life with others, we create our own idea of norms based on what we see, or what others tell us. We fill in the gaps with our imaginations, which are usually more ideal pictures of reality.

I often look at pictures my mom-friends post on social media of their kids playing together or doing exotic crafts (like painting outside). The kids are happy and engaged. I daydream about how quiet and peaceful it must be; how nice to not have any screaming or fighting kids. My mind goes to far away lands where everyone is happy all of the time, and I start to wonder what's wrong with me. Why aren't my kids happy all the time? Why are my boys always fighting? What am I doing wrong? When I talk to those moms, they laugh at the idea that their lives are smooth or their kids never fight. They think it's hilarious that it was even captured that way. Reality is often very different from what we share with others. I take their best moment and compare it to my worst, then wonder what I'm doing wrong.

The final step of hypothesis testing is comparison. We make comparisons between the experimental and control groups to determine how similar or different they are. We, being the experimental group, similarly compare ourselves to those around us, the control group, to determine how close to the norm we are. Do we fit the normal curve? Are we having similar experiences and responses? We compare ourselves to the experiences of others and determine that we don't look much alike at all. We often compare our lows to their highs in order to determine how we are so very different. We compare our breaking point to their moment of strength and determine that there is something wrong with us.

Norms can serve to inappropriately divide us, but it can have an equally damaging effect on smearing everything over and making everything look the same. One struggle scientists have is trying to make the data appear a certain way. We often remove outliers to "make the data fit." We claim that the outliers don't adhere to "normal" population responses and justify removing them to create a clearer picture of what is "normal" or average.

Sometimes when I sit down in her office, which is familiar territory for me at this point, it is hard to talk about deep things of the past because so much is going on in real time. This day in particular was one of those days. I felt like I was losing my mind: a state of complete overwhelm, doubt, worry and more. My eyes filled with tears while talking about all the things weighing me down, asking her if this was normal. Her simple statement moved me, and stays with me daily. "I wish more

people would ask that simple question, 'is that normal?'
Because more times than not, anyone with that amount of stress
and responsibility is feeling the same way."

Removing outliers serves to make the remaining data look like it fits a beautiful curve when it doesn't. Everything becomes a "normal" response, even when it isn't. This can be dangerous to victims when they are looking for something that indicates their experiences are abnormal and dangerous.

"Is this working? Is this right?" "Should we be doing this differently?" We find this type of comparison language, checking in with the norm, all around us and in every day. When we don't have a sense of community with other women, we get lost in the norm-development process, a process that is often established early in our lives when we determine what a "normal" family looks like based on the few dinners or sleepovers we have with friends. True community, where members are open, transparent, and vulnerable is so important to establishing more accurate norms and creating a better sense of awareness.

Sadly, communities where members are open, transparent, and vulnerable are rare. We don't spend entire days quilting together, talking about our lives and sharing advice. We don't spend hours cleaning and canning the harvest while laughing and supporting each other in our struggles. Instead, we have a 45-minute lunch before rushing back to work. Perhaps we have a three-hour girls' night once a quarter (though, if we're being honest, even this is a luxury most women in abusive relationships only dream of). Brief moments don't allow us to get into the deep realities of life. We often stay so surface-level that we don't get to the point of discussing our insecurities, fears, and struggles. Trivia night or in the middle of Chili's isn't exactly the ideal atmosphere for sharing that you feel completely alone in your marriage. Talk about a downer.

It generally takes time and consistent interaction to reach a point where we can be open and vulnerable with each other. We must have enough history and experiences to know that our community can be trusted and that we are safe to share. We also must reach a point where we genuinely care for each other and don't rush to give damaging, generic advice to smooth things over and "lift the mood." True community, real friend-ships, and deep trust are critical factors for establishing more accurate norms and better understanding of our place within them. That said, complete strangers or co-workers can start the conversation. Small inter-actions can build to the point where victims feel safe enough to begin opening the window to their lives. Each of us has the power to make a difference in someone's life regardless of how much we know them or how close we are. A kind comment or smile, checking in or encouraging them when they're down can be a powerful way to let them know you are a safe place, an ally.

Establishing norms isn't just critical for understanding where we fit in. It isn't about competition or curiosity; it is an important part of knowing how to operate within our environment. When we learn how our environment and/or response fits in with the norm, we can then begin the process of making change. It is that knowledge or awareness that gives us the power to do something about it. We may learn that our situation indeed does not fit within the norm and we are okay with that. In this sense, understanding the norm helps us clarify what we want and are willing to live with. When we have a sense of norms or constants in our lives, we can better relate to others. We have a foundation for under-standing and a system of guidelines to help put a framework around our experiences. Despite the often-negative connotation, 'normal,' provides a framework or sense of guidance around what we *should* be experienc-ing. Although we try to avoid the term 'should,' sometimes it is appro-priate. In the case of basic norms, these are experiences that everyone *should* experience because they are basic human rights that we all deserve. They can be very healthy for helping us understand what we can and should expect out of life.

Basic Human Rights We All Deserve

- **Healthy Self-esteem**

It wasn't until the 1980s that the term self-esteem was entered into the dictionary.[1] Now, it has become a household word. For the most part, people recognize the value of having a positive self-image and support efforts to build it up. Anything or anyone that tears down someone's self-esteem is unhealthy and falls outside the norm of acceptable behavior. Sadly, many women struggle with allowing themselves to have a strong, healthy self-esteem. It's not humble to say, "I look pretty today." Why not? Why do we think we need to put ourselves down?

- **Human Rights and Equality**

Basic human rights and "equality for all" is a standard most western cultures have come to recognize, yet somehow, even the most "advanced" civilizations (e.g., United States of America) still struggle to fully grasp the concept of equality for all human beings. We should all expect to be treated with a certain level of respect, dignity, and equality as human beings.

- **Healthy Relationships**

It is okay to want a healthy relationship. In fact, you should have a healthy relationship. Unhealthy relationships are fairly common but should never be the norm.

We should all have basic relationship expectations. Know that you won't be abused. Know that your partner won't hurt you over and over, and that relationships have their downs, but they also have their ups.

Regarding healthy relationships, we often get hung up on what those basic expectations look like. Relationships are often described as roller coasters. They go up, and they go down. What we don't discuss is how far is too far down, and how long before it comes up?

Most of us have been on roller coasters or at least have seen them, and we know that not all are created equal. We don't have to expect the dips to be straight down and plunge into the earth before shooting back up. When we make comparisons such as this, it is important to recognize how far we are departing from the basic relationship expectations we all deserve to experience. If I'm describing the kiddie carnival ride, and you're describing the Texas Cyclone, then we will never have a healthy conversation about the realities of either relationship.

We have the chance to change the norm, the idea of what is and *should* be constant by having conversations with other women by creating community. Many women struggle to find a community where they fit in or feel that they belong. Creating your own community can be a great way to begin breaking down the silos and creating a more open environment of understanding and support. If you don't have an existing community or a trusted circle of friends, counselors and therapists can be a great resource for providing that sense of perspective and balance.

> *I regularly asked my therapist, "Is this normal? Is what I'm feeling normal?" It gave me such a sense of peace when she outlined all of the reasons why what I'm going through is completely normal and okay. She gave me examples of others who are experiencing similar feelings. Somehow, I always walk away feeling a little better. Like somehow, she gave me the permission I needed to feel the way I do. It's a small thing, but it makes a huge difference to know that I'm not alone.*

How many victims could be helped if we only talked about abuse openly? Just like anything else, talking about it brings it to the surface and uncovers realities that often remain hidden. By talking about our struggles, we give others permission and freedom to talk about theirs too. By sharing with each other, we gain strength, confidence, and encouragement. Oftentimes, this is the strength we need to get out of an unhealthy relationship, it is the confidence we need to stand up for ourselves, and the encouragement we need to feel worthy of better.

It can be difficult to get the conversation started, but by sharing your own struggles and insecurities, we open a window for others to feel comfortable sharing as well. It can be scary being the first person, but that may be just what someone needs to open up themselves. We *need* to talk about the things we don't want to; that is how stereotypes are broken down. Maybe not by marching or protesting, maybe not by burning your bras, but by being vulnerable, having conversations with others, opening lines of communication, we are clearing the path for others and changing the future.

We cannot talk about conversations without taking a moment to discuss the different types of conversations that women often experience when discussing their lives, particularly the less favorable aspects. The three different conversations include complaining (often referred to as the 'bitch fest'), venting, and constructive conversation.

Complaining generally involves prolonged griping about a situation or person. There is no attempt to reach any conclusion or resolution. Often, others chime in with their experiences and the discussion ends up several blocks removed from where it began. The same conversation may come up time and time again where the same experiences and emotions are revisited.

Venting is a one-time 'cleansing' of frustrations. It can be useful and appropriate at times to share emotions, release the tension, gather what you learned and move on. Where complaining is revisiting the same situation over and over, venting is a brief release, and then progressing on. There may not be any attempt to find a solution or resolution of the issue, but the intent is to 'get it off your chest' or 'out in the open.'

Unlike the other two types of conversations, **constructive conversations** are those where the intent is to share an issue and find a solution. Someone is seeking support outside of comfort. They are seeking to find solutions, gain a new perspective, or otherwise collect additional input or information.

When having a conversation with someone, the goal is to move them toward constructive conversations. This is the only place true awareness and change can take place. By allowing someone to complain continuously about the same issues, we are enabling them to stay in the same destructive situations. They  not only release their steam or pent-up tension, but they are diving deeper into the comfort of their situation. They have a support system supporting their frustrations and piling on with frustrations of their own. Venting can be a healthy release of some of that pressure, but once the pressure is released, the 'venter' can slip back into a comfort zone. The goal, as an ally and friend, is to move them down the scale toward constructive conversations.

I could hear in her words that she was hurting. This is not the first time we have alluded to this topic during a conversation, but tonight her words are more direct. It's hard when you hear someone hurting, especially when it is similar to your past. I could feel myself so desperately wanting to hug her and tell her it would be OK. However the truth of the matter is that it is only true if she believes and decides it to be true. As she proceeded to vent and release, which was greatly needed, I was diligent to listen to when the need moved to complaining and would remind her of the constructive things instead of the destructive. "Why can't I leave?" she repeated again and again. I focused on directing the conversation back to the truths that she already knew, that she herself had already shared just a few minutes ago. Many times in situations, we know what we need and want, but we need to hear it out loud and have someone point a neon sign to it. "The only person that can answer why you can't leave is you. It really comes down to making a choice and being determined to only look forward. It can take up to seven times for someone to remove themselves from an abusive relationship. Don't come down on yourself so hard."

"I never thought I would be in this situation, and the more I stay the more I become full of anxiety and anger." First, validate her feelings and allow her to express her thoughts freely, then remind her of what she already acknowledged, and then give feasible and tangible solutions that could be implemented immediately. For example, "you acknowledged that... so now let's shift the focus on to what you can control, and start from there."

Engaging in the right level of conversation with someone can be difficult. Heck, even stopping yourself from falling into those destructive patterns can be difficult. During the process of writing this book, we often found ourselves falling back into bitch-fest or venting territory. It's easy to drift down memory lane, rehashing old hurts and pain,  especially when that hurt is still very much real. We are not trying to suggest that every conversation you have must be a constructive, healthy conversation. We are simply trying to increase your awareness of the different types of conversations, and help you recognize when you are engaging in behaviors that don't serve you. Healthy conversations are a great tool for helping you process your experiences and make positive choices.

HAVING HEALTHY CONVERSATIONS

Creating trust is foundational

- Listen without interruption
- Build them up, reminding them of how loved and powerful they truly are.
- Show interest in their life
- Be vulnerable by sharing your experiences (not necessarily similar and not in comparison)

Butt into your friend's business

- Ask tough questions
- Don't stop pushing when the first response is, "everything's fine."
- Ask about specific situations
- Ask pointed questions

Offer support, not always advice

- What are your needs and how can I help you?
- Ask questions that jump-start the problem-solving process
- Don't give immediate advice

Do not compare

- Sparingly use personal experiences or stories of others to highlight a point when appropriate but avoid the temptation to do this as it can distract from the conversation and take the attention off of her.
- Never one-up

We have covered a lot of ground highlighting many of the reasons women get in and stay in abusive relationships. From the history of humans on earth to the things we say to each other as well as ourselves we are fighting an uphill battle. The only way we have a chance of changing the script for future generations is to change our own part. One-by-one, we change the lines we keep repeating. This creates a ripple effect that influences more ripples and those ripples eventually become waves that influence significant change.

How did this happen?
A Breakdown of
Reality

"Even now I still wonder, "How did I let that happen?"

I
t is one of the most common questions victims get asked, and it's one of the most common questions we ask ourselves, even long after the abuse has ended. It is almost inconceivable to think that someone would be berated, abused, hit, talked down to, and/or treated terribly time after time yet not leave. The reality is, it doesn't always start off as obvious abuse. Abusers don't immediately start beating their victims and leaving black eyes, swollen cheeks, and bloody lips. They don't start by locking them in their rooms or threatening their children. Most often, it starts off slowly and builds over time, and it often doesn't progress beyond verbal abuse. It begins with a process of building trust. By listening and learning, by wooing and treating, by wining and dining. By doing everything right, the victim lets her guard down. She *wants* to trust him, *wants* to believe him, and *wants* him to be the person he appears to be.

Even once the abuse starts, it isn't always consistent. It's a roller coaster; wonderful one minute and terrible the next. From flowers and dinner out to yelling and accusations. Anger and hurt, then apologies and promises. The victim is left confused and terrified of what will happen next. Hanging on to the good times and downplaying the bad, she makes it from one day to the next, clinging to the hope that tomorrow will be a better day. In reality, even during the good times, there is often still psychological abuse happening. Those good times are often used for bad later on.

When it was good, it could be great, but it could also be miserable. My oldest daughter, who was old enough to remember during the relationship, agrees with that sentiment. We were spoiled with beautiful things, eating out, and fun activities, especially after abuse. He always knew how to make it better. In the beginning there was a lot of reassurance that he was just stressed, and asking us for reassurance that he'd made up for it: "See? Didn't we just have a fun time?" Even during the good times, he would often get upset about something, ending the fun abruptly with verbal attacks. Sometimes, it wouldn't end in abuse. In those moments, we almost felt "normal." During those times, we felt like there was still hope. He recognized he hurt us, which is an important step, right? If he recognizes he is doing something wrong, then surely, he can and wants to change. Inevitably, even the good times would be used against us in an argument. "See, we had fun together. Why did you have to go and ruin it?" It was a constant whirlwind of a roller coaster. Over time, the lows just kept getting lower and the highs began to flatten out.

The abuser meticulously breaks down their victim's sense of reality and self-worth over time. In tracing back our own situations as well as talking to countless other victims, researchers, and social workers in this space, we have identified a few steps in this process that may help you understand just how an abuser can so effectively slip in and completely overtake their victim.

Decondition

The first step is to decondition the victim. Deconditioning is the process of persuading someone to abandon a habitual mode of thinking, or a way of viewing circumstances. This process is used by abusers in the beginning because not only does it help adhere themselves to the person, the result of deconditioning is that the victim consequently begins to think and view things in many of the same ways as the abuser. In the process of deconditioning, the abuser gains trust and focuses the victim's attention on how good they are compared to everything in the past. Whatever you didn't have before, they will give you now, whatever your ex was lacking, they have in spades. Regardless of how prepared you were to turn over every leaf and look under every rock, you quickly believe that you have found your knight in shining armor. Conversations about the past are: "How dare they, how could they do that to you, I would never do that." Everything before them was horrible, and they are there to make it right.

You *want* to believe they are who they say they are, and you quickly let your guard down. Why wouldn't you believe them? Why would someone intentionally lie to you or hurt you? When a red flag appears, you quickly push it aside. This new person is so great, you mostly only see the positive and quickly release any doubt that may begin to creep up. Any negatives or flaws have a reason, or as commonly said, "That's just how they are."

> *Through my first marriage, I worked all the time. I had no extra money or time to myself. My first husband was trapped in a high school mentality and took on very little responsibility around the home. When I met my second husband, he had a great job, beautifully decorated and clean home, treated me like a queen, and appeared to have it all together, so some of the questions or potential red flags were dismissed. The cherry on top was that he didn't have any drinking or drug problems. I thought I had found the pot of gold at the end of the rainbow in regards to relationship potential. He was the perfect opposite of what I came from. I thought I had done all of my homework. He checked off every box. I had no reason to believe I was being prepped for an even worse relationship than what I had just escaped.*

It's amazing how the brain works. It will literally scan the environment, seeking out information to support what it believes or wants to believe. That's how false news can become so prevalent. As soon as we see something that supports our belief, we cling to it, despite how ludicrous it may sound. To the person hungry for proof, they believe they have just found it. In the face of mounting evidence for the alternative, victims can believe they aren't being abused or that "he didn't mean it."

There are certainly fine lines between being overly optimistic, ignoring the bad, being overly pessimistic, and actually seeking out the negative. It is a dangerous trap we often find ourselves in, and abusers can easily twist our desire to be positive into making us feel bad about questioning anything. "I'm not your ex. When are you going to stop treating me like it?" "You need to move on and not think everyone is out to get you."

Even as allies, we need to be aware and cautious of the things we are saying to those expressing concern. It is easy to get in the habit of normalizing and justifying behavior, which can be dangerous for these women. We will do a deep dive into those things we say to each other in a later section.

Demoralize

The next step in an abusive relationship is to demoralize the victim. To demoralize someone is to cause them to lose confidence, hope, or to break down their morals. Once the abuser has created a sense of trust, the next step is for them to break down all sense of trust in others or even the victim's own sense of self. Slowly, the victim begins to accept things that she never thought she would. She starts questioning her own strength and abilities. *Is this really happening?*

> *He would make me go into the bathroom with him while he went because he claimed "this is the only time we can talk with no kids." At first, I thought he just wanted me to be with him, but the time with no kids never added up to me because he would spend hours playing video games or on his phone with no kids present. As time went on, the demand for my presence when he was using the restroom became harsher. He would even*

show me the poop on the toilet paper and laugh, asking me to
wipe him or make cruel jokes at my expense. Over time, I began
to realize that it was a lack of respect and a show of control. I
didn't need or want to watch him use the restroom, yet I felt
powerless to say no.

By accepting small, more insignificant behaviors, we begin to wonder is *this who I am?* The more we "willingly" engage, we begin to believe this must be who we really are. Just a little more must be okay, or what's the difference? I did it then; this isn't that much different. The behaviors become normalized. Over time, they no longer raise red flags or concerns.

Degrade

The degradation of a victim's self-esteem and sense of self-worth
is one of the first and primary casualties of abuse.

The final step in the breakdown of an individual is degradation or the condition and process of degrading or being degraded. Degradation is a process that renders an object useless or less useful over time. It is the act of lowering something or someone to a less respected state.

The abuser begins to chip away at his victim until there is nothing left. Like a stone statue with pieces starting to fall off, eventually the original statue is unrecognizable. Throughout the degrading process, self-esteem is the first to go. When it's broken, the center of who you are is destroyed. That is very difficult to recover from. The opportunity for someone to abuse you when you have a high self-esteem is greatly reduced. As your self-esteem falls, your standards fall. What was previously unacceptable now isn't so bad. They aren't crossing your boundaries because your boundaries have been removed all together.

When we made the move from our current state to his home-
town in another, I wasn't allowed to bring many of my belong-

ings other than clothes. I justified it to myself that he just didn't want anything in the new house that was from my previous marriage. In reality, he was removing everything that I brought into the relationship until there was nothing left. Everything was his. He owned it all just like he "owned" me.

Abusive relationships can often start with any form and level of verbal and psychological abuse, adding in economic and eventually physical, including sexual abuse. It is a stew. There are so many ingredients, and no specific measurements. Most often, there isn't just one form of abuse happening at a time, but multiple forms. As long as the abuse is getting the job done, maintaining enough control over the victim, the abuser may not escalate to more intense levels of abuse.

Even for the abuser, however, that level of abuse ultimately becomes "boring" or "the norm," resulting in escalation. It may also escalate when the abuse begins to be seen by others.

Escalation doesn't happen overnight. Little slips turn into big ones that become the norm. Despite the new-found recognition that they are indeed being abused, victims may not leave because the environment for abuse has already been established. Abusers then have free rein. The abusive behaviors become a part of "the way things are."

When he started making mistakes, his abuse escalated. Mistakes equal proof. He was angry or annoyed, maybe afraid of getting caught, but when someone else had a glimpse into the life we actually lived, the abuse he delivered advanced. I once caught him taking money from my purse. I noticed after that his anger and yelling became louder and more forceful. My daughter called the police one evening because she was so afraid. After that, I noticed he was much more physical than before.

Self-Esteem and Abuse

There is a direct correlation between victims of domestic abuse and lower levels of self-esteem. So, does that mean that higher levels can combat the violence? No, absolutely not. However, it has been shown that those with a stronger self-image are more likely to be empowered to leave an abusive relationship than someone who feels like they will not be able to do better than their current situation[1]. Additionally, domestic violence offenders have a higher tendency to prey on those with lower levels of self-esteem because they realize that the victim will need them and, as a result, will be less likely to oppose them.

We must have a basic understanding regarding our feelings, what is healthy, and ways to feel better about ourselves. This goes back to the "what is normal" conversation.

To understand the impact of abuse, watch how a chunk of sugar dissolves when liquid is poured on it. The liquid starts to wear it away and melt it down. An abuser does the same with the victim's sense of self-worth. When compounded, lowered self-esteem is stacked with fear brought on by the abuser, and it becomes paralyzing.

Offenders recognize this and use it to their advantage. If the abuser suspects their victim is becoming more empowered or feeling better about themself, thus potentially gaining the confidence to leave, they often turn on the "good" parts (i.e., the charm or caring) to remind their victim of the goodness and love that may still be stirring within the relationship. This is often quickly followed by taking something away, allowing the abuser to reestablish control. Those things could be money, privacy, plans already made, or anything else that is of importance to the victim. Verbal abuse may be used to break them down, reminding them that they are nothing in comparison to the abuser or someone else, ultimately causing the victim to feel vulnerable and fearful in some cases.

When a person doesn't believe they deserve to be treated with respect and dignity, why would they reach out and ask for help? The lower the self-esteem, the more likely a person will start to believe they are truly unworthy of love, kindness, respect, caring, and/or any other human decency or compassion.

As self-esteem drops, standards drop, maintaining control over the victim becomes easier. Just as the sugar breaks down and dissolves, ultimately disappearing, so does the victim's autonomy.

Self-esteem depletes under the chaotic conditions of life with an abusive partner. In a state of abuse, victims are more prone to develop secondary issues like difficulty sleeping, eating habits, symptoms of anxiety, or even self-harming and suicidal thoughts. The marks of emotional and psychological abuse run deep. These marks don't heal like a bruise or a busted lip. They stay, building and compacting each time another cycle of abuse comes, giving more insecurities and self-doubt. Lower self-esteem levels can be seen in many ways such as ongoing feelings of anger, shock, grief, self-hatred, loss of trust, and more.

Abusive relationships have varying degrees of power imbalance, leaving the victim feeling unsure, helpless, emotionally unsafe, and trapped. This can result in a loss of self-love, since giving their abuser everything of themselves often requires the sacrifice of their own self-image. Just like with a career, motherhood, or a hobby, we often pin our identity on something or someone else. Over time, we come to believe we are nothing without that identity. It's not intentional or even conscious, and we often do it to ourselves. As we mentioned, it can also be a conscious process of breakdown by the abuser to the point where we don't even recognize who we have become. When we lose that person or identity (wife, mother, victim), we lose a huge part of who we think we are. Loss of identity and/or purpose is also common in abusive relationships.

After my divorce, I felt lost as to who I was. Setting up a new household, I struggled to make basic decisions without having someone else's opinion to consider. What dishes do I like? What movies do I enjoy? At one point, I was having brunch with a friend when the server asked how I wanted my eggs. I was completely frozen. How do I like my eggs? I hadn't had to answer that in so long; I couldn't even remember if I actually liked them scrambled or not. When that blanket of identity was removed, I felt completely exposed and vulnerable. Freedom is a wonderful thing, but it takes some time to get used to.

Patterns have been recognized through the years, in regard to domestic abuse, anxiety, and depression. It is difficult to determine whether anxiety and depression are preexisting or caused by the abuse. At any rate, mental health struggles are often inevitable in the case of domestic abuse. In situations of current abuse, a victim is less likely to admit to mental health issues in fear that it could be used against them, currently or in future if they try to leave. After leaving, it is not uncommon for a victim to experience panic attacks, flashbacks, nightmares, and/or suffer from PTSD, depression, and grief over the life they had dreamed of, as well as indescribable exhaustion.

When we talk about self-esteem, we must also include self-image. We all have a core level of self-esteem that is unique to us based on our realities of life. While one person may be relatively unbothered by comments from others, someone else may be devastated. Fortunately, resilience can be developed, but it does take conscious and continuous effort.

One of the greatest damages to our personal esteem is our inner shame-voice, which tells us that we are not good enough.[2] In her ground-breaking book *The Gifts of Imperfection*, Brene Brown writes, "Shame loves secrecy. When we bury our story, the shame metastasizes.[3]" In her TED Talk *Listening to Shame*, Brown also said, "If you put shame in a Petri dish, it needs three things to grow exponentially: secrecy, silence and judgment." These are the exact conditions that thrive in an abusive dynamic. The abuser feeds that inner shame voice, backing it up with the reality they create. This manipulation is at the core of an abusive relationship. Abusers utilize this tactic to weaponize fear and doubt against the victim, the driving forces of fluctuations in self-esteem.

If you are struggling to relate to this breakdown of self-esteem, imagine how you would feel if your life was dominated by shame, ridicule, and being made to question your decisions, capabilities, and choices. Then, that same voice doing all of those harmful things will, days or even moments later, profess love, kindness, and support, while at the same time making sure you are super aware that no one else would want you. Where do you think your self-esteem would be?

Feelings of worthlessness and powerlessness are highly interlinked with depression, anxiety, and low self-esteem. Though the victim may understand intellectually that the things the abuser is saying are not objectively true, the primary driver of self-image is emotion. Emotions are the abuser's manipulation currency.

Significant research has been conducted on the physical, mental, and emotional impact of domestic violence on women including chronic health issues and emotional and social complications such as low self-esteem. According to a study done by Papadakaki, Tzamalouka, Chatzifotiou, and Chilaeotakis[4] a bi-product of low self-esteem is self-doubt. As women begin to doubt themselves, their decisions, and their abilities, they are more likely to maintain relations with their abuser.

Additionally, those suffering from low self-esteem often self-isolate from their communities, weakening their ties with others and causing a deeper drop in self-confidence and further reducing their ability to change the situation.[5]Across research, there is general agreement that self-esteem has an inverse relationship with both frequency and severity of all forms of domestic abuse[6].

In the U.S., it is estimated that every year, 1 to 4 million women are sexually, emotionally, and/or physically abused by a domestic partner.[7] Not only may a healthy self-esteem help prevent women from entering and staying in abusive relationships, research shows that it may also help reduce the long-term depressive effects of abuse, which is a common, lingering result of domestic violence."[8]

It is our responsibility as individuals to build self-esteem within ourselves and others. Self-confidence is not a right; it's a privilege. If no one has taught you how to build it, it's easy to lower it and break it. Here are a few tips on building your own self-esteem and flexing your self-confidence muscle:

- Speak kindly to yourself. We are often our own toughest critics. Speak life and love to yourself rather than hate.
- Do something every day that you enjoy and something that challenges you. As you use your strengths and continue to grow, you will gain confidence that comes from achievement
- Accept your imperfections. We all have them, and they make us who we are. Recognizing that you are not defined by your weaknesses will help you see past them to the incredible woman you are.
- Control what you can. In a world where we can sometimes control very little, it is important to grab hold of those things we can. What time we wake up, what we eat, how much we move, what we watch, and the things we say to ourselves are things we can often control that will begin to give us our power back.
- Keep self-promises. Related to the previous tip, keeping promises to yourself, no matter how small, will begin to boost your self-esteem and self-confidence by building self-trust and demonstrating that you are worth it.
- Practice gratitude. Gratitude is a soft concept that has very real and physical implications for overall health and wellbeing. When we take the attention off of the negative and turn it toward those things we are grateful for, it changes the way we experience our reality, thus changing reality itself. We are not suggesting that a practice of gratitude will eliminate the abuse, and we certainly are not advocating that this be used to ignore what is happening. Gratitude serves to boost your self-esteem by reminding you that there is something better, something worth striving for. It actually rewires the brain to see the positive, and we naturally want more of it, which often means leaving or changing the abusive relationship.

In the next section, we will dive into how the words we use (we being the collective we: ourselves and those around us) can influence how we enter abusive relationships and why we stay in them.

LANGUAGE WE USE

The language we use to talk about abuse is a key factor in keeping victims locked in a dangerous cycle of abuse. This includes the things we tell ourselves as well as words others use. Language influences the way we think, defines what is acceptable, and guides our actions.

In this section, we will walk through many of the words and conventions we use when talking about abuse. We will highlight the impact of that language and address how we can begin to break down those myths, stereotypes, and misperceptions that keep so many victims trapped in their own spinning hamster wheels.

Justification

When his mom moved in, I could instantly see why he was so broken, tattered, and torn. That's when the abuse really began to set in. Part of me actually felt bad for him because he was

raised so poorly. I thought I could help make his life easier,
better.

The things we tell ourselves about the abuse we experience extends to trying to find an explanation for the abuser's behavior. It is a natural human instinct to want to understand why or how someone who says they care and love, could be capable of doing and saying the things they do. Constantly making excuses for bad behavior can be exhausting and mentally draining.

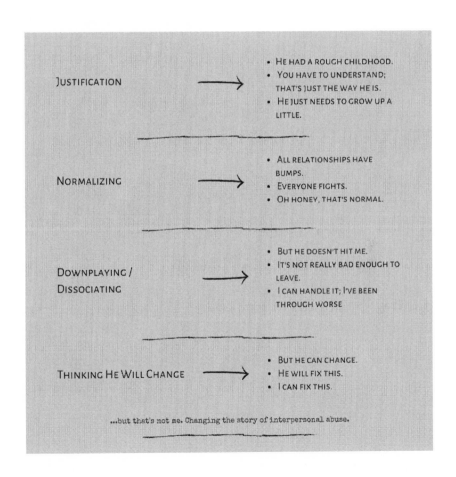

JUSTIFICATION ⟶
- HE HAD A ROUGH CHILDHOOD.
- YOU HAVE TO UNDERSTAND; THAT'S JUST THE WAY HE IS.
- HE JUST NEEDS TO GROW UP A LITTLE.

NORMALIZING ⟶
- ALL RELATIONSHIPS HAVE BUMPS.
- EVERYONE FIGHTS.
- OH HONEY, THAT'S NORMAL.

DOWNPLAYING / DISSOCIATING ⟶
- BUT HE DOESN'T HIT ME.
- IT'S NOT REALLY BAD ENOUGH TO LEAVE.
- I CAN HANDLE IT; I'VE BEEN THROUGH WORSE

THINKING HE WILL CHANGE ⟶
- BUT HE CAN CHANGE.
- HE WILL FIX THIS.
- I CAN FIX THIS.

...but that's not me. Changing the story of interpersonal abuse.

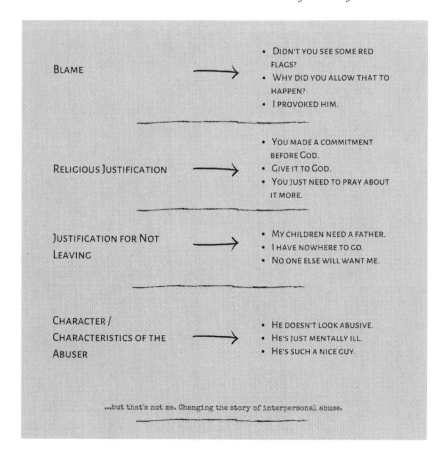

BLAME ⟶
- DIDN'T YOU SEE SOME RED FLAGS?
- WHY DID YOU ALLOW THAT TO HAPPEN?
- I PROVOKED HIM.

RELIGIOUS JUSTIFICATION ⟶
- YOU MADE A COMMITMENT BEFORE GOD.
- GIVE IT TO GOD.
- YOU JUST NEED TO PRAY ABOUT IT MORE.

JUSTIFICATION FOR NOT LEAVING ⟶
- MY CHILDREN NEED A FATHER.
- I HAVE NOWHERE TO GO.
- NO ONE ELSE WILL WANT ME.

CHARACTER / CHARACTERISTICS OF THE ABUSER ⟶
- HE DOESN'T LOOK ABUSIVE.
- HE'S JUST MENTALLY ILL.
- HE'S SUCH A NICE GUY.

...but that's not me. Changing the story of interpersonal abuse.

Some of you may be thinking, well, my man isn't that bad. He doesn't hit me, yell at me, make threats, follow me, or any of that. He's just a child. He takes no responsibility or his actions. He refuses to grow up, hold down a job, etc.

Justification for abuse is commonly used by the victim and those around them. In our experience, the victim's family are prime culprits of this behavior, but we know plenty of victims whose own family will justify the abusive behavior they are experiencing. Although it can involve any category, justification frequently takes place regarding age, maturity level, external stressors, background/how they were raised, or personality.

Age

- He's young; he'll grow out of it.
- He doesn't know any better.
- He's just older and set in his ways.

Maturity Level

- He's just immature.
- He's just making poor choices. He just needs to grow up a little, and it's my job to help him do that.
- He's stuck in a high school mentality.

External Stressors

- He's had a rough day.
- His job is extremely stressful/hard/dangerous.

Background

- That's just the way he was raised.
- He had a rough childhood/ was abused as a child.

Mental illness(es) or disabilities

- He's not an asshole, he's just on the spectrum.
- It's not his fault he screams at me, he's bipolar.
- The amount of pain and stress makes him behave that way.
- He has PTSD, it's not his fault he lashes out.

Personality

- But he's not a bad person.
- You don't know him like I do.
- He's just awkward in public.
- You have to understand; that's just the way he is.

- That's just his personality/style.
- He's just passionate. We're both just passionate people. We both get worked up.
- He's just jealous because he loves me. It's "normal" to be jealous.
- He's just joking around/ a flirt.
- He doesn't mean it/ doesn't mean anything by it.

 There are certainly instances where there is a valid explanation for why an abuser engages in certain behaviors. However it is important to understand that if someone has a legit reason for their behavior doesn't mean it is something others have to tolerate. It is their responsibility to figure out how to handle their condition and not take it out on the people around them. Upbringing, for example, certainly is a contributing factor to what they deem acceptable behavior. That said, it does not make abusive behavior okay. Yes, we now have a better understanding of where the behavior came from and how to begin addressing it, but the behavior itself is still not okay.

When we find ourselves justifying or trying to explain behavior to ourselves or even someone else, it is a sign, a red flag if you will, that something isn't right. It should serve as a trigger to ask ourselves, *what are we trying to justify and why?* Having to constantly justify someone's behavior is a sign that inappropriate behaviors are taking place.

I was regularly embarrassed by his behavior. I would try to explain to the people we were with that he just had too much to drink or was stressed out. When he was exceptionally loud and obnoxious, I would explain that he had been cooped up all week and was just a little excited to be out. At my department Christmas party, someone brought a thong to the white elephant exchange. He put it on his head and wore it around all night. Everyone laughed, at least at first, so I thought I was just being too uptight and was just embarrassed like a teen who doesn't want her parents to show up at school. Eventually, I realized that I was simply trying to be an adult, and he was the one still stuck in junior high.

His mother told me, "That's just the way he is; he's never going to change."

Serial Adolescence

Adolescence is defined as the period that begins with puberty and ends with the achievement of social and economic independence.[1] Extended adolescence is the phenomenon of young people taking longer to reach adulthood than they have in generations past. Many are taking longer to graduate college, returning to live with their parents in their 20s, and waiting longer to get married and start families.

Our contribution to the topic of extended adolescence is that many men do not move out of this stage even *after* settling down and/or starting a family. Even when they achieve some level of social and economic independence prior to getting married, once they have another person to fall back on, they indeed fall back into a stage of adolescence and don't come back out. They take on little responsibility and victims are left picking up the pieces.

Although it does not fit the general guidelines of classic abuse that we have discussed throughout this book, particularly in regard to the intent behind behaviors, the behaviors associated with extended adolescence would absolutely be considered abusive. The impact of this type of behavior is similar to those of psychological abuse, serving to erode the victim's self-worth, creating an environment of confusion and resulting in isolation. Victims with a partner trapped in extended adolescence take on all of the household responsibilities, often in addition to financial responsibilities as well. In some cases, victims not only assume these responsibilities, but they often pick up the school or work projects from their partners because they were either asked to do it or they recognize their partner will not adequately fulfill that responsibility.

Women with partners who provide the majority of the family income may find themselves justifying this extra responsibility because "his job is so important" or "he works so hard all day, he deserves a break when he comes home." Instead of helping with household responsibilities, these men have become accustomed to doing absolutely nothing, sometimes seeing the work around the home as "her job," regardless of how many hours it takes.

> *Like many new moms, when I was pregnant, I joined several baby pages for pregnant women due within the same month. I began to see a strong trend, particularly with women pregnant with their second child, where they would complain about their husbands or boyfriends coming home and not helping around the house. The woman was expected to care for the children all day, cook dinner, clean the house, serve him the meal, and care for the children all night. Many were just complaining with no intention to change anything, others were trying to get a gauge as to whether or not it was normal, and a few were asking what they could do about it. Responses ranged from "get the hell out now" to "if he is working all day, then the home is your responsibility" and everything in between.*

This behavior is difficult to change and often continues to get worse and progress until he has a reason or motivation to change and grow up. Some men will reach this point when they have children. For others, that still isn't enough. For some, an ultimatum works; for others, that only pushes them deeper into their childish behaviors.

> *He always talked about saving money to travel and even living off of one income, saving the other. He said all of the right things, but didn't do the work to make any of it happen. He just pushed it off on me to make more money, find a better job, or turn my hobby into profit. He had big dreams and goals, but very little follow-through. He started expensive new hobbies that were going to be a lucrative career for him that never amounted to anything except more bills. I wanted to be supportive of his dreams. I wanted him to do something that made him happy, so I supported attempt after attempt. In the*

meantime, he wouldn't keep a job. Either the manager was a jerk or they had him doing things he didn't want to do. Either way, he would quit after a couple of weeks.

He would stay up late, sometimes all night playing computer games or watching movies. With nowhere to go and nowhere to be, he would sleep most of the day. He was very talented with construction. We were remodeling our entire house. Instead of working on projects while I was at work, he would sleep or play games all day, waiting for me to get home so we could "do it together." When I asked him to do it while I was working, he would say, "But I want to do it with you," "You may not like where I put the tile," "It's just easier/faster/more fun with two people," "This is our house. Don't you want to do it with me?" When I traveled, he would eat out or eat junk food the entire time. I would make meals ahead for him and come home to a sink full of dishes, dirty clothes strewn through the house, and pizza boxes with slices still in them in the living room. It felt like I was living in a bachelor pad. He took no responsibility for anything. I was his maid, his mother, and his roommate. I had always wanted children, but the thought of raising a child and also raising him felt unbearable. Fortunately, he kept pushing it off any time I would mention it, so I hung that dream up.

He would get angry when I served the children first. "Why do I have to wait? They always need something. I want my food hot." Eventually, I just served him first so that I didn't have to hear him fuss.

Some trends of extended adolescence may include:

- Spending significant time playing games, "hanging out," or partying rather than taking care of responsibilities.
- General disrespect of or disregard for the feelings or rights of others.
- Victim mentality. Everything is always someone else's fault.

- Does not participate in general household responsibilities including cooking, cleaning, taking out the trash, mowing the lawn, or household maintenance.
- Has to be asked multiple times to do something.
- Makes frivolous purchases at the expense of necessities or saving for the future.
- Inability or unwillingness to keep a job or provide adequate financial support.
- Seeking inappropriate attention from others.
- Engaging in risky behaviors: risky to self or others.
- General disregard for the safety and health of others.
- Lack of appropriate future vision.
- Inability to do basic activities like chores without the victim being present or 'helping.'
- Not taking responsibility or pushing responsibility for all household duties on others.

To be fair, many people, men and women, may display some of these behaviors from time to time. When we are tired, stressed, worn out, or need to let off some steam, we may revert back to childish behaviors for a moment or even much longer. Generally speaking, when brought to our attention or when we recognize it ourselves, we snap out of it and pick back up where we left off. Others display a few behaviors fairly consistently (i.e., when men can't seem to get their dirty clothes *in* the hamper). Although that really isn't okay either, when the majority of their behaviors reflect responsibility, adulthood, and partnership, the behaviors are likely not associated with extended adolescence, which is more of a general inability or unwillingness to grow up.

One night, I woke up to the smell of smoke. We lived in a two-story apartment. I ran downstairs to see the bottom floor filled with smoke. I saw him lying on the couch, a fondue pot burning on the woven straw stool in front of him. The ceramic pot had cracked; cheese ran everywhere. Somehow, the flame was still burning. I wasn't sure if he was dead or passed out. If he was passed out, I wasn't sure if it was because of the smoke or the alcohol. I opened the doors, put out the flame, and cleared the smoke. I tried waking him several times. Once the smoke was cleared and the cheese cleaned, he finally woke up. I explained what had happened, and he didn't even remember making fondue. He simply laughed and said, "I guess I wanted some fondue." He went upstairs and fell asleep.

One common justification is that "he is not a bad person; he is just making bad choices" or "he's just inconsiderate." So, when does a bad choice turn into abuse? When someone, especially someone who is supposed to love you, is made aware of the fact that they are hurting you with their behavior and is still unwilling or unable to change it, that behavior is abusive. They are making the *choice* to not change, *knowing* that you are being hurt by it. By any definition, that is not love.

I still struggle, ten years later, with the idea of intent. Even today, I truly believe that he did not intend to hurt me the way he did. I can't bring myself to believe that he intentionally manipulated me, degraded my sense of self-worth, and isolated me for control. Maybe I just don't want to believe I would have fallen for that, but I still can't bring myself to believe it. In all honesty, I don't believe he spent that much time thinking about me at all. I believe he was inconsiderate, childish, irresponsible, lazy, selfish, disrespectful, and rude. I believe he took advantage of the good situation that he had. I am even tempted to ask, "who wouldn't?" Even though I know the answer to that. Most healthy adults would not take advantage of that situation. I know that, but a part of me still struggles with naming it abuse.

Because I couldn't see him as the bad person I pictured when I said the word "abuse," I just couldn't justify leaving. It took me a long time to realize that, even if I wasn't being abused (according to my mental definition at the time), it wasn't my responsibility to change him or wait for him to change. I gave him eleven years, including eight years of marriage. I begged and pleaded with him. I cried with his family, begging for their help. I laid it all out, yet he refused to change. All the while, I was being deeply hurt. My self-esteem plummeted; I doubted myself, my abilities, and my judgment. I was living a nightmare. Regardless of whether he meticulously planned it that way, he was abusing me by refusing to acknowledge my needs and make an effort to change.

 Focusing on intention rather than result is one of the key ways our culture downplays and justifies abuse. In reality, we can't know anyone else's intentions, we can only observe their behavior and whether or not it changes once they're made aware of how it's affecting us. That's where victims must make a conscious effort to shift their mindset around abusive behavior. Even if they aren't *intending* to hurt you, they still *are* hurting you. You may never be able to accept the reality that someone intended to hurt you, especially someone you love, and that's okay. If you need to, separate the behavior from the person. Just like a mother who must cut ties with their drug-addicted adult child in order to protect herself and give the addict any chance of recovery, victims must often remove themselves, regardless of how much love and hope may still exist. At that point, it is about the behavior (which is abusive) whether or not you are ready to label them and write them off as an "abuser."

Normalizing

I began to open up a bit to women I worked with. All were quite a bit older than me and had been married longer, so I valued their perspectives. As I shared about his immaturity and partying, his inability to hold down a job, and my overall dissatisfaction with our arrangement, they responded with, "Oh honey, that's normal" or "get used to it; that's marriage."

Things we say that normalize abuse behaviors:

- All relationships have bumps / All marriages have trials.
- It's not healthy if you don't fight every now and then.
- Jealousy is a good thing. He must really love you.
- We're just getting the kinks worked out, that's all.
- But you look so happy together.
- All marriages go through rough patches.
- Oh honey, that's normal.
- Marriage is all about compromise.
- It's not that big of a deal.

According to Merriam-Webster, the definitions of normalize are to conform to or reduce to a norm or standard, to make normal, or to bring or restore to a normal condition. Normal is defined as conforming to a type, standard, or regular pattern, or according to constituting, or not deviating from a norm, rule, or principle.[2] "Normal" is considered acceptable or even desirable. In the case of "normalizing" behavior or experiences, this language serves to downplay the victim's experiences as "normal" therefore okay.

Even if this behavior and experiences are normal, that should never, in and of itself, make it okay. Thinking this behavior is normal and therefore okay or to be expected is what keeps many victims in relationships for far too long. We tell each other that this is normal, that "everyone fights," but in reality, we know very little about what the victim is actually experiencing. What they describe is often just a piece of a very large, very complex puzzle. We do ourselves and each other a disservice by downplaying what they are going through, especially when we know very little about the reality of what is going on.

I didn't know I was being sexually harassed until years later.

Normalizing is not just a phenomenon in cases of domestic abuse. Through our language and what we come to accept, we normalize all types of behaviors including sexism and sexual harassment.

Did you know that reports of sexual harrassment go way up after employees or students receive training? This is because they now know the process for reporting this type of behavior, but also because victims now have language to use to describe what is happening as well as recognition that it is indeed *not* okay. Language is key to normalizing behavior. When we don't have the words to use to describe it we tend to downplay it and think that it must be normal.

How people talk about marriage and relationships in general differs significantly across people and across families. I have heard adults reflect on hearing their parents fight at the dinner table or through the walls as they tried to fall asleep at night. Others almost praise their parents for never so much as arguing in front of them. What we let our kids see regarding our relationships matters. It's important for us to model healthy tools for working through crises and settling disagreements as a team, rather than as adversaries. If children grow up thinking their parents naturally agree on everything or rarely disagree, it sets up unrealistic expectations of what marriage will or should look like.

> *They made it look so easy, and I just assumed that's what marriage was. We grew up in a very loving and kind home, so when my brother and I found ourselves with abusive partners, we didn't know what to do. We didn't have a functional toolset for building a strong and healthy marriage.*

Not everyone has a healthy marriage. In fact, most people don't, which is why the divorce rate is higher than 50%. We go into it with unrealistic expectations and think it's going to naturally work itself out. It doesn't. Both partners need to be willing to do the self-work necessary to show up as the best partner they can be, as well as the teamwork to take on the problems that inevitably come up as allies rather than adversaries. Nobody can fix anybody else, we can only fix ourselves. So if your partner is unwilling to do their own self-work, no amount of counseling or support from you is going to solve that underlying issue.

If you are raising children, talk to them about the realities of relationships. Don't be hesitant to show them what a healthy disagreement looks like, and certainly don't hide it. This is how children learn to have healthy discussions across all types of relationships.

It may also be necessary to surround yourself with others who do have strong marriages. We are most like the five people we hang out with the most. If you want a strong marriage or relationship, hang out with other couples who have strong relationships.

> *How far do we go to "make a marriage work"?*
>
> *Growing up, I was taught, and truly believed, that you do whatever it takes to make a marriage work and keep the family together. This was the number one priority.*

In many faith-based and secular beliefs, this is a common standard. Living with someone else can be challenging, but when you enter into that commitment, you do what it takes to make it work. Well-meaning people often tout this idea without realizing that it is based on the expectation that both parties are in agreement and willing to do whatever it takes. Those who get divorced are often accused of treating their marriage as "disposable" and giving up too soon. Divorce is frowned upon as an "easy out." Although many couples do give up without learning to grow together, many more women (and men) are trapped in a relationship where they are the only one trying to make it work while the other half is sucking the life right out of them. Many wait far too long, trying too hard, putting their lives and the lives of their children in danger.

> *I was trying to live up to an example that I didn't fully understand with someone who was never on a similar level. Seeing my parents, I didn't realize that they were both on the same level before they got married and then continued to grow on that solid foundation. I didn't even realize there were different*

levels. I just thought that people were all made ready for marriage. I understand how naive that sounds, but there really is no other way to describe the mentality I had at the time. Instead of growing together, we grew further apart. I had always wanted a family, so maturing to meet the responsibility of a new family was part of who I was. Sadly, that wasn't part of who he was. Whether he was incapable or not interested, he didn't grow. Committed to keeping my husband satisfied and making our marriage work, I began making compromises that I should never have made.

Don't get me wrong, making compromises is a natural part of marriage. When both parties have the best interest of the other at heart, compromises can be healthy. But when you feel the need to compromise your beliefs, integrity, or boundaries, you are headed down a dangerous road. I felt such immense pressure to keep it together that I agreed to things I never should have. I was taught to be the submissive wife, but I wasn't taught that this only works in a relationship with mutual love and respect. I was living up to my end of the deal, and he was taking full advantage of it. I gave up too much of myself to be the picture-perfect wife I saw growing up and always wanted to be.

I finally accepted that I wasn't going to change him, so I decided to just roll with it and make the best of a bad situation. Everyone else apparently had terrible marriages anyway. It's not like there was something better waiting for me. So I put everything I had into making this one work.

In order to balance the cognitive dissonance I felt between my beliefs and actions, I began to change my beliefs. That's what happens in the beginning - just a little bit more, and I can do this. I can push through this.

"Everyone goes through this, right?" Everyone says their husbands suck, their marriage sucks, everyone hates it. Even

Christian women talk negatively and complain about their husbands. Others go on business trips and seek out affairs, flirting, and seeking attention from others. Most of these women were 10 to 25 years older than me. They weren't simply young moms dealing with immature men. These were grown women who were still putting up with this behavior from their husbands. I started to think that this was just normal behavior that I was going to have to put up with.

Where did this concept come from that women believe they just have to make it work and take responsibility for people in their lives, show mutual respect, or show up? At its core, it's a mix of society and staunch religious beliefs. We somehow believe we have to put up with it and just keep praying and go to church more. We have heard story after story of how, through the faith and patience of one partner, the other partner eventually turned into the most loving, faithful, dedicated spouse. When that happens, it is beautiful. More often than not, however, prayer and regular attendance at church, in itself, is not going to get them to change. They have to want to, then they have to make a continuous effort to change. Neither of which comes easily.

Yes, marriage has challenges. What we need to be discussing is what reasonable and acceptable challenges look like, as opposed to unnecessary and unjust ones.

Do I have to have sex with that man because my husband wants to sleep with his wife? What do I have to do to keep my family together? How far? Where is the line? Are you okay with that? Do you have a choice? What does a committed relationship look like?

What does it mean to have a choice in a marriage? Did you know you are allowed to tell your husband you don't want to have sex with him? If he forces or coerces you, that's rape. As long as it is your choice and you are doing it because *you* want to do it, then the parameters of what is "okay" and "normal" can be fairly wide. No judgment here. As long as you are into it and not going along with it just to keep the peace then the boundaries of your relationship are purely your own. There are many healthy relationships that fall within a variety of different lifestyles. If it's working for you, then that's not what we're talking about, and only you get to decide what works for you and what doesn't.

Let's just take a moment to pause and recap this section:

- When you are doing something against your beliefs, betraying your own integrity, or allowing your boundaries to be trampled, that is unhealthy.
- It is not your role to just "make it work."
- Marriage can be hard, but it shouldn't always be *that* hard.

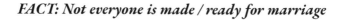

FACT: Not everyone is made / ready for marriage

One thing we need to realize is that not everyone is ready for or even *made* for marriage. Just because they *say* they want to get married or because you are ready, doesn't mean they are actually ready. Make sure you know the person before you get married. Don't expect marriage to fix it and certainly don't fall for the idea that children will fix it.

> *My mom used to always say, "Those things you think are cute now will probably annoy you later, and those things that annoy you now will only get worse." Why do we think at 20 years old we know so much more about love than those women who have been married 30 years? I'm still trying to figure that out.*

Those bad habits will only get worse. Some men change drastically when they get married or have kids. For the most part, though, the bad habits don't go away completely. If they tend to be lazy or controlling, they will continue to be. If they party too much, they will continue. Most young men begin growing out of these behaviors by about 25 years old, or when they start their first "real" jobs.[3] That is about when the frontal cortex is fully developed and maturity takes over. We just want to encourage you to not overlook these behaviors early in your relationships. Give yourself time to fully evaluate them and determine if that is the type of person you want to be around for the rest of your life.

Downplaying or Dissociating From the Abuse

Regardless of the type or severity of the abuse, victims will often downplay or even dissociate from the abuse entirely. This language is closely related to normalizing the behavior we discussed previously in the sense that if we downplay the behaviors enough, they will eventually fit into what we would consider "normal" behaviors. From there, we would only need to make a few tweaks like adding a date night or a little counseling. Otherwise, we have a perfectly healthy relationship, at least that's the lie we tell ourselves.

Stories we tell ourselves:

- But he doesn't hit me.
- But that's not me.
- I wouldn't still be in this relationship if it was abusive.
- I wouldn't have married an abuser -- I'm not stupid!
- It's not really bad enough to leave (especially in marriage).
- It could be worse.
- I can't be abused. I'm not even worthy of being abused. Who would want to abuse me?

When we downplay the behavior, we experience a disconnect between what we are experiencing and what we feel. "If it's not *that* bad, why do I *feel* so bad about it?" We then begin to wonder, "What's wrong with *me* that I'm so unhappy in this fairly "normal" relationship?"

When we experience this cognitive dissonance, our brains start trying to level it out. Instead of adjusting our perspective on the behavior, we try to change how we *feel* about it. As strong as our brains are, they just can't trick our hearts into feeling different. Now, we start doubting ourselves, our feelings, experiences, and even judgment.

Although not exclusive to abusive situations, victims often engage in the practice of dissociating. We don't want to associate with the stereotype that we ourselves have assigned to abused women, a.k.a. *"...but that's not me."* We don't want to believe we made a poor choice, but we don't want to think of ourselves as fitting all the other stereotypes that come to mind. Perhaps you think of them as uneducated, lower class of poor upbringing, using foul language, making poor choices or anything else. In an effort to separate ourselves from these stereotypes, we tell ourselves stories that downplay and dissociate ourselves from the abuse. So, we put as much separation between us as possible through our language, actions and ultimately, beliefs.

This phenomenon doesn't exist only in cases of stereotypes associated with abuse. We see this with a number of marginalized groups, whether by people within certain racial groups separating themselves from the stereotype by dissociating from their own race, women in the workplace separating themselves from working moms, working moms belittling stay-at-home moms, and on and on . This dangerous and unhealthy practice may give the individual leverage and improve their reception by their peers in the moment, but in the long-run, it further perpetuates the negative stereotypes of that group because it has been promoted by someone with authority on the subject: someone from the group in question.

> *I have seen women in the workplace criticize moms for being home with their sick children or needing to leave early to attend a function. They use it as leverage to boost their own status. By differentiating themselves from the other working moms, they separate themselves from the stereotype in hopes of being accepted by the primary group, which is typically the males and higher status women in the office.*

Stories Others Tell Victims:

What makes this pattern even more dangerous is when *other* people begin joining in on the subject. We often turn to others for a reality check. *"Am I crazy? Do I have a right to feel this way?"* We may not always phrase it like that. It may come out sounding more like, *"I know I'm blowing this up, but..."* or *"I'm just overreacting, but it really bothers me when...".* It may sound like, *"Am I crazy to think..."* or *"I just need to get it together."*

Post on Social Media: *Do you think this is true?*

Reference Quote: *Cheating is a part of the ups and downs of a relationship. Every man is gonna hurt u, u just gotta find that one worth hurting for. Millions of happy wives have been cheated on & abused but they fought for their marriage to work. If you're not willing to fight for love then stay single.*

First Comment: *Yes it's true.*

My Response: *I think it's telling that this is coming from a man. This is absolutely NOT true and not okay. It is NOT normal to be cheated on and abused in a relationship. Saying that putting up with this behavior is "fighting for love" is a lie. It's a way of normalizing and justifying the behavior, making women feel wrong for thinking they deserve better. Ups and downs are one thing. Cheating and abuse are NOT part of ups and downs. You deserve better. Keep setting your standards higher and you will have the relationship you want. This is not an area to settle or accept this type of thinking.*

Victims frequently reach out to others trying to get a sense of reality, only to be told that what they are experiencing is totally normal, not that bad, and they just need to accept it. Again, it doesn't always come out that way. It may sound like, "Oh yeah. So-and-so's husband does nothing. You should be glad yours works." "Girl, you just need a drink. Everything's gonna be fine." "I know. My husband does that all the time. Drives me crazy." We may think we are supporting each other, but we are actually promoting a very dangerous belief that normal relationships are fairly abusive, and that those abusive relationships are therefore healthy. Instead of getting the support she needs, the victim walks away downplaying the abuse even more.

The reality is, others can't possibly know exactly what you are going through because they don't live in your reality. Every time you doubt yourself or say you're crazy, *you* aren't living in your reality either. You are living in the *context* of a healthy relationship, but you are not actually *in* a healthy relationship.

Behaviors that may be fairly normal in a healthy relationship are not healthy in an abusive relationship. A partner encouraging you to fight for a promotion or commenting on your choice of outfits, when out of a place of love and support, is very healthy and positive. When those same comments come from a place of manipulation or criticism as a play for power, that is not healthy in the least.

When it comes to recognizing abusive relationships, sometimes we can't see it until someone else points it out to us and/or we actually see it on paper. Seeing the behaviors stacked up, one after another, we can more clearly see the pattern emerge. It can be more difficult to downplay when we see one example after another. Single incidences rarely tell the complete story, especially from the outside looking in. As tempting as it may be to downplay someone's experiences,, we encourage you to listen to their experiences, validate their feelings, and offer to support them however you can.

Another concept that downplays or even normalizes abuse is comparison. It is physically painful to hear someone belittling another's experience by comparing it to someone else's. The sad part is, we often don't even use our *own* experiences to devalue someone else's. As soon as someone starts talking, our brains begin scouring history to come up with anything that tops what the other person is going through. We will talk about trauma stacking a bit later, but abuse doesn't all have the same impact on individuals. Someone experiencing early stages of abuse for a limited time may have fewer internal scars than someone experiencing abuse for years and potentially multiple relationships. Giving someone advice based on a totally different situation can be damaging, especially if it is not realistic for them to apply those same principles successfully. They may already feel like a failure, and hearing how someone else overcame in ways that they can't is further damaging.

Examples of comparison statements we use:

- Here's my experience and how we pulled through it.
- So-and-so went through something way worse.

Ten years and I was completely and utterly spent. I was supporting our entire family working three different jobs all from home. I had given up pursuing my dream career that had great traction because he could not sustain a job. His priorities were not our family, our marriage or really anything other than drinking, doing heavy drugs, partying and playing music in the studio. (It was a huge outdoor shed that he had convinced me to use part of my retirement for so that he wasn't playing music in the house anymore and waking the babies. We had two with a third on the way at that point.)

Needless to say, his choices and behaviors had greatly and continued to impact our lives daily. It was not conducive to raising children and I was so drained carrying the load of everything.

In one of those moments where I could just feel it so heavily upon me, I spoke about a few things to a dear friend at the time. I remember just crying on her couch as our kids played. I know I divulged way more than I probably intended to but once the floodgates were open, and I felt safe with her just listening. I shared the dark things, the shameful things, and my raw heart.

I don't recall her giving me too much advice, but most of her responses had something to do with someone she knew, her experiences or Church. Although, she did listen and I didn't feel judged.

She remained a dear friend, as our children were close in age and we both loved scrapbooking. Her family was dear to me and still to this day cherish the friendship we had.

As time went on my life situations were not improving and quickly sliding down major slopes I knew I needed to get myself and my three children out of. We were separated and I was trying to figure out life and build a new foundation for myself. Things were complicated and overwhelming. My friend was aware of a good majority of the details.

After my husband had reached out to them (bear in mind he didn't like them the entire time we were together and they didn't care for him either), my friend showed up at my house. I wasn't aware of his actions at this time so I was for sure caught off guard. As she was talking to me and telling me how he had gone and cried out to them and pleaded for their help, she felt called to come talk to me and give me a copy of a movie called Fireproof that would be the answer and solve all of my problems. Not his problems; my problems.

"*Oh my gosh I would just leave, if my husband ever did that.*" Even in the greatest of relationships, ending it is not an easy thing where you can "just leave," but when someone says that to you in response to hearing or seeing just a brief snippet of how you are being treated, it feels like the person saying it thinks that "just leaving" is easy and simple to do. "Just leave" isn't a choice some have.

This pattern of comparison of one-upping perpetuates the idea that victims don't have a right to their feelings, to feel bad about a certain situation because somewhere in space and time, someone has it a little worse than them. Instead of living in their reality, they are told to go live in someone else's for a while to see how bad it could be. Equally as bad, victims are berated for feeling that way and told to "count their blessings." As much as we believe in the power of gratitude, training your brain to focus on the positives is not going to change the fact that you are living with an abusive partner who takes every opportunity to hurt you, take advantage of you, and make your life miserable. Although there is always *someone* experiencing a worse situation than you, it does not take away from the fact that yours may be pretty bad. It isn't fair to downplay that experience, and that practice perpetuates the dangerous thinking that the victim's situation isn't serious enough because there is someone who has it worse. It's just ridiculous.

> *When I would see a movie with a scene of a husband throwing his wife against the wall, kids cowering in the corner, I would sigh and think, it could be worse. My mantra was always, "At least he doesn't hit me." When someone would explain why they were getting a divorce, they could always point to a single, powerful thing. "He cheated on me." What did I have to complain about? I had a nice house, food on the table, and a comfortable bed. I mean, he did cheat on me, but that was early on. He was drunk. He thought I was okay with it. Anyway, that was years ago. If I had a problem with it, I should have left him then. I just needed to let that go and move on. He didn't throw things or yell. When I tried to list it off in my head, imagining that I was explaining it to someone else, the list was endless, but everything seemed so small. One thing wasn't big enough to be the thing. I couldn't pinpoint exactly what was wrong. Since I couldn't explain it with a single, powerful thing, it didn't feel valid.*

As humans, we have a need to quantify our experiences, to know how they stack up and fit into the bigger picture and to know how we should feel about it. We use comparison to do that. As long as there is someone farther along than we are, especially if that person is handling it well, then we aren't justified in feeling bad about it. It's really difficult to put  abuse on a sliding scale. It's impossible to compare experiences from two different people and say which is worse than the other. Worse how? How do you compare physical and mental scars? How do you compare manipulation and threats? It's all so different, and however it makes you feel completely valid. Regardless of how far down the hypothetical scale you may be, anything above 0 is abuse. Abuse isn't continuous; it's categorical.

When I was pregnant with my oldest, someone asked me, "How pregnant are you?" I simply replied, "Yes."

It is very difficult to put abuse on a scale. Either you are abused or you aren't. The degree to which that abuse affects the victim differs, but it is less based on the degree and type of abuse itself and more so on various other factors: mental state, length of abuse, incidences within a given timeframe, involvement of children, pets, others, etc.[4]

Trauma stacks. How many occurrences and time frames of traumatic experiences play a significant role in the intensity of the trauma. There is no magic formula to know the severity of the impact of abuse. To make any kind of comparison is unhealthy and dangerous.

We need to talk about our experiences, but not to compare notes. We need to normalize experiences by sharing that it happens, not that it's okay. When we don't talk about it, we remain in a bubble, thinking we are alone. It creates an environment of doubt and confusion, keeping us locked in the crazy within our own minds. We need to be able to share with each other safely. When we are silent, our abusers hold all the power.

Thinking it/he will change:

- But he can / will change.
- I can fix this.

For years I prayed that my husband would change. I just needed a little change to make life more bearable. All I needed was a glimmer of hope. When I threatened to leave, he promised he would change. Of course, any change was temporary and not nearly enough. As soon as the real threat was gone, he was back to his old ways. Still, the idea that he could change was enough to keep me holding on. It's that hope that you can still make it work; the hope that he cares enough to change, to try.

Yes, many men can, and do, change for their families or to maintain a relationship. The reality is, most do not, especially if you are still there. Pain or the thought of the pain of loss can be a portion of what convinces a person to change. If we take on our abusers' pain, in their stead, not only do we take on that which we can't do anything about (since it isn't actually ours), we deprive them of the pain they need to motivate them to change. If you are there, serving as a buffer between them and their pain, why would they feel the need to change, when they can just manipulate you into changing to accommodate their needs and whims? It often takes a true breaking point for someone to bring about real change. In the case of addicts, family members are often called enablers when they provide the addict with money, a place to stay, or a back-up plan. Addicts often don't make the effort to change until they are at rock bottom, out of options.

Why do we use analogies like these? Because we know them. They are familiar to us even if we have never experienced it. We've seen it play out like this in media and community experience. It brings a visual story to your head instantly. Take a moment to see what comes to your mind. Now, keep it there as we make the tie in.

Abusive relationships are very similar to addictive patterns. One person will stay, thinking they can be supportive and help the other become better. Unfortunately, when they are no longer at rock bottom, the motivation to show up differently is gone. Regardless of how deeply they may want to, they have lost a critical component of implementing those actions. Rather than waiting around while the person decides to turn things around, it is imperative that you get out. Remove yourself and your children from the home if necessary and go somewhere safe. If the person is truly willing, they can seek help, hold onto the improvements for a while, then and only then can you discuss getting back together. There is nothing wrong with giving someone a chance to turn things around and holding onto that hope, but do not put your life on hold, and potentially in danger, waiting for it to happen. The reality is, it rarely works that way.

I begged him to change for years. I shared my feelings, explained why it hurt me, and offered rewards to replace what he was giving up. He would agree to change and would even appear to sincerely try, apologizing when he would mess up. It didn't take long before I caught him doing things behind my back again, and eventually he wouldn't even try to hide it anymore. When I left, he called me for a year, telling me about his efforts. He talked to the pastor, saw a counselor, joined a church, got a job, changed his entire look and wardrobe. He admitted to his addictions and joined several different programs. He contacted my family members, asking them to pray for us and had the ministers at church praying publicly. He joined various groups he knew I would approve of. He sent me gifts and wrote sweet notes; things he had not done since we first started dating 10 years before. If I had been meeting him for the first time, I would have probably fallen for him all over again.

For certain, the moment a victim starts to stand up, showing signs of leaving, abusers begin to see the potential consequences. They will plead for another chance, maybe even apologize and beg for forgiveness, show overt kindness, and make promises to change. Think about how many times they have already made these statements. Abusers may even believe what they are saying, thinking they really can and will change. Generally speaking, the ultimate goal is still to remain the controlling partner, keep the victim from leaving, and avoid facing any consequences for their behaviors. When the victim remains, promises and/or caring behaviors continue for a time, but more often than not, the abuser returns to the abusive pattern previously established. How long it takes for an abuser to return to their abusive behaviors can vary, but typically, the abuser returns once they feel like the victim has forgiven them, let their guard down, and stopped showing signs of leaving.

Talking about these things gets it out in the open, allowing both partners to have the opportunity to **calmly** discuss the situation. Journaling your experiences gives you tangible things you can reference when having those conversations. Addressing the situation and creating a plan gives you a sense of control in the situation. Rather than feeling like a helpless bystander, you are taking the reins of your own life and directing where you want it to go. Hopefully, your partner will come along with you. If not, be prepared to take the outlined action. Following through on this step is critical for the last chance of change.

Although we don't want to spend a ton of time on change, we do want to take just a moment to discuss propensity, or capability, for change. Because it is often our default to think abusers can change, we want to give you just a little more guidance and direction when it comes to working through it.

Identifying Propensity to Change

Believing that the abuser can and will change is a common reason victims stay in abusive relationships. Can people change? Yes, absolutely people generally *can* change. However, change can only happen when the person takes full responsibility for their behavior and stops blaming their actions on you, childhood, stress, work, drinking, temper, or anything else. Some changes even require professional support. Until that is happening on a regular and consistent basis, the likelihood of lasting change diminishes. Abuse will likely continue because abusers have deep emotional and psychological issues that need to be addressed.

Signs that your abuser is not changing:

- Abuser minimizes the behaviors or denies the seriousness of how it is/was
- Abuser continues to blame others for their behaviors
- Abuser claims the victim is the one who is abusive
- Pressures you to go to couples counseling
- Abuser tells the victim that they owe them another chance
- Victim has to keep encouraging the abuser to get or continue getting help

- Abusers says they can't change without their victim staying and supporting them
- Abuser seeks sympathy from their victim, children or anyone else close or around
- Abuser expects something from the victim in return or exchange for getting help
- Abuser pressures the victim to make decisions about the relationship, therefore alleviating themselves from the responsibility and putting themselves in the victim role to outsiders and new people they bring in. (The pattern continues)....

Tips on how to identify propensity to change and plan for change:

Journal and look for patterns.

- Journaling is a great way to document the intensity and frequency of behaviors. It can serve as a reality check, providing clear evidence of your experiences
- Include behaviors, context, and how it made you feel.
- Example: The last five times he came home, he was grumpy. I tried talking to him about it, and this is what happened...."
- Journaling isn't about rubbing his face in it but rather for you to look back on and see patterns in behaviors and feelings.

Determine / Examine if this is what you want.

Tell him how you feel.

- It is important to talk to your partner about how their behaviors are making you feel. Using scripts like, "When you _____, I felt _____. I don't like feeling that way."

- Example: "When you stormed in, I felt scared. I was walking on eggshells, and I don't like feeling that way. Let's talk about that."
- Say "no" or set a boundary and observe how they respond. If they accept the no/respect the boundary, awesome, if not and they get angry or try to convince or coerce you into retracting and going along with what they want, pay attention
- It is important to have these conversations, test the water. If you don't talk to your partner about their behavior, you don't know how they'll respond. If he yells at you and blames you or tries to justify it away rather than acknowledging your feelings, it will give you good information on their intentions.
- Taking the risk and having the conversation can help save potentially healthy relationships that just need to be guided back on the right path.

If you are in a dangerous situation, leave immediately.

If your partner acknowledges your feeling and their role in this feelings and is willing to change, outline a plan for change.

- Include the behaviors that need to change
- What those positive behaviors would look like
- Timeframe for change
- Clear consequences for no change
- You should both understand and agree to the plan. It isn't fair to have expectations that your partner isn't aware of. If you truly want to give them a chance to change, you need to make sure they understand the rules of the game.

No one can *get* someone else to change. It is not our intent to get you through the change process. It is recognizing the problem and getting help, whatever that help is. If you want more information on this topic, we encourage you to look at other resources specifically designed for behavior change.

He talked about his past abuse, bad relationships, and greatest fears. I wanted to help him, and I knew I could fix this. At least I could if I was any good at what I was trained to do. I could fix this, right?

We want to reiterate that some people will not change until they have reached the bottom, and others will only change when it suits their needs. It is not your job to wait around. If they are hurting you with their words, actions, or behaviors, you have the right to step aside. When you follow through and leave, they may be left with no option but to implement real change. Don't give in too soon, or if you have left, return too soon. Abusers often make changes just long enough to gain control again. It must be real, true change. Otherwise, you have walked right back into the same, abusive relationship, maybe even worse this time around.

Blame

External Blame: Placing the blame on the victim

When presented with a challenge or problem, it is a natural tendency for people to attempt to fix that problem. In order to do that, they often must establish the cause, or what (who) is to blame. Once the cause or blame is established, only then can they proceed with telling the victim how to fix said problem.

In addition to trying to fix the problem, in many situations, it somehow makes us feel better to place blame, like we have a level of control in our own lives if we can see where the victim went wrong or how they did something to bring it upon themselves. *We* would never put ourselves in that situation, so we don't have to worry about it. Our loved ones would never put themselves in that situation, so we know they are safe.

Have you noticed how when you hear that someone passed in a car accident, the first thing you ask is, "Were they wearing their seat belt?" Or perhaps, "Were they drinking?" Or even, "Were they driving too fast?" We are wired to look for the cause and find a solution. What we're really finding comfort in is the fact that we are somehow protected from bad things happening to us because we are safer than that. Placing blame is assigning responsibility, and that gives the facade of protection.

It also protects us from the pain of knowing that bad things happen to good, innocent people. It is painful to watch a child suffer from cancer or another terminal illness. We can't understand why it would happen to them or how in the world it is fair. They are innocent, free from guilt. There is no reason it should have happened to them. We ache at the thought that it could possibly happen to our own children. We can't even fathom it. When we can find a reason for someone's suffering, it allows us to have less negative emotion around it. We don't have to imagine the horrors of an innocent soul being harmed at the hands of an abuser. It hurts when we can't find a reason for it. As soon as we can find one fleck of fault, a portion of that pain is released and we begin to feel better. Our brains are wired to escape the pain, and blaming the victim is often the way we handle intense pain like observing the suffering of another.

In the following pages, we will discuss some phrases outsiders use that place blame on the victim.

- **Didn't you have some red flags?**

Of course we see red flags. We all do. Didn't you see flags that your spouse was out of shape or didn't like exercise, or that they were a compulsive shopper or any other numerous character flaws? Of course you did. Even so, early on they can be hard to recognize or we ignore them altogether. We are often focused on the wrong things. Abusers take full advantage of those insecurities or weaknesses in previous relationships. We are so focused on those areas that we don't pay attention to the things that may be more important.

Questions like "Didn't you have some red flags?" are actually pretty insulting to the victim. The implication is that we saw the red flags, recognized them as such, and completely ignored them. Or, we were so ignorant that we didn't see them at all. As we mentioned earlier, it is actually somewhere in between. It's like trying to beat a train at the railroad crossing. No one ever tries it thinking they won't make it. Even when they see the train, they either don't think it's coming that fast, or that maybe the train is slowing down. There are any number of things going through their heads. On occasion, a true daredevil believes they only have a slim chance of crossing the tracks, but for the most part, they see the train and think, for whatever reason, that the threat isn't as "real" as it is.

That's what red flags in relationships are like. Maybe we actually didn't see them. It's possible the lights were off and our music was too loud to hear the horn, but most likely, we saw the train and thought we were faster. We didn't recognize it as the threat it actually was until it was too late.

Sprinkled throughout this book, we have been alluding to red flags. You probably even noticed the flag illustration indicating those sections. So, what exactly is a red flag? The term is used to indicate and draw attention to danger. It is a symbol that an environment has become unsafe, whether an alert on the control panels of an airplane or a flag placed on the beach. Red is the universal sign for danger or alarm. When a red flag is waving, it signals the highest level of threat. It is indeed to draw your attention immediately and cause you to begin seeking additional information regarding the target of the alert. In relationships, they aren't always as obvious as the person asking the question "*Didn't you have some red flags?*" is suggesting.

In dating relationships, red flags are very rarely waving so boldly. There isn't necessarily a clear sign that says *this thing needs attention, pay attention to me or warning!* It can be something that makes you uncomfortable, doesn't line up with previous expectations, or something that just doesn't sit right with you. Rather than one big flag, there are often just a bunch of little ones, none measuring up to much on their own. In hindsight, it seems like that should be even *more* obvious with so many flags. In reality, they are often so small that you don't even notice. Rather than a flag waving high above the water, it looks like a few sticks or blades of grass barely poking above the surface. It isn't until you've waded out into the water that you realize how many and just how big they really are.

Patterns of behavior can also be red flags, but again, they are often difficult to identify and only emerge when you recognize the pattern. Abusers get away with it for so long because they are cunning. They aren't waving huge red flags and they certainly aren't outlining a pattern. Instead, they are drawing the victim's attention where they want it, which is away from the red flags. They capitalize on the victim's insecurities, past relationships, and desires to highlight exactly what he wants her to see. Sadly, recognition of red flags and patterns arise mostly only in hindsight.

> *Recently, my husband and I were going on vacation. Packing before a vacation is always a little stressful and difficult, especially with five kids. Amid the swimsuits, toiletries, emergency kit, suitcases, books, headphones, activities, and snacks, I suddenly realized that this time felt different. I didn't feel the stress and anxiety I used to feel. I didn't feel the pressure to have everything just right, to make sure and not forget anything yet not pack everything. This time, it felt almost too easy. No yelling or fighting, no throwing clothes around the room. I was so struck by the stark difference in the experiences that I actually journaled about it afterward. How did I not know that my experience was so abnormal? How did I not know it was wrong? In the moment, sometimes you just don't.*

Additionally, red flags are unique to each person. What's important to one person might not be important to another because they don't relate with that particular concern or it may not be part of their moral compass. It's hard to say what should and should not be important to someone, especially from the outside. It's hard to come up with a specific list of red flags, but below is a list of things you can begin considering and asking yourself if it's truly okay with you.

How they respond to situations of stress or pressure

- Life will always present challenges. How they respond to pressure now will likely not change. If they get aggressive or completely shut down, it will likely get worse, not better.

How they treat other people

- Are they kind and patient with hospitality workers? How do they respond when their order is wrong? Do they make fun of people with disabilities or get impatient with someone who doesn't understand? This says a lot about their true character.

How they handle being confronted or critiqued

- No one enjoys being critiqued, but it can be a valuable part of growing. If they get agitated, angry or super withdrawn after criticism, it may be difficult to grow together in their future.

How do they handle "no" or the setting of a boundary

- If a person freaks out when you refuse to jump when they say jump or ask them to stop doing something, that's an indication of controlling/manipulative behavioral patterns.

Trends or issues in past or current relationships

- We so badly want to believe that the fault in previous relationships rests solely in their previous partners. If you see a pattern emerge in your partner's past, be aware of the common denominator. Issues are rarely one-sided. If he can't point out how he contributed to the relationship's demise, he is likely hiding, or failing to confront something.

- Be particularly wary of men who describe their exes as "crazy."

Missing information; parts of their life that they don't talk about or where there are significant gaps/information that doesn't line up.

- Sure, we will all have parts of our pasts that we don't want to talk about, especially on a first date. When you begin getting serious with someone, these skeletons should generally begin falling out of the closet. If there are big chunks of time missing or parts of his past that are completely off limits, this could be a sign that he is hiding something that could significantly and negatively impact your relationship.

 Keep in mind that everything we have discussed in this book, no matter where it falls on the pendulum, should be a red flag. That doesn't mean you need to get hung up on it, but it is something to be aware of. Consider it, discuss it, address it. If you choose to continue to move forward with the relationship, make that conscious decision with full awareness of the behavior. However most people in these situations are making a decision based on justifying the behavior, thinking they can change it, thinking it isn't that big of a deal. They aren't paying attention, and when they are, they don't fully consider the implications. We know because we have been there too. If your gut is yelling, listen. Patterns emerge and we can see them more quickly when we become more diligent with our hearts and mind. Intuition is often simply a matter of our unconscious mind picking up on these patterns faster than our conscious mind. Learning to trust it is a huge piece of self-trust and self-esteem.

- **Why didn't you say anything?**

After my divorce, my family would often ask, "Why didn't you say anything? We had no idea." I remember one time I did mention my marital struggles with my mom. I was crying and asking her for advice. I remember being so incredibly lonely and had absolutely no one else to turn to. It had never been my intention to say a thing. I knew that my mom would never forget. If I wanted my marriage to have a chance, if I wanted my family to ever see my husband the way I did, then I couldn't tell them about the ugliness of our marriage. Besides, it was private between the two of us. I remember between sobs hearing my mom speak from a long silence. She simply said, "I'm going to kill him." After spending the rest of the call trying to convince her that I was overreacting and highlighting all of his good qualities, she decided not to get in her car and drive 900 miles to kill my husband in his sleep. It sounds supportive, but when a victim is not ready to admit they are in an abusive relationship or aren't ready to give up their relationship, this can push them deeper into the isolation. I vowed that day to never say anything negative about my husband or our marriage again, at least not to my family. I was still trying to convince everyone we were okay.

Oftentimes, victims *do* say something, but those around them aren't listening. When a victim opens up a little, perhaps testing the waters, they are often met with many of the responses we are discussing here. Normalizing the behavior, encouraging them to power through, downplaying the behaviors, comparing their situation to someone else's, and changing the subject discourages victims from speaking up again. Rather than feeling heard, they feel judged. It further reinforces the doubts they already had, and they are even less likely to say something next time.

Sadly, it isn't just others who aren't listening. At some point, victims stop listening to themselves too. We stop trusting ourselves and start believing what others are saying. It takes someone hearing something seven times before it sticks.[5] When it comes to victims sharing their experiences, they often don't make it that far.

There are many reasons why victims choose to keep their abuse to them-selves. As we have discussed, they often don't even realize they are in an abusive relationship. As abuse gets more extreme, even recognizable to the victim, the reasons for not saying anything intensify as well. Even once the victim knows they need help, the risks are often far too high to say anything. So often, victims report the abuse and are returned to their abuser after a slap on the wrist or a lengthy "trial" that rules in the favor of the abuser. The victim is hand-delivered back to the abuser, and the abuse continues, more intense than ever.

Another reason is that many victims don't recognize abuse for what it is. They think they can try harder or make the abuser love them more. Maybe if they were a better wife or housekeeper, then things will get better. *If only I am _____ enough, things will improve. Or, if only he loved me more, things would change.* Victims often see the situation as their own fault, so why would they say something?

Finally, many of us are taught to keep private matters private, and to not speak negatively about our partners. We know that once our support circle sees our partner in a negative light, the relationship is doomed, so we keep it locked inside.

On more than a few occasions the local police were called to our home and each time a similar scene would play out. "Hi, we are here about a call. Can you step out here Sir and talk to us? If it's ok, these two officers are going to stay and talk here." As he is walking out the door I can hear them already chumming it up, because of course he leads with, "Hey I'm one of you. A 20 year military police officer, US NAVY," and so on and so on. By the time they reach the driveway they seem to be old pals, laughing it up and sharing war stories.

The other two officers would ask simple questions like, "Are you bleeding?" and then nothing else. They would say, "You are two grown adults, you can work this out right?" "You don't look hurt ma'am." It never felt like they were actually there to help me or my children.

As the abuser comes closer to getting caught, it doesn't "scare them straight," it does the opposite. The abuse often intensifies, escalates. Either types of abuse are expanded or the current abuse moves along the sliding scale to a more extreme level.

- **Why didn't you just leave?**

Fortunately, most people don't ever experience the true horrors of being in an extremely abusive relationship. It's hard to comprehend how dehumanizing and terrifying it can be. Nonetheless, more women than not experience domestic abuse in one form or another. Many never reach the point of sheer terror and physical abuse, but psychological abuse can be equally damaging and make it extremely difficult to leave.

Additionally, most people don't understand the difficulties and challenges associated with leaving an abusive relationship. This isn't too surprising, though, because we often speak flippantly of divorce in general. It is a strange dichotomy. On one hand, those suffering in bad relationships are told to "tough it out" and reminded they "made a commitment," on the other hand, they are told to "just leave the bastard" or are held as responsible for what happens to them because they stayed. As a society, we speak out of both sides of our mouths creating a whirlwind of confusion for victims.

The realities of leaving a bad relationship, especially when a marriage is involved, are much more complex and difficult. Most people on the outside of the relationship don't experience the fear of losing everything or face the reality of themselves or their family, friends, or children being hurt by their abuser. They don't experience the psychological damage that accompanies years of abuse and how feelings of unworthiness can drive them to stay. Abusers hobble their victims in every way conceivable, and yet people still have the audacity to ask, "Why didn't you just leave?" It sounds so easy: just leave.

Even on the outside, I still ask myself that same question. "Why didn't I just leave? Why did I stay so long?" When you aren't living in a moment, it is impossible to fully understand the decisions made in that moment. Even after the fact, and after writing this book, it still sometimes baffles me.

Economically, leaving a relationship can be devastating or impossible. Psychologically, victims are often too damaged or weak to even consider the possibility. Physically and logistically, victims may be too weak or unable to leave, whether physically restrained or the abuser having removed all forms of transportation or communication with anyone. Oftentimes, victims have been so isolated from others that they have no one to reach out to for support. Their leaving and standing up for themselves activates muscles that haven't been used. If you don't walk for ten years, how are you going to get up and go run a marathon?

- **I would never let that happen to me.**
- **Why did you allow it to happen?**

This is where we get the idea that it's our fault because we allowed it to happen. We didn't stop it, we didn't put our foot down, we trained them that it's okay. All of these ideas don't mean we are to blame. Each person's behavior is no one's responsibility but their own. The abuser's reliance on abusive behaviors is their responsibility alone. We remove the blame and responsibility from them when we take it on ourselves. Sure, we may have made choices that "allowed" the behavior to continue by not leaving or by putting up with it. That choice is our responsibility, but that doesn't mean it is our fault, and it certainly doesn't mean we have to stay in that situation forever. To allow something to happen under stress does not mean you should take the blame. Like prisoners of war, they do things that are against their morals because they are in a state of distress and feel they have no choice. We excuse it or justify it away, just to survive.

It is also possible to "allow" one abusive behavior in an attempt to reduce the likelihood of even worse behaviors or to avoid a different result. In this sense, victims are making choices between two bad options which means it isn't really a choice at all. Victims can get so used to the abusive behaviors that they simply begin doing what the abuser wants before they even ask. Rather than wait to be told or wait for the argument, they preemptively engage in behaviors that they know are expected of them. In this vein, victims are abusing themselves before the abuser can.

> *I was watching the show, Little Fires Everywhere, when I heard the words, "You didn't make good choices, you had good choices." In one small statement, my heart broke open. This! These words captured so much of what I try to acknowledge all the time. I can not compare my life to others because of the trauma I faced, the circumstances of my reality, and the fear that held my body. I didn't have good choices available; the only options were bad or worse. Say yes and maybe extend the length of the good time; say no and suffer unknown consequences. It was a constant balance of knowing that I couldn't really choose what I wanted because the consequences would be worse. So, I would go along with what he said and do whatever I could to keep the peace.*

As we mentioned before, often people assume that the victim has a choice between a good option and a bad one. Between an obvious right answer and an obvious wrong one. In reality, there often isn't a good choice. It is between a horrific choice and a terrible one. Even the "choice" to stay is not choosing abuse over paradise. It is like choosing a situation you think you can handle with losing your children, being unable to feed them, being homeless or even being hunted down and killed by your abuser.

We all have choices, but that doesn't make what they did to you right. It doesn't mean we deserve it because we put ourselves in that position. No one has the right to take advantage of you because of your choices.

It is not your job to train an adult man. In healthy relationships you grow together. If not, it feels like you have to raise them and if you don't, you are "letting" them get away with bad behavior. No. That's not true. It is not your fault and it is not your responsibility.

Accept the amount of responsibility that you should, but not more. When it's in the past, we need to let it go and forgive ourselves, but in the moment, we need to increase knowledge, awareness, and power to help women take control back. We need/want a certain amount of control so that we can fix it or figure out how it happened so we can avoid it. We need/want a cause and effect. We are constantly in that need. In the victim's head, we take on all of that. It's a natural desire to need to figure it out. Responsibility versus Blame = circular. This could also be called a victim cycle. You must take responsibility for your actions and the role that you played in your circumstances. It's part of healing. That does not mean you are at fault and take blame. It means you are human. Stop apologizing.

- **I thought you were stronger/smarter/raised better than that.**

My mom once said, "I thought you were stronger than that." The reality is, I did too. I still wonder how in the world I allowed that to happen. I feel like a failure, but it happened so slowly. I didn't realize what was happening at the time. I wish I hadn't allowed my naivety, love, and guilt to drive my decisions. I wanted so badly to be the ideal wife; I never once saw the situation for what it was. I just knew I was "smarter" than that. I didn't have any red flags because I thought I was too smart for that. I am educated, I have a great job, great savings account, and a great life, how did this happen? People ask me all of the time, "How did you let that happen to you? I thought you were stronger than that." I thought I was stronger than that too. Now I question my own intelligence and ability. If I let this happen to me, then how can I be successful in anything? I must be a complete and total idiot. I still catch myself falling into those same thought patterns.

Related to how victims "allowed" this to happen, assuming that a victim should be strong, smart, or raised well enough to avoid abuse reveals how little we actually understand about abuse. Such as, the process of psychological breakdown, the cultural influences, and the deliberate intent of the abuser. Additionally, it is a round-about way of placing blame right back onto the victim while simultaneously continuing the destructive mental abuse and gaslighting that got the victim there in the first place. Victims blame themselves and take full responsibility. *How did I let this happen to me?* As a society, we promote this mentality.

You aren't an idiot. You aren't lower in society. You aren't dumb or damaged. What happened to you and against you is not who you are. Someone took advantage of you. You have nothing to be ashamed of. Abusers take your strength, intelligence, and compassion, all that makes up who you are, and use it against you. You are smarter than that, but your confidence in yourself is being broken down while your compassion and love for others is being built up and taken advantage of.

> *I was a kickass caretaker and homemaker. I loved taking care of people. He capitalized on that and used it against me.*

> *I was getting my doctorate in psychology. If he was manipulating me, I would see it.*

> *That's what abusers do. They use who you are to abuse you.*

Internal Blame

It is human nature to try to understand the world through cause and effect. We want to know what caused a situation so we can avoid the same mistake. This often comes out sounding a lot like blame.

> *Who did it? Whose fault is it? What did you do wrong? We want to know where to point the finger.*

When it comes to understanding someone's behavior, we engage in what psychologists call attribution. Attributional theories attempt to answer the question of whether or not the behavior or response was due to an external, outside factor or something inherent within the individual. Said another way, did something cause that person to act that way, or is he just a complete jerk?

Although men and women apply internal and external attributions to situations regularly, research shows that women *more frequently inappropriately* assign internal attribution to their own mistakes or downfalls and external attribution to the mistakes of others. They are also more likely to inappropriately assign external attribution to the mistakes of others, seeing it as outside of their control.[6] What this means is that when it comes to abusive behaviors, we are more likely to contribute external factors (justification) and place blame on ourselves (internal attribution). We are already wired to do this to ourselves. When society supports it by saying the same things, it serves to further embed this faulty way of thinking into the fabric of our minds.

- **It's my fault because I provoked him**

Even if we manage to not immediately place blame on ourselves, the words of others become part of our own belief system, part of our own language. Why did I let this happen? Maybe I am just an idiot for allowing him to act that way. That's just who he is, and I made the choice to stay. I provoked him too much. As we mentioned within each of the above statements, there is a level of control. We *need* to have some sense of control over our environment and our lives. If we truly believed we had no control or *choice*, there would be no hope left.

We can take responsibility for our choices, for our role, but we are never to blame for their actions. This is where it sometimes gets confusing. When a woman is walking home late at night and gets attacked, the first response is often, "she shouldn't have been out so late all alone." When a woman gets raped, the first question is often, "what was she wearing?"

- **When the victim starts victim-shaming**

Victim-shaming has become an all-too-common occurrence. Our first response is to find a way to blame the victim. We perpetuate this mentality in schools where females must follow strict guidelines so as not to be a distraction to the males. We have taken the blame off the perpetrator and placed it squarely on the victim. It is no wonder that we do the same thing to ourselves in abusive situations. Because we take the blame, we also believe it is somehow our responsibility to stay and fix it. *I got myself into this situation; I can or need to get myself out.* As a society, we prompt this thinking with phrases like, *You made your bed, now lie in it.* As long as victims keep believing these lies, giving abusers excuses, and staying stuck in broken patterns of thinking, they will never free ourselves of the physical and mental prison of victimization.

> *I have to constantly remind myself not to use phrases like, "you made me angry," or "why did you make me do that?" You cannot make someone feel a certain way, and no one can make you do something. It has become such a part of our language, though, that it just comes out naturally. When my son bumps into me and spills his drink or bounces off of me and hits the wall, he snaps, "see what you made me do!" He may have even hurt me in the process, but his first thought is to snap at me. It is a human tendency to blame, and to justify our own actions by recasting those we've harmed as having brought that harm on themselves.*

Abusers are adept at deflecting the blame back onto the victim. Over time, the victim stops questioning it and either begins to believe it herself or grows too weary to fight it. What we hear and tell ourselves over and over creates a neural pathway in the brain. Like a river carving a deep groove into rock, with repetition it becomes easier to follow that pathway and harder to create a new one.

Since the ultimate goal of the abuser is to control their partner's behavior, thereby achieving and maintaining power over their partners and getting their own needs and desires met quickly and completely, convincing a victim to blame and punish herself for doing anything that does not align with that goal is among the most diabolically effective tools in the abuser's arsenal.

There are also many secondary benefits of abuse for the perpetrator. An abuser may choose to be abusive because he finds it fun to terrorize his partner, because there is a release of tension in the act of abuse, because it demonstrates manhood, or because it is erotic for him. Abuse is a learned behavior that must be deliberately unlearned.[7] While it's always a good idea to self-reflect and take responsibility for one's part in any interpersonal dynamic, the abuser must be held accountable for their abusive behavior. Whether these behaviors are calculated or the result of a repeated failure to confront and correct abusive habits, the abuser is making the choice to leverage these behaviors to get what they want.

In the midst of abusive relationships, victims use words along with actions to create a "manageable" environment where they can have the best chance of getting through each day with as little disruption as possible. These words become shields used to deflect or deter the abuser from becoming abusive.

How often do you automatically agree to what is asked of you without taking the time to consider whether it is aligned with your values, interests, and integrity? Do you ever catch yourself using affectionate language even when you're feeling exactly the opposite of affectionate toward your partner? Victims are well-trained not only to jump when told to jump, but to ask "how high?" even before the word "jump" escapes their lips. This survival mechanism may keep victims safe initially, but it also opens them up to accusations (both internal and external) of dishonesty, manipulation, and failure to follow through on agreements.

For the sake of organization, we divide blame into external and internal blame, but the reality is, we don't need someone to help us place blame on ourselves. Victims repeat these same blame-directing phrases all the time. When effective, these phrases can serve to keep the victim in the abusive relationship because it keeps it manageable. *See, I can* handle it. It really *isn't* that bad. Because the blow-ups are reduced, it is easier to say, "See, he is a good person, or at least he can be." It is easier to justify or downplay the abuse because it feels almost bearable. It also makes it easier for the victim to blame themselves when a blow-up does occur. *I just didn't respond correctly* or *I really did provoke him. Had I just said/done the right thing, this all could have been avoided.*

Religious Justification

- You/I made a commitment before God
- God put you/us together
- You/I just need to give it to God
- "You just need to watch [religious movie] / read [religious text] / talk to [religious leader]"
- You/I just have to have enough faith and hope
- You/I just need to stick it out

Let's take a detour for a moment and talk about something that we've really struggled with and know that many of you probably have too: the Christian perspective of marriage. If you are not a follower of Christ, then feel free to move past this section, but you may have some of these beliefs as they are often ingrained into our society and part of your reality, whether you are a believer or not. Two people stand in front of an ordained minister, before God, and vow to love one another for better or worse, for richer or poorer, in sickness and in health, 'til death do you part.' It is not only a commitment to each other, but more significantly, a commitment to God. That promise is held over our heads like Moses holding the stone tablet with the Ten Commandments on it.

> *I felt like Ariel from The Little Mermaid closing my eyes and signing a magical scroll that God was holding in his clutches somewhere, opening it and waving it at me any time the thought of divorce crossed my mind.*

We are berated with this commitment from the pulpit with annual sermons on marriage and in marital seminars, where we are often sitting alone as the sole person trying to make our marriage work. Many marriage vows still emphasize *duty* rather than *equality*, and the final proclamation of unity is, "I now pronounce you man and wife."

Prior to the marriage, men attend parties celebrating their last days of freedom and are encouraged to sow their wild oats, while wedding and lingerie showers are focused on helping the woman satisfy her new husband's appetites and expectations. We are seeing a trend toward couple parties and showers celebrating union and preparing the household, and we do recognize that many bachelorette parties get just as wild as bachelor parties. That said, these are new trends combating traditions that date back to the 5th century B. C. when the Spartans would celebrate the groom's last night as a single man.[8]

When struggling in our relationships, we are often reminded to draw a circle around ourselves and commit to changing the person within the circle (ourselves), allowing the other person to do the same so both can come together in a stronger, more loving relationship. These are good sound practices to engage in for generally healthy individuals and relationships. However, when we are talking about a significantly unhealthy relationship or partner, these techniques can do more harm than good, keeping victims locked in a cycle of self-blame and false hope that they can fix the relationship if only they can transform themselves into the perfect partner. As we have mentioned throughout, many of these *good* principles only apply when *both* partners bring a certain level of maturity and willingness to the table. There are countless examples of relationships that have pulled through very dark times by engaging in these practices. We encourage you to evaluate the character of your partner in determining whether or not "making the relationship work" is either possible or desirable.

As an ally, be cautious of pushing these tactics on someone without a deep understanding of their unique situation. Encouraging a victim to stay in a mentally or physically abusive relationship and continue working on themselves in hopes that the abuser will change is not only irresponsible, it can be devastating to the victim and/or her children.

> *I was once "gifted" the movie Fireproof when I was going through my divorce by a well-meaning believer, trying to remind me that I could save my marriage through prayer and by focusing on my actions alone. She knew nothing about my story, my marriage, and how I had spent eight years sacrificing myself, hoping and praying for him to change. I had kept my commitment as long as I could. It had taken everything I had just to admit that I needed out. I was not*

willing to put my life on the line to give it another forty days.

More couples are eliminating the line about "wives submit to your husbands" from their wedding ceremonies because they don't like the idea of the husband lording over the wife. In reality, Biblical submission, in context, can be a beautiful representation of love and respect between both partners. In a healthy relationship, you don't have to *tell* people that it is an equal partnership. You don't have to *tell* them to love and respect each other, putting the needs of the other above your own. In a culture of faith, victims are often told they simply need to "soften your heart," "forgive," and "give it to God." Where these can be good suggestions for many relationships, they are not healthy for victims in abusive relationships. We must stop telling women to sit back, pray and wait for his heart to change. We are advocates of prayer, but prayer alone will not keep women safe. Keeping victims trapped in an abusive relationship, clinging to hope that things will change and making them feel that somehow it is their duty or responsibility to wait around until things change is ridiculous. Hope often keeps us trapped far beyond where we could, and should, have gotten out.

For so long, I hated the phrase "Faith, Love, and Hope." When all you have is hope that things will get better, that he will get better, it quickly turns to hopelessness. I was told, God is not so happy with divorce. I didn't say it at the time, but wish I had: God is not so happy with adultery either.. Or any kind of abuse.

What is not often discussed among Christian marriages is that the commitment you are making before God is a commitment to Him, not to that person. You are committing to love them, care for them, nurture them, and give it everything you have, as an act of service to God. If you have done that, you have upheld your commitment. Their life is not on you.

This is the biggest lie that Christian and other religious women believe: that to leave an abusive marriage is to break our commitment to God.

This is a significant reason the female race is still oppressed as we are today: we buy this lie that we must stay committed to a man that is not committed to us, or to God.

Your abuser broke the commitment, not you. You committed to love, serve, and respect. You did all of that, and so much more. *They* broke the commitment, but we take the blame for leaving and "giving up." We sentence ourselves to a life of unhappiness because of one decision.

Emotional Abandonment

> *He was more enthusiastic about any football game than spending time with me, that is just one example. He was unavailable on all levels, barely engaging in moments that should be shared. At times it felt like any reaction, even a negative one, would be better than emptiness.*

Not necessarily exclusive to religious justification is the topic of emotional abandonment. It is a good fit here because many believers struggle to see their freedom in leaving a marriage that isn't overtly abusive. Their partner is emotionally unavailable, but is that enough of a reason to break a commitment?

Again, you kept your end of the commitment to love, honor, and respect your spouse, regardless of circumstance; He did not.

Emotional abandonment or neglect by a partner is when they simply check out of the relationship. They stop investing time or energy into connecting with their partner or simply place other things first. They may have the expectation that being married or in a relationship simply means you are just there, waiting for them to be ready to engage with you on their timeline. Empty relationships may not be technically abusive, but neglect is certainly an abusive behavior, and their failure to love, honor, and respect you constitutes a clear breach of the specific terms of your marital agreement.

Justification for not leaving:

- **But my family loves him/they wouldn't understand.**

- **But I made a commitment/choice and need to stick it out.**
- **I can't just leave him with no job, home, or way to pay the bills.**

Even after victims recognize that they are in an abusive relationship, it is often still difficult to leave. Even if a victim can overcome the logistic or economic challenges, which are significant obstacles to be certain, the psychological challenges of leaving an abusive relationship are there to reel the victim back in. Despite obvious abuse, we find ourselves questioning, doubting, and coming up with justification for *not* leaving the relationship.

- **But I have nowhere to go**

Logistic and economic challenges are very real. Many victims indeed *do not* have a place they can go if they were to leave their abuser today, tomorrow, or in the foreseeable future. Some friends may let them crash on their couch, but many victims have been isolated from their friends and even their family for so long that it isn't a viable option. Add children to the mix, and the challenges pile higher. Even if they *do* have a place to go, they often have no way to get there, let alone with their children, pets, and belongings. Owning or even having access to a vehicle or money for other transportation is a privilege many abused women only dream of.

Finally, if they did manage to get out, they would then have to start over from scratch, potentially in a new town. Many of them have no bank account in their name, no vehicle in their name, no credit card in their name, no job, or a job that wouldn't come close to covering their expenses, and children at home that can't stay by themselves while the victim works. All of these very real issues deter many victims from ever making a real effort to leave their abuser.

The advocate asked, "Do you have somewhere to go?"

"What? Go? What do you mean?"

"Sweetie, do you have a safe place to take yourself and your children? He is going to be very mad when he is served. It can be a pretty dangerous situation."

"Where am I supposed to go with four kids? I barely know anyone..."

This is why it's essential for victims to rebuild their broken support network, or build one anew, as soon as they recognize their partner's behavior as abusive. More to the point, this is why it's essential for allies to offer victims tangible support instead of simply encouraging them to leave on their own. Chances are, if they could leave on their own, they would have by now.

• But my children need a father

Another factor that regularly keeps women with their partners is this drive to keep the family unit together. Women often believe that being with their abusive or unsupportive spouse for the sake of their children is better than raising their children without a father. We put so much emphasis on the family unit at the cost of our own health and safety. Just like everyone else, victims want the very best for their children, and are making the best decisions they know how. Those decisions are, again and again, tainted by their experiences, psychological abuse, and fear. Although some of those decisions are flawed, victims truly do want the best for their children, just like any other mother.

In many abusive situations where a mother stays in the relationship with her children, it is often because she has gotten so caught up in what she is taking away from her children by leaving rather than what they will gain. *My children need a father. My children need two parents. I don't want them having to go back and forth. Without him, I can't maintain the lifestyle they need.* It is not the abusive situation she is choosing to keep them in, but rather everything else that comes with it. The abusive situation is the unfortunate rider.

When children are raised in abusive homes, they are learning how to behave themselves, what relationships look like, and what they deserve in their own relationships. You are setting the example they will likely follow. Mothers of daughters, your daughters are watching you and learning what they should and should not accept. Mothers of sons, your sons are watching you and learning what is acceptable treatment of women. Yes, both parents are important in the home. Growing up with self-respect and a healthy understanding of relationships is important too. Remember to consider both sides of the equation when determining the best action to take for your children.

- **But no one else will want me**
- **I don't deserve better**

Victims of abuse can also be so psychologically damaged that they actually think they may be better off *with* their abuser. From the outside, it can be difficult to understand this way of thinking, but the abuser has potentially spent years breaking down every belief system the victim brought into the relationship. Beliefs about their own self-worth, what they are capable of, and even their own sanity. They may also have taken time to reinforce the idea that they made a commitment or choice and must "stick it out," though victims often bring this idea into the relationship themselves for reasons we've already talked about.

> *But no one else will ever want me... he made sure of it! Those were the words that would spin on repeat in my mind. He made sure of it and reminded me of it frequently, though never actually taking the responsibility for what he had done. I was ruined and tarnished by him, ashamed and less of a human. That's what I believed. It was my fault. It was all my fault.*
>
> *In reality, it wasn't. None of it. He knowingly and willingly infected more than a handful of other people that can be traced, most of them women he was trying to trap into his control.*

- **Grass isn't always greener on the other side**

Clichés are so dangerous when used ignorantly. People often say "the grass isn't always greener on the other side" to encourage women to stay where they are and not jump ship too soon. This saying implies that the victim is simply coveting the few blades of her neighbor's bright-green grass she can see poking between the fence. Like she went searching for something better when she grew bored of her current shade of green. A clever rebuttal to that is, "The grass is greener where you water it," further implying that the victim isn't doing enough to keep her own grass bright and plush, choosing to throw in the towel and chase someone else's beautiful yard rather than tend to her own.

What this clever quip is failing to note is that it's not just the woman's responsibility to water the yard. Unlike a true lawn, one person cannot be solely responsible for keeping it alive. Both partners must take an active role in fertilizing, watering, and trimming. One person cannot do it all.

Additionally, in many abusive relationships, not only is the grass not being watered, but it is completely dead. No amount of watering will bring it back. To guilt a victim into going back in the house and keeping her eyes on her own lawn is irresponsible. Sometimes, the grass really is greener on the other side. Sometimes, it's also safer and healthier too.

Character or Characteristics of the Abuser:

- **He's such a great guy, I never would have pegged him for an abuser!**
- **He doesn't *look* abusive.**
- **He's only ever been nice to me.**

It is amazing just how pervasive the stereotype is around what an abuser *looks or acts* like in public. In one sense, it's insulting to a victim to suggest that abusers should have a certain "look" about them. If it was so easy to peg, why would we find ourselves in those situations? If abusers were total jerks, disheveled, alcoholics who went around punching cashiers, I assure you far fewer women would find themselves as victims. The reality is, abusers are con artists. They often don't fit the stereotype at all.

> *How I pictured abusers is how you see them depicted on TV.*
> *That was my only frame of reference. The men I saw around*
> *our family growing up were not all innocent and perfect, but*
> *my step-father was respectful and kind, firm and caring, and I*
> *was kept safe from a lot of things I am sure. So my skewed*
> *perception of what a "bad" guy looked like was not the best*
> *basis to start from.*

Many abusers are con artists. Not only do they con their victim into trusting them, but they often con their family and friends into believing they are upstanding as well. Just like hackers or scam artists have made vast improvements over the years and are able to scam even the most watchful eye, abusers are able to take a woman who was previously abused and bring her right back into a similar or even more abusive relationship. How do they do that? How are they able to slip in and wreak havoc time after time? Well, because abusers don't all have a certain "look."

They often are generally nice and even charismatic. They have a lovable personality that draws people in, and it can take a while to really see their true character. Most people outside of the relationship wouldn't spend enough time with the abuser to see their more sinister side emerge. They are able to reel it in when they need to so that most people never see who they really are.

The term "abuser" often conjures up images of haggard looking druggies or alcoholics. Maybe they look disheveled or are missing a few teeth. Maybe we don't go that extreme and anticipate someone who has the rough, mean look or has an obvious short fuse. With that image, we think, "Of *course* he is abusive. Just look at him." Or "Did you hear the way he talked to the cashier?"

> *The terms abuse or abuser were never really in my vocabulary,*
> *but growing up, I imagined "bad guys" looking and acting like*
> *villains in Disney movies. They were charming, but you could*

tell they had a sinister side to them. I mean, how could the princess really be fooled by that? We could all see it. From the "predator eyes" to the slow, sly grin, the evil side should be pretty easy to spot. Life isn't a kid's movie, and villains aren't always accompanied by minor-key theme music. Without the evil laugh and strumming, bony fingers, it's easy to miss it altogether.

Many abusers do indeed display red flags, but they aren't always as obvious as we would expect. As hard as it is to believe, they are often even less obvious to those in the relationship. Why can an outsider often see the abuser for what they are before the victim? Because the outsider is not emotionally attached to the abuser. They aren't seeing the good sides that the victim sees; those sides that keep them clinging to hope that he can and will change, that there is a good person underneath all of the layers of abusive behavior. Outsiders are not being constantly manipulated and controlled, they haven't been deconditioned, demoralized, and devalued to the point where they have no self-esteem or standards. Outsiders aren't trying to justify the behavior or convince themselves that they made the right choice.

"Local stabbing three blocks from the Common Place." When I heard the news I was shocked, no, I was dumbfounded. There is no way that he could have done that. I knew him. We had hung out frequently for a six month period of time not too long ago, but he didn't seem or look like the type of person to do that.

The reality is, as we have mentioned, abusers come from all socioeconomic backgrounds and come with various addictions, some of which are difficult for even their partners to detect. There are no tell-tale signs from the outside, only stereotypes that mislead us into believing our situation doesn't fit "the mold" and can therefore be overlooked, not only by ourselves but by others. The truth is: there is no mold, there is only abuse in all its myriad forms.

There were characteristics that I loved. I wouldn't have married him if they weren't there, right? I would never have intentionally gone right back into another abusive relationship if there weren't.

When we find out that a neighbor is a pedophile, we are shocked. "He didn't *look* like a pedophile." What do we really mean by that? Do we expect them to walk to the mailbox naked or lick children in the mall? If we are honest with ourselves, we could come up with our own ideas of what a pedophile *looks* like to us. Perhaps we imagine them being homely and disheveled. Images of a forty-year old man with a potbelly living in his mother's basement may come to mind.

In turn, we naturally apply these stereotypes to people who *do* match that description, whether they are actually pedophiles or not. What that often results in is unwarranted discrimination of people who do fall more closely into those stereotypes. When a stereotype eventually matches up, we use that as evidence to become even more set in our beliefs. This applies to all types of stereotypes influencing racism, homophobia, sexism, discrimination related to weight or socioeconomic status.

This is a slight detour, but we want to take a moment to talk a bit more about stereotypes and the role they play in abusive relationships. In the United States, where this book is being written, there is a racial division. There is a strong bias against black and brown men, in particular. They are often viewed as more violent and dangerous. They are given the benefit of the doubt significantly less frequently than their white counterparts whether they are being pulled over for speeding, jogging through the park, or sitting peacefully in their own homes. Although that is not the discussion of this book, it does feed into an important factor when it comes to domestic abuse.

When a woman finally gets the courage to call for help, it is rare that she wants her abuser to suffer or be locked away forever. She simply wants the abuse to stop; she wants help. In the case of the suburban housewife who is being abused, the stereotype of an abuser often results in her abuser having a nice conversation with the reporting officers before turning back to the house with barely a slap on the wrist. In the case of a victim whose partner more closely fits either the stereotype of an abuser (whatever that looks like in the mind of the receiver) or the stereotype of a more violent individual (in the case of the American black male), she may be less likely to even call for help in the first place. Knowing that her abuser (her boyfriend or husband), is more likely to be thrown to the ground, hauled away in handcuffs, or even shot on the spot is enough to deter her from making the call in the first place. She is more likely to continue to suffer in silence because she knows the result of her cry for help will be much more dramatic than the white victim.

At first blush, this may appear as a positive thing. *Don't you want a dramatic response?* We want an *appropriate* response. In both cases, the response is extreme: too much or too little. There is a balance that must be found.

Now, we can argue all day about what an abuser does or does not deserve, but the reality is, equal abuse should result in equal response. It is hard enough for victims to cry for help. It is natural for the brain to default to a stereotype when we are faced with unfamiliar situations or until we have enough information to create a more accurate map. What often happens, though, is we never update our mental map and push off the new information as an exception. That's where the idea behind "He didn't look like a murderer" comes from. If we asked ourselves "What does a murderer look like?" we would start to peel back the layers of our own stereotypes and biases. It doesn't feel good, and it won't be pretty, but we must push past our own stereotypes and biases in order to form new paths and better recognize the signs. Whether or not you care about the inequality of treatment of abusers, these biases continue to hurt victims the most. Victims often get wrapped up in these stereotypes themselves. *I don't look like an abused woman. I don't fit the stereotype.* Instead of seeking help, we don't even recognize that we indeed are abused. Even when faced with evidence to suggest that we are, we still push it off thinking, ...*but that's not me.*

Despite what our initial stereotypes may tell us, the most dangerous abusers may actually be surgeons, construction workers, mechanics, military, teachers, ministers, police officers, or an executive wearing a suit to work every day. It may be the man who takes his wife to nice dinners, is well-known in the community, attends the neighborhood New Year's Eve party, and plays basketball with the kids in the backyard. Those most *obvious* candidates for abuse are often physically abusive. They are reactive and operate in an environment of hostility. Those who don't fit the mold are often calculated, planning attacks and intentional about where and how. One is not worse than the other. One is not necessarily harder to leave because so many factors beyond recognition go into that. But one is certainly harder to detect, especially early in a relationship.

- **He's just mentally ill**

Mental illness is often used as a scapegoat for a number of bad behaviors. We often see this in the case of mass violence. When searching for an explanation, to understand how someone could possibly engage in such heinous acts, mental health is inevitably brought into the discussion. The hallmarks of a number of mental illnesses involve low empathy, lack of understanding regarding what is socially acceptable, impulse control, and excessive mood swings, all of which provide fertile soil for abuse. Additionally, many violent individuals do indeed display signs of mental illness. That said, it is not fair or appropriate to make blanket connections between the two, and it is certainly not healthy to use mental illness as an excuse for behavior.

One practice that runs rampant in our society is labeling. We label children, job applicants, and even different types of people in the grocery store line. We make sense of the world by categorizing things, events, and people into buckets. From there, we apply known stereotypes, so that we don't have to spend as much energy trying to get to know them or understand them. We base whether or not we even do engage with them solely on the stereotypes we have put in place around that bucket or label.

The labels we assign people can also influence *how* we interact with them. In any case, labeling behavior can be dangerous. Studies conducted on teachers and school children have clearly shown the power and influence of a label. When students are labeled as intelligent, they perform better on standardized tests compared to those labeled as less intelligent. Students labeled as coming from a higher socioeconomic status are viewed as more intelligent, perform better on tests, and are considered easier to teach as compared to those labeled as coming from a lower socioeconomic status.[9] It is interesting how many are beginning to see the damage this type of labeling causes, yet we are so hesitant to see it elsewhere.

Associating abuse with mental illness and labeling abusers, or anyone, as mentally ill is flawed thinking. It is unfair and can even be dangerous. As a society, we tend to flippantly use labels, particularly when it comes to mental illness. "She's so OCD," "That's his ADHD," or "I'm so depressed." Not only does this diminish the severity of the illnesses for those who truly do suffer from them, but it downplays the behaviors themselves, allowing the abuser to fly under the radar. "He's a narcissist; what do you expect?" There are several other reasons why we must be cautious when it comes to blatantly associating abuse with mental illness.

First of all, mental illness is never an excuse for abusive behaviors and should never be a justification to excuse it. Mental illness may play a role in some behaviors, but victims should never feel *responsible* for staying in a relationship that is abusive, even if it is due to a chemical imbalance in the brain.

Secondly, not all abusers are mentally ill, and everyone who is mentally ill absolutely is not an abuser. In true mental illness, one cannot "turn off" certain behaviors at will. Abusers, on the other hand, know when to turn it off in public or around others and turn it back on when they are behind closed doors. Someone can have a mental health disorder or personality disorder and still choose to not be controlling, manipulative, or abusive. In all things, there are rarely absolutes. Some abusers get so comfortable abusing that it becomes a habit and "leaks out" in public. Others are under the influence of alcohol or drugs and have reduced impulse control. In those cases, the habitual behaviors will make their way to the public setting, potentially creating additional confusion regarding their mental state.

Thirdly, labeling an abuser as mentally ill can give the victim hope that they can be "fixed" with the right medication or support.

> *I would often find myself thinking things like, if he could just get diagnosed and get the help he needs. I would dream that medications and therapy would be the answer and that life could return to the "happy days."*

Medication is rarely a "fix all" and is not appropriate for everyone or all mental health disorders. Medication certainly is not a treatment method for abusive behaviors. It may help to balance out moods or improve underlying imbalances that could lead to abusive behaviors, but the behaviors themselves often don't change, even when imbalances are addressed. Abusive behaviors need to be addressed specifically, often through therapy or counseling. Abuse is not the result of a chemical imbalance; it is a choice that someone is making, even if that choice is choosing not to address an ingrained habit. Ironically, mentally healthier individuals are often the ones that don't see the abuse coming.

The most powerful impact of labeling abusers as mentally ill is that it can lead victims to excuse or justify the behavior. Blaming mental illness for an abuser's actions, victims often excuse them of responsibility for their own behavior. "It's not his fault; he's sick." Victims may even begin to blame themselves for the way they are treating their abuser or somehow causing the abuse by not engaging correctly with the abuser's illness.

It is very common for abusers to use mental illness or mental health as an excuse for their behaviors, whether they are actually managing mental health disorders or not. The reality is, in most cases, abusive partners are in control of their actions.

Below are some ways to tell if your abuser is making a conscious choice in how and where he demonstrates abuse:

- **They choose the limits** of how far abuse goes, when it happens, and how.

He would sometimes threaten physical abuse, even to the point of almost slapping me before stopping. Sometimes he would laugh at my discomfort and say, "I'm just joking around," other times he would point and say, "Next time, I won't stop there." He knew how far to push or how to hurt me so as to not get caught. "You know, a phone book doesn't leave any marks."

- **They only behave abusively towards specific people.** An individual who was managing a personality disorder would exhibit behaviors in other areas of their life and with less specific intention. Similar behaviors would be seen at work, in social environments.
- **They choose behaviors to escalate.** This book isn't about diving deep into personality disorders or mental illnesses and we understand that the vast dynamic of a person's mental health can alter over time and with circumstances, behaviors are generally consistent over time. An abusive partner can choose to not abuse during periods of time, gradually intensify the abuse, back off or start back up. The abuser manages how their behaviors are presented not only over time but during specific periods.

You may be thinking, *"Yeah, but my man really does have a mental illness."* Regardless, it is not your responsibility to sit around and be hurt by him, physically or psychologically, while he gets help. It is not your place to give up your well being because he "can't help it."

Just because a mentally ill person's behavior isn't their fault doesn't mean it isn't their responsibility. We are each responsible for managing our own condition, even if that means ceding our decision making to someone more competent. If an abuser genuinely wants help in curbing abusive behavior, there are plenty of resources available. Statements like "he can't help it" or "his mental illness makes him...," promote this flawed thinking. Don't fall into that trap.

Narcissism

Although mental illness is not necessarily related to abusive behaviors, and it is never an *excuse*, there is a mental state or personality disorder that shows a greater correlation with abuse. That mental state is called "narcissism." We by no means want to encourage straight labeling here, as we discussed previously. Taking that risk into consideration, we do need to give attention to narcissism because many of the characteristics of narcissism lend themselves well to potential abusive behaviors.

If you find yourself in a relationship with someone who appears to possess some of these characteristics, it could help you understand behaviors you are witnessing and the abuse you may be experiencing. There are always exceptions, but if you find yourself in a border-line unhealthy relationship with someone who  meets these profiles, we would encourage you to take a good, close look at your relationship and not blow off any red flags that you may see. Chances are, those red flags are flares telling you to get the hell out as quickly as possible. Unfortunately, it will be very difficult for someone with these characteristics to change..

> *If I had taken more time to think about it, maybe I would have seen it sooner. I was just sucked in so quickly. I knew something was off, but I was clueless as to how off.*

In a clinical sense, we must differentiate between narcissistic personality disorder and narcissism. Although similar, the clinical definitions are slightly different. Narcissistic personality disorder (NPD) is one of many different personality disorders. According to the Mayo Clinic, NPD is a "mental condition in which people have an inflated sense of their own importance, a deep need for excessive attention and admiration, troubled relationships, and a lack of empathy for others. But behind this mask of extreme confidence lies a fragile self-esteem that's vulnerable to the slightest criticism."[10]

This specific personality disorder causes many to misunderstand what is really going on inside the individual. Someone who possesses this disorder will seem to be arrogant and highly confident. This confidence is often very attractive at first. Beneath the surface are layers of shame, humiliation and low self-esteem. They are generally unhappy, highly disappointed when they don't receive attention, favors, or admiration they believe they are deserving of, and may find relationships unfulfilling.

Some with NPD do not function well. They will alienate friends, family, and others, normally feeling socially isolated and depressed. They will not believe or admit that anything is wrong because they are stuck between a belief of superiority and the darkness of depression all in the same moments. We want to reiterate that having narcissistic personality disorder does not automatically equal abuse.

A person who has NPD, as described in the "Diagnostic and Statistical Manual of Mental Disorders" (DSM-IV), shows extreme, rigid, and consistent expressions of narcissism, including:

- Expectations of superior treatment from others.
- Fixations on fantasies of power, success, intelligence, attractiveness, etc.
- A belief that they are unique, superior and associated with high-status people and institutions.
- Needing constant admiration from others.
- A sense of entitlement to special treatment and to obedience from others.
- Exploitation of others to achieve personal gain.
- An unwillingness to empathize with others' feelings, wishes or needs.
- Intense jealousy of others and the belief that others are equally jealous of them.
- Pompous and arrogant demeanor.

The term "narcissist" is an informal label for egotistical, self-serving individuals who do not acknowledge the feelings of others. It is based on the characteristics of narcissistic personality disorder but is a less formalized, non-clinical diagnosis.

> *During one of the many tearful phone calls during our divorce, he said, "This would be so much easier if you had died instead." In another conversation, he told me that he would never find someone else like me. I wasn't sure if he was referring to someone dumb enough to put up with him for so long or someone capable of carrying his weight. Either way, it was all about him and the suffering I was putting him through, never acknowledging the pain he caused me for years.*

The most common characteristics of narcissists:

1. **Grandiose sense of self-importance - some say this is the defining characteristic of narcissism.**

- Grandiosity is more than just arrogance or vanity; it is an unrealistic sense of superiority. They believe they possess something unique or special and can really only be understood by others of their "special" level. They possess an attitude that they are "too good" for the average or ordinary. Most want to be associated with or rub elbows with other high, elite status people, places, possessions and more.
- Self-importance is a belief that they are better than everyone around them and expect recognition, even when there is a lack of earning. Achievements are exaggerated or lied about. Talents are faked. They speak mostly of themselves, and how they "contributed," "gave," or did right in a situation. They fail to acknowledge the support they have received and make you think that you are lucky to have them in your life.

"I don't sweep floors."

> *We were taking a walk and, for some reason, he said, "If someone put a gun to my head and said 'you or her', I would*

tell them to shoot you because I wouldn't want you to live without me." I thought he was trying to be sweet but just didn't know how to get his point across. That was three years before we got married. It should have been a red flag, but somehow, it wasn't.

2. They build a life that supports delusions of grandeur.

- Frequent lies and exaggerations about themselves and others.
- "Since reality doesn't support their grandiose view of themselves, narcissists live in a fantasy world propped up by distortion, self-deception, and magical thinking. They spin self-glorifying fantasies of unlimited success, power, brilliance, attractiveness, and ideal love that make them feel special and in control. These fantasies protect them from feelings of inner emptiness and shame, so facts and opinions that contradict them are ignored or rationalized away. Anything that threatens to burst the fantasy bubble is met with extreme defensiveness and even rage, so those around the narcissist learn to tread carefully around their denial of reality."[11]

"I'm a MENSA member."

"I carry a gun every day."

"I could have attended any college I wanted."

3. Large need and desire for praise and admiration.

- Sense of superiority can be described as a balloon. In order to keep it fully inflated it needs a steady access to air. Ego needs a steady stream of applause and recognition to stay inflated to a level they feed off of. Occasionally is not enough. They seek out people to cater to their craving for attention, creating one-sided relationships, all about what others can do for them.

4. Sense of entitlement

- Believe that they should get whatever they want, that favorable treatment is owed to them.
- Expect others to automatically comply with their whims and wishes. When you don't anticipate and meet their every need and demand, then you are useless, selfish for asking for something in return or defy their will, aggression, outrage, or cold shoulder could result.

"I'll take out the trash, if you...."

"What are you going to give me if I do?"

"You'll owe me."

5. Exploits others without guilt or shame.

- General lack of empathy and struggles to identify with the feelings of others.
- View the people in their lives more as objects there to serve their needs. Taking advantage of others becomes part of their nature to achieve what they want. It can be malicious but often oblivious to them. Simply put, they do not think about how their behavior affects others. Even when it is addressed or pointed out they will still not truly get it or believe it.

Even during midterms and finals, he would stay out late, sometimes until three in the morning. I was working in my office on campus. It was late and he was drunk. He called to tell me he was going to walk to the bars a couple of miles away. I begged him to just stay put. The last thing he said was, "I'm going to go; I'll be back later." By the time I got home, he was gone, so I drove around looking for him for about an hour before finally giving up and trying to finish my work from home. Worried that he was either dead or in jail, I tried my best to study. He finally managed to stumble home around five o'clock in the morning. He never apologized for making me worry or causing me distress, particularly in the midst of such an important time. He never acknowledged that it caused me any distress at all. Whether he even recognized it, I'm not sure. He wanted to have fun, and it didn't matter how it impacted me.

6. Frequently demeans, intimidates, bullies, or belittles others.

- Threatened by others who appear to have something they lack or by those that aren't subservient to them or who challenge them.
- Defensive mechanism is contempt - neutralizing the threat and propping up their ego is only done by putting others down, using patronizing or dismissive mannerisms and words.
- Attack mechanisms are insults, name calling, bullying and threats to force the other person "back in line."

7. Magnetic and charming by creating a flattering self-image to draw others in.

- Set up the image to fit the fantasy of themselves they created and then find people who fit into that or will be appealed to with it.
- Set the stage of lofty dreams to help establish the vision that others fall prey to. This is a technique used by successful leaders throughout history. However, effective leadership qualities can be used for both good and evil.

Always the life of the party.

Witty, clever, funny, fun

A narcissist defined by psychologist Stephen Johnson is an individual who has "buried his true self-expression in response to early injuries and replaced it with a highly developed compensatory false self.[12]

There is so much more information when it comes to narcissism and gaslighting, which we touch on briefly throughout. If you are interested in learning more, we have provided an ebook that you can access at www.butthatsnotme.com.

The 3 C's

In family care programs for addiction recovery, family members are taught the three C's: I didn't cause it, I can't control it, I can't cure it.[13]

As a family member supporting someone through addiction, it can be easy to take the blame for their actions and behaviors, therefore thinking you can somehow control it or fix it. This flawed thinking keeps them in a painful cycle of guilt and frustration. By learning the three C's, family members are better able to understand the addiction and step into the appropriate role they are able to play. These principles can also be applied to victims of abuse struggling to accept that they are helpless to change their abuser's behaviors.

1. **I didn't cause it.** Your partner's actions are not your fault or your responsibility. You did not do something that caused him to behave in an abusive or even emotionally unavailable way. It is their private battle, and theirs alone.
2. **I can't control it.** We so badly want to take hold of the situation. If I'm just _____ enough. If I just behave in a certain way, then he will respond differently. We have no control over the behaviors of someone else. Though we may see temporary results by walking on eggshells or responding just right, this is not a permanent change.
3. **I can't cure it.** It is not your place to cure or fix his anger, depression, or behavior resulting from any other mental or emotional state. He and he alone can fix or change his behavior.

The words and language we use to describe our experiences serve to shape our reality. It can be a very powerful tool to create the life we want, but it can also be a very powerful source of imprisonment. That's why we spent so much time talking about it. We want you to fully understand the influences of the words you use. Sticks and stones may indeed break bones, but words can keep you trapped in a dangerous cycle of blame, self-doubt, justification, and normalizing.

In the next section we are going to dive deep into each category of abuse. This is in depth and necessary in order to properly equip ourselves against these pendulums of behaviors and actions we are up against. Grab a cup of coffee or tea, take a walk, and join us back here.

PART TWO
ABUSE DEFINED

Types of Abuse

The reality is, there is only one category: abuse.

Before we get into the specifics and types of abuse, we want to clear a few things up.

There are endless ways to categorize abuse. Instead of picking one, we organized abuse in categories that make sense to us. You likely won't find this particular way of sorting anywhere else, and that is okay. We have organized this book in a manner to make it easy to digest based on how we wanted to share the information with you.

Abuse is messy and doesn't fit nicely into any box. Physical abuse affects you psychologically. Psychological abuse is often verbal. Sexual abuse is physical. Threats of physical harm have psychological implications, and so on – it's just hard to organize it. Therefore, you will see types of abuse pop up in more than one category. They will wind through the different themes, which allows us to talk about it from a different angle. It is our hope that it will shed light on the abuse you or someone you know may be experiencing, so that you can recognize it for what it is. Knowledge and recognition are powerful tools. Until you recognize the harm, you cannot act on it.

One more thing about categories: different states may categorize types of abuse differently for filing and "charging" purposes. That is the only reason it even matters if abuse is categorized "properly," though it often leads us to believe there is a hierarchy of importance. Because you can't press charges if no one else can "see" it or an outsider wouldn't recognize it, physical abuse often rises to the top of the hierarchy.

Whether anyone else, especially an outsider, would recognize what you are experiencing as abuse should have no bearing whatsoever on whether or not you are able to get help in an abusive situation. You are the only one who needs to recognize it as such. You do not need to justify it to someone else or explain it. You might need to in a court of law, which is the only reason it even matters to "define" it or put it in a nice, pretty package.

In reality, abuse isn't nice, it isn't pretty, and it isn't clean. When it comes to getting out of an abusive relationship, you do whatever it takes to get your abuse classified in a meaningful way. We are by no means advocating lying, but we encourage you to do whatever it takes to get the protection you need.

The reality is, there is only one category: abuse.

Verbal Abuse

It was us against the world.

My parents and family didn't understand how much he believed in me and supported my big dreams of being an executive. I was so glad he helped me see that those were my dreams, because I didn't even realize it until then. They didn't understand how our relationship worked. Sure, he didn't work, but he supported my dreams. Sure, he wasn't a gentleman, but he was funny and engaging. Sure, I didn't feel loved at times, but that was my issue, and we were working through that.

Everyone else loved him. He was the life of the party, the class clown. He made everyone laugh; they wanted to be around him. Of course, he would occasionally make jokes at my expense, but I was just so sensitive. I needed to work on that.

We were so excited about our future. I felt pressured when he would heap all of those goals on me, but big dreams are scary sometimes. Right? Sure, he would embarrass me in front of my family, our friends, and people we didn't even know, but that's just his humor. When I did something wrong, he would make a joke about how I was so smart yet so dumb. He wondered how I could have gotten my doctorate, but measured the space for the tile wrong three times. Always with a laugh; always with a smile. I smiled too. I knew he was just joking and didn't realize the insecurity I felt in my new job, trying to do something challenging, knowing that I carried the weight of our future. If he saw through me, surely my boss would too. My imposter syndrome was fueled.

Early on, he would only make me look like an idiot in front of his friends, then my friends, then his family, but rarely my family. Over the years, he got more comfortable making fun of me around them. I knew they didn't like it, but they didn't see that it was just his personality. That was just his style. He didn't mean anything by it; that was just the way he showed how much he loved me and how "connected" we were. They didn't know how he texted and called all day just because he missed me and wanted to know how I was doing. He would check in before doing anything at all because he wanted my thoughts and opinion. What should I eat for lunch? Where is the extra toilet paper? When are you coming home? He would text me constantly to tell me what he was up to. I'm about to order pizza. I slept until 11:30. The cable is down. I just got the high score on my game. I just watched this video about a woman having sex with a horse. I'll show you when you get home. They just didn't realize how much he missed me and was thinking about me constantly...at least when he wasn't sleeping, playing his games, or watching television.

As little as he did around the house, he always had opinions about what I was doing, eating, or wearing. "You said you wanted to lose weight. Should you really be eating that?" "That outfit doesn't look right." I thought he was just helping me out, because he loved me and wanted to see me succeed. Over time, it began to wear down my self-confidence. It also agitated me, which I then felt guilty about.

I wished he would stop being disrespectful to me in front of other people, but I didn't think they really noticed. No one ever said anything to me or even to him. I convinced myself it wasn't that big of a deal and kept smiling through it. When my family would say something to me, I was incredibly defensive. How dare they butt in on my relationship?! They didn't know him and didn't know what we had.

I would mention it to him to try to get him to tone it down, but that just led to him using it as ammunition to further solidify that our relationship was the only "true" relationship worth investing in. "They don't get us. They're butting in too much." In order to get him to stop talking badly about them, I stopped mentioning my family altogether. And in order to keep my family from talking badly about him, I stopped mentioning any struggles all together. I eventually withdrew completely, not talking to them unless they reached out first.

When we did talk, everything was sunshine; everything was wonderful. I exaggerated the positive to make sure it didn't sound questionable and quickly changed the subject to my job, activities, or even the weather. My relationship was off limits as a topic of conversation. I even did a pretty good job of convincing myself it was okay. I had to. What other choice did I have? It wasn't "bad enough" to talk about leaving. We just had different communication styles. As long as I didn't talk about certain things, everything seemed to be okay.

When I mentioned that I was unhappy, he would say all the right things. "I'll change. I know I messed up. I'm so sorry. I love you more than anything. I will never find someone like you. I moved across the country for you. I gave up my job for you. I gave up my family for you. I have nothing without you." I couldn't bear the thought of leaving him jobless, homeless, and a thousand miles away from his family. If he was so good, I thought that was a problem with me, my attitude, and my perspective. We were just going through a rough patch; nothing that a little time and persistence couldn't heal.

With only his words, he kept me trapped in a relationship that I couldn't escape. With only his words, he made me a slave in my own house. With only his words, he made me solely responsible for our livelihood and lifestyle. With only his words, he isolated me from my family and friends who no longer wanted to be around us. With only his words, he held all of the power and none of the responsibility. With only his words, he left me a broken and ashamed shell of a woman who wore a smile on the outside, but was constantly crying on the inside.

When I did finally decide to tell my mom how unhappy I was, she was immediately ready to help me move forward. I hadn't even told her what was wrong; I didn't need to. I cried saying, "But he doesn't hit me." I will never forget the look she gave me as she said, "He doesn't have to." She knew he was verbally, psychologically, mentally, and emotionally abusive, and that was enough. I still thought perhaps I was overreacting or "giving up too soon." I was so relieved to know that someone else could see it and it wasn't just in my head. For years, I thought I was crazy. I thought I was a terrible person for feeling the way I did. It haunted me for years and still does, more than ten years later.

Verbal abuse is a daunting category because it happens so frequently and in so many forms. In reality, we have all been guilty of it at one point or another. We verbally abuse ourselves and others without even a blink. It occurs in family relationships, socially, on the job or anywhere people are conversing. Maybe we feel guilty about it later and apologize, or perhaps we didn't even realize the hurt in the words we spewed in a moment of anger.

As I write this, I know several of my own responses to difficult situations result in borderline verbal abuse from time to time. Whether this stems from my upbringing, my own history of abuse, or bad behaviors that went unchecked for too long, I can't say for sure. That does not excuse the fact that they are abusive behaviors and need to be changed.

That is the difference between an abuser and a slip up that resembles abusive behavior. Serial abusers use words as weapons to inflict pain and maintain control well beyond any one argument or "having the last word." That said, even non-abusers who display these damaging response patterns need to develop more productive and healthy ways of communicating, otherwise they risk inflicting serious harm on their own partners, children, or others with whom they interact. Just because lasting harm wasn't intended doesn't mean that wasn't the result. Abusive behaviors result in abuse whether it was the intent or not. That said, in this context we are focusing specifically on those who repeatedly use words to demean, frighten, intimidate, or speak in a manner with the intent to control someone else.

Verbal abuse is tricky. Although it is characterized as such because it comes out of the abuser's mouth, it is often intended for psychological or emotional abuse or even a threat of physical abuse. As children, we all learned the phrase, "sticks and stones may break my bones but words can never hurt me." Or how about my personal favorite, "I'm rubber; you're glue. Whatever you say bounces off me and sticks to you." To this day, I still can't say the words without bouncing them rhythmically in my head. We often give these words to ourselves, our friends, or our children as encouragement. We are reminding them that they have the power within them to ignore those words or let them eat at their hearts.

These phrases can be powerful sources of strength and inspiration to ignore and move past the bully and focus on the encouragement from those who love us. In abusive situations though, these same tactics don't always work. For a while, we put up our guard and bounce those words right back. Regrettably in most cases, when someone is in an abusive situation, they can't just walk away. They can't go home, cry, and be filled with positive words of encouragement from their mother. Their abuser is the person who is supposed to love them the most, the one who is supposed to speak truth and life into them. Their home is *the* unsafe place. If they are saying these terrible things, it's easy to start believing that they are actually true.

More Than Words: Why verbal abuse is so dangerous

The effects and toll of a verbally abusive relationship can have long-lasting effects on physical and mental health, including leading to chronic pain, depression, or anxiety. Because of the intricate way our minds work, verbal abuse has the ability to deteriorate the healthy mechanisms we've developed. Repeated exposure can make one question memory of events, asking "Did that really happen?" intentionally changing behavior out of fear of upsetting them or in opposition, acting more aggressive or more passive than you would normally. Verbal abuse brings on the feelings of shame, guilt, constant fear, feelings of powerlessness and hopelessness, manipulation, and the sense that you are used, unwanted and controlled. You may be left feeling that you need to do anything in your power to restore peace and kindness, and that you have to go above and beyond to accomplish those. This environment and state of mind is stressful, overwhelming and detrimental to overall health.

> *My fourth pregnancy was hard. Despite my difficulties, I wasn't allowed to slack. He would yell at me for being lazy if I needed to rest, follow me around the house harassing me for not doing exactly as he expected. When he was tired or cranky, he would scream for me and the kids to "get the hell out." I was hospitalized for a period of time for complications. I hated being away from my other children. At the same time, it was a relief to have a little physical distance from him.*
>
> *Unfortunately, in the age of technology, physical distance isn't enough when your abuser engages in verbal abuse. He would call me frequently to yell at me while I was in the hospital. "Why the hell can't you come home?" He would complain about not being able to work out or play his games. He would complain about having to take care of the kids. It was relentless. I would catch the side-eye of a nurse checking my blood-pressure, as she could overhear the language he was spouting out through the phone. Between the threats, expressions of anger and wanting to save my children from more abuse, I*

begged my doctor to allow me to go home. The risks I was taking
seemed like an easier task to handle than his anger at the time,
so I did what I needed to do to keep the peace for the moment.

What does verbal abuse look like?

In the majority of cases, we can see that abuse starts on an emotional (psychological) level, the vehicle being verbal abuse. Verbal abuse may begin with simple name-calling or "joking around." Sometimes it is obvious and sometimes it is disguised as a pet-name or teasing, but habitual name-calling is a method used to belittle, diminish and condition the victim. In some cases, abusers will cease to use the victim's birth or preferred name altogether, which is a psychological tactic that removes their identity and any human characteristics. Most abusers, especially men, do not even comprehend the vastness of their behavior because it becomes so ingrained into them that it behaves like instinct.

> *My oldest daughter was on the phone with her biological father*
> *discussing what was new in her life. As per usual she spoke of*
> *our family and in particular what I had been working on,*
> *mostly because it's just facts, but also because she is proud.*
>
> *"I mentioned that you were pretty deep into writing a book*
> *when he asked 'about what?' I try to stay pretty generic with*
> *him because of who he is and how he behaves so I just said, 'It's*
> *about abuse.' His reply somehow didn't shock me. He chuckled*
> *with disdain and said 'yeah, she liked to toss that word around*
> *when we were together. I thought it was funny then too.'*

Abusers don't typically start out full-on verbally assaulting their victims. Instead, they start out behaving adequately long enough for their victim to let their guard down. Early on, they may give intentional love and attention including compliments and requests to see the victim often. It may even feel a bit excessive at times, but this is all very normal at the beginning of healthy relationships, which can make these early signs extremely difficult to identify. In most new relationships, partners want to spend time together to learn more and grow as a couple. Abusers take this to an unhealthy extreme of trying to make the other person feel strongly bonded to them, as though it is the two of them "against the world."[1]

As time progresses, the abuse advances. The abuser may begin to insult, joke, or use embarrassment. Sadly, this behavior still doesn't throw up major red flags because it remains fairly socially acceptable. We blow it off as humor or "goofing around" when it really should be identified as abusive. We must begin standing up to this type of behavior and calling it out for what it is. By normalizing this behavior and allowing it to continue, society as a whole is being conditioned to see past this behavior and treat it as a normal part of a healthy relationship. This is no different than accepting slang as words in the dictionary, it becomes commonplace.

 Sometimes, verbal abuse hangs out at the early stages including joking at the victim's expense, using unflattering "pet-names", or embarrassing her in front of others. Abusers in this phase may be stuck in immaturity, which is a bigger problem than disrespectful name-calling. This should be a red flag. If you notice one sign, be on the lookout for other clues of immaturity that can lead to struggles with family responsibilities, holding down jobs, and more. Some people engage in these behaviors because they weren't raised in a manner that taught them respect for others, or this was simply how their family interacted. In these cases, they may not even be aware that the behavior is harmful. Although abusers may certainly be able to reverse these behaviors, serial or extended adolescence is a major problem among young American men and not something to overlook.

As victims of this type of abuse, we recommend taking time to calmly express how the behaviors make you feel. Provide specific examples and outline how it impacts you. Pay attention to how they respond to the recognition that their behavior is hurting you. If they are sincerely remorseful and express shame or regret for behaving that way, it is a good sign that the intent was truly not to belittle you. There may be hope that they can change. If that is the case, it may still take time and repetition for the behavior to truly change. Consistently and patiently remind them when they slip.

Just like changing an old habit, it takes time and practice. Don't give up on them, get too frustrated, or decide that they don't mean anything by it and let it go. Just because they aren't intentionally inflicting lasting harm on you, it is still harmful. It is still abusive behavior. Unchecked, over time, these behaviors can easily slide into more extreme behaviors. Even if they don't, you deserve better and your relationship deserves better. Do not allow this behavior to continue. Whatever the justification, it is not okay and must be addressed. Call him out. He's a big boy. He can take it. If he can't, get ready to move on, especially if you are dating. Whatever you do, do not marry someone who displays these tendencies. Make sure they have stopped these behaviors before you agree to marry them. They are much less likely to change for the better after the fact.

We spent a great deal of time talking about the early phases of this entry-level abuse because it is such an easy entry-point to abuse. Many abusers slip in unnoticed because victims simply let them get away with making jokes, calling them names, and embarrassing them. It may look obvious that these behaviors are not okay, but they are slipped in so slyly that we often wonder what just happened. "Did I hear that right?" It's easy to miss. They are indeed harmful in themselves, but they are particularly dangerous because the abuse rarely stays there. Even within verbal abuse, the abuse escalates. Let's dig into some specific categories we particularly identified with in regards to verbal abuse.

Accusations

Accusation means   repeatedly and unjustly/inaccurately accusing someone of doing bad things. Abusers often engage in this behavior out of jealousy, envy, because they are guilty themselves, or to taunt and torment the victim. Accusations create doubt, confusion, and insecurity, making the victim question whether they are doing something inappropriate or wrong. It is easy to begin doubting your own words and actions.

Did I say something wrong? I thought I did tell him that? Did I say some-. thing inappropriate to my co-worker? I hope I didn't lead him on. Maybe it was my fault.

Similar to gaslighting, which we will discuss below, this type of verbal abuse can be a form of torture, making the victim unable to discern what has or has not happened. Accusations of cheating based on jealousy are common among abusers. Just being in the room with a male co-worker or having male contacts can result in accusations against the victim. The result of this is potential for massive confusion, doubt and uncertainty.

- "I saw the way you looked at them. You can't tell me there's nothing going on there."
- "Why won't you give me your cell phone if you've got nothing to hide?" "Whose number is this?"
- "Why did you 'like' that picture?"
- "Where were you? Don't lie to me!"

Accusations can be paralyzing. In a healthy relationship, when a concern is mentioned, both parties try to understand what happened and they work to uncover the truth. In an abusive relationship, the abuser is not trying to explain exactly what it was the victim did wrong so they can understand and either explain, correct or apologize. The abuser is judge *and* jury, and the verdict has already been reached.

I was taking a shower one evening when he came rushing in. He swung the door open, holding onto the door frame and balling his other hand in a fist accusing me of something I couldn't recall because I hadn't done it. I couldn't even escape or get some distance from his anger. It was easier to agree and cower down than to deny and stand firm on the truth. Looking back now, that describes a lot of what I experienced. It was more beneficial to agree to false accusations than it was to defend the truth. That is a hard place to be because eventually the mind believes the falsehoods too.

The victim is left confused and unsure of what they did wrong and how to fix it. In these situations, the abuser has control and often uses this state for his benefit, making the victim do things to "make up for it" later. Whether the accusation was based in any reality at all is irrelevant, and the abuser often continues to bring it up long after the alleged event took place.

Sadly, victims often find it easier to cower and agree to the accusation because it is easier and safer than standing for the truth. Things they would never agree to under "normal" circumstances become common-place in these relationships because it is necessary to survive. The victim is left feeling like they "allowed" the abuse to happen and were somehow an active participant in their own abuse.

> *I would agree that I was wrong just to stop the argument from getting worse. Sure, I did that. Yes, I was wrong. Whatever it took to move past it.*

Blame

Blame is, on some level, a natural part of being human. When we are children, we learn to place blame to avoid getting into trouble. As we get older, we place blame to reduce the feeling of shame or to protect our image. It can quickly become a dangerous habit.

In an abuser's hands, it is a tool of deflection and belittling used to protect themselves from an undesired outcome. Constantly accusing the victim of messing things up or being the reason things aren't working out is a common pattern of abusers. Abusive individuals may blame others for their own actions or call attention to behaviors that have very little to do with the situation in discussion. This type behavior is often used to make the victim believe they are bringing on the abuse they receive.

- *"I hate getting into fights, but you make me so mad!"*
- *"I have to yell because you're so unreasonable and thickheaded!"*
- *"It's your fault I can't keep a job. You keep moving us around."*
- *"If you would just listen and do what I told you to do..."*

- *"Now look at what you made me do!"*

> *The kids were in the living room under his care. When he left them alone, the baby burned her hand on the fire. He began yelling and blaming the older kids for not watching when they weren't even in the same room. "You should have been watching them!" When I came down to see what was going on, he said, "You are a terrible mother," and wouldn't let me care for my crying baby.*

Abusers will often avoid taking responsibility for or engaging in activities or decisions within the home. At first, it can feel like a trusting, loving relationship where the victim feels a sense of ownership and control. Abusers then have no reason to take accountability for any part when things go wrong, thus placing blame on others. Blame may be verbal or non-verbal, but the message is received loud and clear.

This lack of participation in basic responsibilities, constant critique of those choices, and the full burden of responsibility if things go wrong amounts to incredible pressure. Even if fear of repercussions is not involved in the abuse, the sole responsibility and pressure alone, along with the psychological implications of that pressure for the victim, is damaging and painful.

> *He would say, "you just need to be the CEO...," "One day when you are making more money...," "You just need to ask for a promotion," or "Go schmooze your boss." It's difficult to spot verbal abuse. At the moment, it looks like he's just trying to be encouraging, but it feels like a lot of pressure. It was his way of putting the responsibility and expectation on me. If, when things went badly, it would then be my fault because I didn't get the promotion, work hard enough, or choose the right career path. There was so much pressure on me to produce that I didn't enjoy my job at all. Our dreams and entire livelihood were solely dependent on my ability to be promoted and do it quickly.*

Circular Arguments

Circular arguments are not uncommon in healthy relationships. It is not unusual for a disagreement to arise about the same thing more than once until a common ground or compromise can be reached. When used as a tactic, the abuser will reignite the old argument over and over again not to resolve it, but to provoke the victim, start a new argument, or even escalate.

- You've talked about not wanting children yet, but your partner brings it up every month or even more frequently
- You are both aware that your job requires overtime, sometimes at a moment's notice. However, every time it happens, he starts in on you about your absence, and it feels like the argument will never end.
- When you want to go out, he reminds you that you worked late or went out with friends last week instead of spending time with him.

Condescension

Condescension is an attitude of patronizing superiority or disdain used to belittle. Comments, words used toward someone, can be sarcastic, disdainful, and patronizing. It is all designed to make themselves, the abuser, feel superior while making the victim feel "less than." Name calling fits into this category as well (e.g., ugly, bitch, whore, dumb, fat, stupid). Abusers may tell them they are unattractive, undesirable, dirty, or worthless without them. The intent is to demean them, make them feel that they are unworthy of anyone's affection and the abuser is doing them a "huge favor" by just being with them.

- *"Well, aren't you just the smart one in the room?"*
- *"You should be happy I took you in."*
- *"You're lucky I'm so patient."*
- *"Why did you do it that way? I could have told you..."*

I would make dinner, of course at a very specific time and based on very specific food requests, dish up his plate first, because how dare I feed anyone else before him? I served him his plate where he sat on the couch, another way to incite division for me. Then the kids, seated at the dining room table. By this time if I was lucky and everyone had what they needed, it was my turn to plate food for myself and eat. Many times he would beg and plead for me to sit with him, because didn't I love him? And he hadn't seen me much, the kids are fine, they don't need you. Maybe I got half of my plate finished, but most times not. It felt as if I had barely swallowed a bite before the demands would come. Give me attention, ignore the kids, and rub his feet, while he continues to eat or finish his plate. There were times where words were no longer used and he would just force-fully place his bare feet in my lap, trying to play it off as cute, touching my plate or messing with me so I couldn't eat and instead had to attend to him. I became so accustomed to it that I would anticipate his demanding needs and not even get a plate of food. He would yell, "Can't you fucking sit still?" Or any other of the numerous ways he would belittle me if I moved around too much. How dare my seven month pregnant body get in his way?

Criticism

Criticism can also be a verbal abuse tool when the intent is to break down rather than build up. When it is not constructive, criticism takes on a whole different meaning. It is a particularly harsh and persistent way to wear the victim down and chip away at any confidence they may have. Criticism is another form of abuse often experienced outside of romantic relationships such as parent/child, friendships, co-workers, or supervisor/subordinate relationships. Criticism may also manifest itself in abusers deciding things for you like what to wear or eat because they don't like your choices or think you are incapable of making a good choice.

- These reports are always wrong.
- You just keep saying the wrong thing.
- You have terrible taste in fashion.
- Don't wear that; wear this.
- No, that's a stupid choice. Let's go here.

Very specific items had to be stocked in the house or all hell would break loose. He would actually take offense to it, as if I was not attending to his needs. Even at times when it was an honest mistake and left off of the shopping list. "Where are my nutty buddy bars? Can you do anything right for fuck sake? I don't ask for much so why can't you go to the store and not forget what I want?"

His request for me to make him his lunch wasn't really a request because no was not an acceptable answer. I would have to get up at four or five in the morning to make lunch for him, even while pregnant and then when nursing. Often before I could go back to sleep, he would call me to complain about the sandwich or whatever was in the lunch that day. This is a crappy lunch. You call this a lunch? What the fuck am I supposed to eat? Where's the napkin? How could you forget the napkin? I got to the point that I would record and take pictures of what I had packed so that when the accusations and criticism flew at least I knew the truth in my head. There were times when he was so forceful with the criticism that I really had no choice but to agree just to move on. It was 5:00 am and I had a baby crying to be fed, I didn't care anymore to fight.

Degradation

Degradation is a verbal tool used to make someone feel bad about themselves. They employ humiliation and shame to degrade you and eat away at any confidence that may be there. In addition to psychological damage, degradation, along with other forms of verbal abuse like condescension and criticism, there can be physical implications as well.

For example, degradation can result in preventing the victim from receiving medical care they may need. *"Oh come on. It's not that bad. I didn't realize you were such a wuss. You don't need to go see a doctor for that. We can't afford for you to go."* We will discuss this type of abuse under psychological abuse and isolation, but the verbal aspect makes it a worthy topic to mention here too.

- These reports are always wrong.
- You just keep saying the wrong thing.
- You have no fashion sense at all!
- Insulting or attempting to humiliate you, shortly followed by accusing you of being overly sensitive, saying that it was a joke and you have no sense of humor or that you need to lighten up.

I can't begin to count the number of times I heard the words, "You would be living in a box behind Walmart, if I hadn't come along." "I saved you from living in a ditch." "Before me, you were nothing. Without me, you will be nothing again." "Nobody else would want you." "You are dirty and worthless, no one else will love you." There are more, but honestly does it matter? They all have the same purpose. He wanted me to feel and believe that I was worthless. The sad thing is, I did. I bought into the brainwashing because after hearing it over and over, I thought he must be right.

Dismissive Language

Dismissive language is used by abusers to downplay or belittle feelings, emotions, or opinions. Like many verbally abusive behaviors, dismissive comments are widely used outside of romantic relationships. This type of response or comment is a demonstration of disregard for the victim. Dismissive language is frequently used when a victim is attempting to tell her abuser how his behavior made her feel or asking him to stop certain activities. Dismissive language leaves the victim feeling unheard and devalued.

- *"I didn't mean anything by it."*
- *"That's not what happened."*
- *"You're too sensitive."*
- *An insult followed by an accusation that you are overly sensitive or a brush off saying that it was a joke, you have no sense of humor or that you need to lighten up.*

He would stay up all night, every night, drinking, playing games, or watching movies. The master bedroom was right above the level with the TV. I woke up many nights to the sound of the music playing, bass thumping through the bed. I went down to turn it off, and he was fast asleep with a pizza box open on the floor and a drink spilled in his lap. The TV was so loud, it was hurting my ears.

The next day, I confronted him about his behavior, explaining how it was disrespectful to me and kept me up. I asked him to get onto a schedule and do some things during the day instead of sleeping all day. I also told him how it hurt my feelings that he didn't sleep with me and only came to bed when he wanted sex. He simply explained that the TV wasn't that loud, that the only reason he fell asleep was because he had stayed up late helping me with the remodel, and he would eat the pizza in the morning, so it made sense that it was left out. No apology, no recognition that he heard me, no plan to change.

Gaslighting

Gaslighting is a systematic effort to make a victim question their own version of events. Victims may even begin apologizing for things that weren't their fault or that never happened. Gaslighting can also make a victim more dependent on the abuser, since they can no longer trust the evidence of their own senses. Gaslighting can be common in non-romantic relationships as well. If you have ever felt like you are losing your mind or have just entered the "Twilight Zone" after having a conversation with someone, you may have just been "gaslit."

Gaslighting is another tool abusers use to maintain power and control. When a victim is questioning her memories and perspective, she is more easily manipulated. Gaslighting happens over time, and you may not even notice it at first.[2]

> *Since our divorce, the court order assigned specific responsibilities, particularly over school and medical care to me as the residential parent. On more than one occasion, I have been sure to discuss topics and come to even further detailed agreements pertaining to specific situations.*
>
> *Over a period of time, after coming to an agreement of how things were going to be handled, I learned that he had completely disregarded that agreement. It may feel simple, but it is an example of a play for control and complete disregard for an agreement that was made. It left me wondering what happened. Didn't we have this conversation? Do I mention it or just let it go? Will it just be something else next time or even something else for him to take me to court over? Even court documents say that I will handle these decisions, yet he and his new wife disregard it.*
>
> *For a while, I was mad about it. I was left with doubt. Am I even sane? It's easy to feel like you aren't having rational thoughts. Being in that mental state of fighting between logic and confusion constantly leaves you with the question: Am I crazy?*

Examples of gaslighting include:

- Denying an event, agreement, or argument happened at all. Perhaps telling you that it's all in your mind, you dreamed it, or are making it up.
- Calling you crazy, overly sensitive, or emotional.
- Telling you that you are blowing it out of proportion.
- Describing an event as completely different from how you remember it.

- Telling other people that you're forgetful, unstable, unreliable, or have emotional problems.

When we were preparing to separate, or more accurately when I was trying to, I had made a list of major possessions in our home. I knew this was the most important thing to him, so I figured it would be a good place to start so that he would see I just wanted to get away. I left the list on the kitchen counter so that he could mark all of the items he wanted and expected. At least this would be a movement forward, since it had been ten months of me begging for him to let me go.

Not long after indicating to him that I had completed the task, he stormed up to the bedroom I had been ordered to inhabit, telling me I had lost my mind. What list was I talking about? I calmly repeated what I had already communicated, and he insisted he didn't know what I was talking about. There was no list on the counter. He followed me around the house saying, "You're crazy" and harassing me about the list. I made a note in my journal when he actually started harassing me about "there must be ghosts then, cause you say you're not wrong and I didn't take any list. I don't even know what it looks like." This went on over and over for 24 hours. I never knew when he was going to start coming back at me. When he finally admitted to moving the list, because he was tired of the game, he said, "I will do whatever and say whatever I want to you because I can. Don't forget that."

When being gaslit, it can be easy to lose track of reality. In good times, it can be easy to forget the bad. If you aren't already, we highly recommend journaling your experiences, particularly the negative ones. This will not only help provide evidence if you should ever need it, but it will help you better recall the negative experiences when you start to wonder why you feel disconnected or lack trust in your partner. For more information on this topic head to our website at www.butthatsnotme.com and download our free resources.

Manipulation

Manipulation is the attempt to get someone to do or feel something without directly communicating that desire, ideally making it seem like it was their idea in the first place. Its purpose in an abusive context is to control and keep the victim off-balance.

- "If you do that, it proves you don't care about your family and everyone will know it."
- "You'd do this for me if you really loved me."
- "Don't you want me to be happy?"
- But you're never home, so the least you could do is do this for me.

The fish and all that goes with them was his idea. He wanted them, yet I was the one standing here cleaning, scrubbing and changing the water every week. It started shortly after we got them, though the promise was this was his hobby responsibility and his alone. The first time the tank needed to be cleaned he called me over, "Aren't you going to help me? Let's do this together." and within minutes he was yelling and screaming at me to do it this way or that, or I was doing it wrong. Within a short period of time, it became "Why haven't you cleaned the tank yet? Can't you take care of it yourself 'cause if I have to get involved you know what will happen." He was right. He had manipulated me into taking on this responsibility, even though with 4 kids, 2 under the age of 3, I really didn't have the time, but it was easier than being made to do it with him, while he yelled at me.

I took over doing the nightly dishes after he deliberately broke two glasses and suggested that if I didn't want more to break I should just take over.

He would whine and complain worse than the toddler about every ache and pain. It was so excessive and unnecessary, continuing on and on and not stopping until I offered to help alleviate the pain.

Threats

Threats **are verbal** abuse used to frighten victims into compliance. They are a tell-tale sign that the verbal abuse will escalate. For this reason, we want to take a moment to discuss threats in a little more detail.

Threats are often verbal, but they also fall within several of the other categories depending on the specifics of the threat issued. Rarely is the intent to threaten the victim with more words. Demands fit into this category as well; the intent being that if the victim doesn't meet the demand, something negative will happen. Although the threat itself is verbal, that is simply the vehicle for something much more menacing. Threats may also be non-verbal: a look, picking up a weapon, holding up the back of the hand, pointing, stalking, etc. Any time the intent is to control or instill fear based on the idea that something else could happen, a threat has just been issued. This is another common type of abuse outside of non-romantic relationships that everyone should be aware of.

In the workplace, threats are often used to get employees to focus on specific projects or reach particular goals. In parenting, threats are frequently used to get children to behave. When someone breaks into our home or puts us in a dangerous situation, we use threats to scare them away and appear bigger and more powerful than we are. It is no different with an abuser except the victim isn't the one creating a dangerous, fearful environment. Threats instill fear and fear is the basis or foundation of power and control.

- "When you come home tonight, you might find a 'for sale' sign on the lawn, and I might just be gone with the kids."
- "If you did that, no one would blame me for how I'd react."
- Threatening to call the authorities to report you for wrongdoing.
- Threatening to harm themselves when upset with you.

- "If I can't have you, then no one can."

Threats are particularly effective if the abuser has done things to make the victim believe they would actually follow through, whether directly related to the threat or not.

As the physical abuse increased, in the forms of pushing, shoving, bumping into things, or stepping on feet, the threats became much more effective. Because he built the foundation of trust, that he would indeed hurt me, I knew the threats were real. One time he looked at me and said, "I know how to kill a man with the snap of my fingers." His eyes and military background assured me he was telling the truth. The response of fright was embedded into my body as I felt the instant need to retreat back a few steps.

There were weapons all over our house. I knew when I met him that he liked to be protected. I assumed this was due to his military training. Early on, it made me feel safe knowing he could protect us. On each side of the master bed, a knife was placed right under the mattress, close enough to reach easily. He was very aware of and acknowledged many times their existence, so that I wouldn't forget their presence. It didn't take much for his threats to stick.

Once, we were talking in the kitchen and the conversation got heated. He looked at me with those intense eyes and said, "If you think you can get to that knife faster than I can while we sleep then you're dead. I would get there faster than you and slit your throat before you even pulled it from under the mattress." His eyes bore into me for a long moment before softening and crinkling with his laughter. "Haha. That's so funny. I'm just kidding, but don't let me catch you moving them. I'll know if they are out of place."

I laughed, but as he walked away, I wondered, "Did he just say he'd kill me? He loves me, right? Doesn't he love me?" No wonder I felt crazy all the time.

Threats and verbal abuse are such a mixture of every type of abuse. Additionally, they are hard to prove, to others and even ourselves. It's easy to justify, "He's just a jerk." By the time a victim realizes they're being threatened, sometimes it's too late.

Withholding

Withholding is when the abuser refuses to talk with or withdraws from the victim. The "silent treatment" if you will. It is another tactic used to dominate and control and takes a psychological toll on the victim, just like the more verbal categories of abuse.

Remember when we said matter of factly that we all have been verbally abusive at one point or another? This is one of those areas where many of us default to abusive behaviors, particularly within an argument. By developing better, healthier argument tactics, we can begin to eliminate this damaging and abusive tool.

Refusing to talk, looking the victim in the eye, or even being in the same room, the victim must work harder to get the abuser's attention, communicate, or interact. The abuser's refusal to discuss the problem or allow the victim an opportunity to be heard is a power-play aimed at demonstrating dominance and further belittling or isolating the victim. At a friend's house, you say or do something they don't like. Without a word, they storm out and sit in the car, leaving you to explain and say goodbye to your hosts.

- They know you need to communicate about who's picking up the kids, but they refuse to answer your calls or texts.

We were headed to a party that one of his coworkers was throwing. We hadn't been to a party in a long time, and he hadn't had coworkers even longer, so even though I was an exhausted introvert, I was looking forward to getting out and meeting his new friends.

On the way, a discussion turned into an argument. He was angry and we both just stopped talking about it. When we arrived, it was dark. We had to park pretty far away from the house. Before I got out of the car, he had already started walking down the street toward the house. I caught up with him at the door as the host was letting us in. He didn't even acknowledge me, much less introduce me, as he made his way through the crowd. I spotted him intermittently for the next several hours until I found him completely drunk and having a great time on the back porch. At that point, the party was slowing down, so he begrudgingly agreed to leave with me. He didn't speak to me again until sometime the next afternoon.

In the case of withdrawing, victims often overcompensate by talking more, trying even harder to engage the abuser in some type of conversation. "Tell me what I did wrong?" Apologizing, but not knowing what it was that upset them. In this type of situation, the abuser holds all the power as the victim is left replaying the tape, trying to figure out what went wrong and how to fix it.

Yelling

Yelling, screaming, rampaging, finger-pointing, or terrorizing is a common form of verbal abuse. Abusers will often attempt to overpower and intimidate their victims by raising their voice and creating an overall environment of chaos. This is a category of abusive behavior that may be experienced outside of romantic relationships. It is often experienced in parent/child relationships and even employment. No one deserves to be yelled at.

We became so accustomed to yelling that the versions and variations started to be very clear, even the children learned how to interpret them. So much so we would alter behaviors to try to prevent the yelling or avoid it. Yelling became a language we had to learn, interpret and also speak. It was all part of surviving the day.

- Stomping around the house yelling, arms waving, knocking stuff off the table.
- Griping about everything or anyone who walks in the room.

- Family walks on eggshells, not sure of when he will get angry or start yelling.
- Victims feel as though they can't do anything right.

Years later, when in a healthy marriage, I witnessed my husband experiencing abuse from his boss. I recognized it immediately as verbal abuse and was surprised when others didn't call it out, since it wasn't reserved to just behind closed doors. It wasn't uncommon to hear loud voices over the phone when his boss called. That man rarely spoke to his employees at what anyone would consider an acceptable level. As I was working in the dining room, the noise that was coming from the master bedroom was alarming. I could clearly hear the words screaming through the phone at my husband, three rooms away, and they were not kind, respectful or what children should hear, much less how an employee should be spoken to. Hell, no human should be spoken to that way.

Part of what makes this category so hard and dangerous is that we often don't recognize the difference between verbal abuse and a "normal" disagreement or discussion. As we grow up, adults, including our parents, frequently resolve conflict in private. Unless they are screaming and yelling, we don't often learn how the disagreement was resolved. We may think they magically get resolved or don't even have a thought about it. Either way, we are ill-prepared for how to handle our own arguments in our relationships. We aren't even sure what "normal" is.

I remember the first healthy disagreement I experienced a few years after leaving my abusive relationship. I was shocked. I was confused. How could an argument be so calm? Why weren't they yelling? Where was their cursing and name-calling? After years of unhealthy relationships, it was difficult to not engage in those same behaviors. Ultimately, I had to learn what a healthy disagreement looked like. It also took a while to feel safe and okay after an argument, because what I had come to rely on was not the calm and peace that was before me. Still to this day, 6 years into the aftermath, I have to remind myself that a disagreement or even an argument doesn't equal fear.

There are many people that have never seen or experienced a healthy disagreement, so there is no basis of understanding because there is a lack of foundation. We use the term *healthy* instead of *normal* because sadly, "normal" disagreements or arguments often lead to verbal abuse and personal attacks. Disagreeing in a healthy way does not come naturally. When we are hurt or feel attacked, it is normal to want to lash out. It takes a great deal of control to not intentionally hurt someone with our words. That is why it is so important to begin raising children to have these healthy disagreements and role play with them. We cannot allow the next generation to grow up not knowing what a healthy disagreement and discussion look like.

Generally speaking, in healthy relationships, true arguments don't happen every day. Issues are discussed but don't regularly turn into arguments. They also don't have a winner at the detriment of the other person, who feels like the loser at the end. In fact, healthy disagreements more closely resemble discussions rather than arguments. When the discussion is resolved, it is over.

Participants in healthy arguments (discussions):

- Address the relevant issues or concerns, ask for what they want, and set healthy boundaries. They don't stoop to name-calling, personal attacks, or character assassinations.
- View the problems raised as something to be tackled as a team, not a competition that one will win and one must lose.
- Listen to each other and try to understand the other's position and empathize, even when both are upset.
- Use calm voices and respectful language. Although raising your voice in frustration is somewhat natural, yelling or saying something awful out of frustration is an unusual occurrence.
- Know when to pause and restart at a later time to allow tempers to cool but still resolve in an adequate time period.

Neither party is forced to stay against their will, or denied re-entry after stepping away for self-care.

- Can come to a compromise even if you can't agree completely, with the ability to move on without punishments or threats.

Examples of *un*healthy disagreements or arguments and signs that you may be in an abusive relationship:

- Frequent yelling or screaming.
- Arguments that take you by surprise and seem to come from out of nowhere, but the blame for starting them is pushed toward you.
- An initial disagreement sets off a string of accusations and dredging up unrelated issues to put you on the defensive quickly, which then in turn fuels the fire they are lighting or trying to light.
- They try to make you feel guilty and position themselves as the victim, bringing up all the things that have been done to them or how they have been wronged. Refusal to take responsibility.
- They save their hurtful behaviors or those that would be more alarming to outsiders for when you are alone, typically utilizing embarrassment and jokes at your expense in the presence of others.
- At some point, the argument can start to cross physical boundaries by getting into your personal space or blocking you from walking away from the discussion. They may hit the wall, gather their hand into a fist, throw things and express a high level of anger, typically used as a fear tactic to keep you from talking anymore and just submitting.
- Telling you that they should get credit. "At least I didn't hit you" or "at least I hit the wall instead."

Most of these examples sound like things we would never imagine putting up with, but it is possible that verbal abuse is happening so subtly that you don't recognize it.

How is that possible? According to Patricia Evans, author of The Verbally Abusive Relationship, in more than two decades she has counseled some 40,000 people about verbal abuse, many of whom didn't realize that what was happening to them by someone they loved is/was abuse.[3] The fact is, abusers have significant influence on how their victims perceive reality. They know how hard or how far to push before their victim breaks or recognizes the abuse for what it is. Over time, abusers do begin pushing their boundaries, but the behavior has become normalized for the victim and they are often too far in so that leaving the situation doesn't feel like an option.

Interestingly, abusers aren't always intending to take victims down this path. They aren't necessarily plotting it out and calculating their next move. As in all types of abuse, calculated actions or intention is not a requirement for the behaviors to be considered abusive. What makes the behavior abusive is the negative effect it has on the victim, regardless of intent.

> *They're being put down constantly by a boyfriend, girlfriend or spouse. These abusers are defining their reality for them. Which is, in essence, insane. But people who experience it may just start to think, 'I'm an awful, stupid person.'*

> *The effects of this self-worth tear-down tactic, combined with gaslighting statements like, "You're being too sensitive" or "That never happened," can be emotionally destructive for years to come. It can be worse than physical abuse. I know some [survivors] would rather get hit because things like bruises can heal.*[4]

Is There a Pattern?

How can we determine if what we are experiencing is abusive behavior? The number one way is by establishing whether or not abuse is the pattern of behavior.

In her book, Evans identifies ten patterns verbal abuse may take, and seeing them all laid out like that really helped us identify them in our own relationships. Abuse by means of verbal attacks will typically include some element of many of these, if not all of them.

He would tell me "this is a bedroom conversation" to stop me from talking any more. I learned to know what that meant, and it wasn't good.

What happens at home stays at home. The worst verbal abuse often occurs out of the public eye. This serves a double function by isolating the victim and catching them at their most vulnerable, and protecting their public reputation. If your partner continually waits until you are alone together to unload on you, rather than bringing up concerns in the moment, that is cause for concern. However, it can also be a warning sign if behavior that you once experienced only in private starts to leak out into public spaces. Evans notes that "going public" with blatant verbal abuse is "usually a sign of escalation and/or impending physical abuse."

Where did that just come from? If a verbal onslaught catches you off guard with some frequency, especially when everything seems to be fine in the relationship and you couldn't have predicted or pre-empted it, it is important to acknowledge this quickly. If one minute he's telling you how happy you make him, and the next how miserable, that's an indication of a pattern of verbal abuse.

But (we, you, I) are/were just so happy. If you notice that when you gain or express enthusiasm and/or success in some area of life--career, health/wellness, school, etc.--and your partner seems even more stressed and angry, with arguments escalating even more quickly than usual, pay attention. That's an indication that your partner is using verbal abuse to suppress your joy and detract from your achievements.

Verbal attacks as a form of communication begin to feel normal in abusive circumstances. Though it may take on different forms, it just seems like the same thing over and over. A good example of this is when you express basically any thought on something and the other person constantly argues against it. The feeling of being the enemy no matter the specific details just becomes part of reality.

Diminishing the interests of the other person or expressing complete disdain toward them is another tactic used to belittle, degrade, and maintain control..

> *My career was going at a steady pace and it felt like a manage-able place to stay for a bit so I started to pursue my passion of crafting, particularly paper crafting and scrapbooking. He was always so deep into his music/band hobby it was nice to have something of mine to fill the void of his absence. Plus I knew I was capturing memories for generations to come.*
>
> *At first, he didn't seem to have much issue with it and would even seem somewhat interested in the details, gracing me with his "artistic eye." I would laugh it off most times because I didn't need the help. I was fairly confident in my artistic abili-ties since I was a child. For almost the entire time of my full-time career, I made sure to find ways I could improve my graphic design skills and learn more about how to use the "elite" programs like the professionals because I knew those skills would be invaluable in my position. So as I got more into it, so did my confidence, and more so, how happy it made me. It was my escape time to just be me. I didn't have to be mom, housekeeper, cook, maid, or employee. Just me, paper and glue (and a lot of other fun things, if you know, you know).*
>
> *The side comments like calling it "child's play" or a waste of time compared to his hobby of playing music that could make him money and fame would come out of the blue, but usually after having a layout published or having a "pro" comment on my submission. (Interestingly enough his "band" never made a single dime in almost a decade before I even attempted to*

pursue my own hobby.) His comments started off snide but became even more hurtful the more I expressed joy in what I was doing. By the time I was teaching classes, holding and organizing weekend-long retreats and venturing into a full business all centered around my joy of memory keeping, I would avoid talking about it around him altogether unless I had to.

Does not instigate reconciliation. A person with a verbal abuse pattern most likely will not be the primary person to seek reconciliation. They don't try to apologize and may even indicate they don't believe there is anything to talk about, even after clear examples are brought up. If they fear they are losing control of the situation (for example, if the victim threatens to leave them), they prefer dramatic "grand gestures" such as expensive gifts, trips, or public declarations of love, rather than a simple and specific acknowledgment of and apology for their behavior.

It feels okay. Outside of these verbally abusive communications, it can be common to feel like the relationship is really OK because overall things seem to be functioning well. Victims often believe they can handle the abuse because, after all, it's just words. Abusers need to keep your sense of "it's not that bad" under their control.

Frequent feelings of isolation creep in until it becomes a full-time reality. Things don't necessarily feel right, but you would rather not talk about it, so instead of discussing it openly, or acknowledging it, it is easier to just pull away.

Inconsistent description of the relationship. How a person defines their partner, the relationship, and many of the interactions will be very telling. These descriptions are often very different from how the abused experienced them. For example, if your partner, who has an explosive temper, describes their temperament as "pretty easy going; I rarely raise my voice." Or if, when asked about your communication style, he paints you as crazy, unhinged, and bent on his destruction.

Despite the abuse received, the victim does not engage or return abusive behavior. This is an interesting element to the pattern. People who are consistently blamed and confused via verbal abuse wouldn't even think of saying the things that are frequently thrown their way.

My career was going at a steady pace and it felt like a manage-able place to stay for a bit so I started to pursue my passion of crafting, particularly paper crafting and scrapbooking. He was always so deep into his music/band hobby it was nice to have something of mine to fill the void of his absence. Plus I knew I was capturing memories for generations to come.

At first, he didn't seem to have much issue with it and would even seem somewhat interested in the details, gracing me with his "artistic eye." I would laugh it off most times because I didn't need the help. I was fairly confident in my artistic abili-ties since I was a child. For almost the entire time of my full-time career, I made sure to find ways I could improve my graphic design skills and learn more about how to use the "elite" programs like the professionals because I knew those skills would be invaluable in my position. So as I got more into it, so did my confidence, and more so, how happy it made me. It was my escape time to just be me. I didn't have to be mom, housekeeper, cook, maid, or employee. Just me, paper and glue (and a lot of other fun things, if you know, you know).

The side comments like calling it "child's play" or a waste of time compared to his hobby of playing music that could make him money and fame would come out of the blue, but usually after having a layout published or having a "pro" comment on my submission. (Interestingly enough his "band" never made a single dime in almost a decade before I even attempted to pursue my own hobby.) His comments started off snide but became even more hurtful the more I expressed joy in what I was doing. By the time I was teaching classes, holding and orga-nizing weekend-long retreats and venturing into a full business all centered around my joy of memory keeping, I would avoid talking about it around him altogether unless I had to.

Abuse often starts as verbal, but can quickly escalate. Once the verbal abuse loses its effectiveness, the abuser often has to prove that their threats are not empty to remind you of their power and your reality.

Verbal abuse doesn't always *feel* negative at first either. Constant contact can feel like love, not control. Critiquing your clothing can feel like support, not criticism. Pushing you in your career can feel like encouragement, not responsibility. Joking around can feel fun and not humiliating, degrading, and disrespectful.

 At one point or another, we have all been or have the propensity to be verbally abusive. The first person many of us, especially women, verbally abuse is ourselves. We say things to ourselves that we would never say to someone else. We tear ourselves down for making mistakes, we call ourselves *stupid* and *ugly*, and question why anyone would give us a chance. The things we say to ourselves are the most powerful influencers on our own self-image and often perpetuate the cycle of abuse. This tendency to speak without thinking or tearing down with our words creates a petri dish to grow abuse that is always available. The average person has 60,000 thoughts a day, and 95% of them are the same as yesterday.[5] As incredible as the brain is, it will believe whatever we continually tell it: good or bad, true or false. We need to take responsibility for feeding our minds positive, uplifting truths.

> *I was a bully at times in high school, but I didn't continue and I didn't mean to hurt people. People apologize when they realize it or don't intend to hurt people. In the moment, I was passing my pain onto someone else. Even so, it wasn't and still isn't okay. Just because I didn't mean to hurt them, especially long-term, doesn't mean it didn't.*

We encourage you to be aware of and not downplay the words used and how they make you feel. Although they may not be able to physically hurt you, they do affect you psychologically, especially when used over and over. It may very well end there, but likely won't. Even if it does, you deserve so much better.

What to do if you believe you or someone you know is experiencing verbal abuse:

- Keep a small, hidden journal and document examples of verbal abuse, especially threats. Better yet, if you can do so safely, secretly record examples and keep the recordings in a secure dropbox or send them to an ally. Make note of the situation, exactly what was said, and how it made you feel.
- Be honest, acknowledging your actions and words as well.
- Talk to the abuser, letting them know how their joking, name-calling, etc., makes you feel. Ask them to stop. Their response will tell you quite a bit about their intent.
- Whenever possible, disengage from arguments with your abuser. They only serve to fuel the flame of abuse and accomplish little. Anything you say will be used as a weapon. Like an attacker who finds that knife you hid under your pillow in hopes that it would keep you safe and turns it against you, an abuser is far more adept at wielding words as weapons, and far more ruthless in exploiting any weaknesses you betray. The less material you give them, the better.
- As soon as you can do so safely, just walk away.
- Don't stoop to their level.

ECONOMIC ABUSE

I worked hard. Like really hard. I'm talking two to three jobs at a time. Early on in our relationship, I moved in with his parents, launching our relationship ahead a little more quickly. Though we were young, I had no desire to live with someone else's parents. I was an adult and wanted to behave as one. Now, I know many people who live with parents/in-laws. When an active choice is being made to live in that situation, or when it is intended to be temporary, it is different than when you financially can't afford to get out from under it because one of the partners isn't responsible with money and is making poor and selfish choices.

What started out as a temporary situation out of necessity turned into our "normal." The more I worked, the less money it felt like we had. He had no control over his spending and priorities to him were having fun, which included alcohol and drugs. In the beginning, he was a contributing partner for the most part, but it was never very balanced.

Financial dependency was more of a lack of finances, so I had to keep working, often at jobs I didn't really want and which led away from the direction my heart and goals wanted. The more progress I made in my career, the more he would slack off, job-hop, or try to find a fast way into money.

In the early years of our relationship, I would wait tables or bartend while also holding a full-time career. It was not uncommon for him to come to my place of employment to just "hang out." Whether it was a lack of social skills, the ability to know when enough was enough, jealousy, or a power struggle, his actions quickly affected my job, the relationships at work, and ultimately my desire to continue to show up. I dreaded the days I needed him to pick me up because for sure he was already wasted or would get that way while I was working.

Naive as it may sound, I really thought things would change, that he would grow up and mature. I had compassion because we were young and he was already a dad when we met at 19 and 20 years old. I knew he needed time to let loose and just be a young adult male.

Life was a roller coaster and any stability during that time was provided by me working hard for it. We moved into a town-house, again secured by me, and from there I was able to buy a house within that first year. We had been married for a few years, had a two-year-old and an almost six-year-old. Life was starting to look up in some ways. I managed our life, worked full-time on salary, went to college at night full-time, and started my own organizational administration outsourcing on the side part-time, all while taking care of all of the home management. He was around and participated when he wanted to, but for the most part he lived as if he had no responsibilities or people who depended on him.

Within a four year period of time, I lost my salaried job, partly due to his constant calling and showing up, was convinced to refinance our home to use the equity for various expenses, and had my retirement cleaned out for "this is a good idea for our family" expenses. Sadly, those expenses ended up meaning a large backyard shed to hold his music equipment and band practice. He sat out there for hours drinking and not participating in our home.

Almost ten years in, I wanted a solution. This was my constant. He would work a job and within months find a reason to quit or get fired. The longest period of time he held the same job was three years. And to top it off, my birth control had failed yet again and I was pregnant. Even though at this point I felt like the situation was helpless and he wouldn't change, I didn't see a solution except to keep working as much and as hard as I could.

Our second son was born with a disability, so this added on a new element of responsibility. Again thinking, okay he will grow up now, so I stayed and continued.

A few years later, after 13 long ones, I was done. I was exhausted, financially depleted beyond what I could comprehend, and knew this was not what my life was supposed to be, should be, or what I wanted. Still to this day, more than a decade later, I am still in financial recovery.

Looking back, I can see that economic abuse was one of the first ways I was conditioned. I grew up being taught that when you were married you "became one" with your husband in all things. Many of us have been taught similarly. And why wouldn't you join everything together? Doesn't it make it simpler, build trust, give you a common goal and foundation, encourage the team mentality and less selfishness?

After a marriage with several elements of what I would refer to as mild abuses (now that I have experienced much worse), I was desperate for security, for a partner, for stability, work ethic and a decent financial foundation. The economic abuse in my first marriage primed me for future abuse because I was desperately looking for someone who would contribute, pay bills, and provide stability. My first marriage wiped me out and made way for the "all American" predator to step in.

With my first marriage, it may not have had the impact that it did because my second husband just picked it up and took advantage of it.

Economic abuse may be the least-discussed type of abuse, yet it remains one of the most prevalent. Between 94-99% of domestic violence survivors have also experienced economic abuse.[1]

Economic abuse or financial dependency is defined as making or attempting to make an individual financially dependent by maintaining control over or limiting access to shared or individual assets and/or financial resources, withholding one's access to money, forbidding one's attendance at school or employment, and/or limiting the current or future earning potential of the victim as a strategy of power and control.[2] Victim(s) are separated from their own resources, rights and choices, ultimately isolating them financially and creating forced dependency, which is the desired result. Economic abuse allows the abuser to quickly establish, maintain, and increase control at their discretion.

Sad fact: Survivors often cite financial manipulation as a primary reason they stay with an abusive partner.[3]

Financial Torment

Financial torment is a way to exert control through the manipulation of economic resources. Finances or even the talk of money is hard for everyone, especially so when experiencing many of the forms of financial dominance and control listed below. The reality is that this is such a huge topic of life in general that there is no way to include examples of everything. In addition, most cases experience numerous tactics within the same category and financial abuse is no exception. Economics of your life can be impacted by financial abuse on varying levels of the pendulum at any point in time. This may include, but is not limited to:

- controlling the family income and either not allowing access to money or rigidly limiting access to family funds.
- keeping financial secrets or hidden accounts.
- putting the victim on an allowance or allowing the victim no say in how money is spent.
- making them turn their paycheck over to the perpetrator.
- causing the victim to lose a job or preventing them from taking a job, e.g. by making them late for work, negatively affecting their work performance by breaking down their confidence, hiding resources, etc., refusing to provide transportation to work, or by calling/harassing/embarrassing them at work.
- spending money for necessities (food, rent, utilities) on nonessential items (drugs, alcohol, hobbies.)
- forbid attendance that would help them gain financial independence - school, work, social interactions.
- preventing you from keeping or getting a job.
- making you ask for money.
- interfering with work or education.
- using your credit cards without permission.
- not working and requiring you to provide support.
- keeping your name off joint assets.
- making you pay for his attendance at a behavioral change program.
- borrowing money from you and not paying it back.
- removing, stealing, and/or selling your assets without your knowledge.
- forging signatures to have access to your funds.
- making you dependent on their income.
- routinely checking and criticizing your expenditures.
- unfounded litigation to incur legal costs.
- having to pay relocation expenses to avoid further abuse.

Economic abuse may be the least-discussed type of abuse, yet it remains one of the most prevalent. It is often not recognized as abuse and is often the most difficult to identify. Victims themselves may not even recognize this as abuse, which makes it an easy entry and escalation point for abuse. If you think you are alone, consider the evidence. Between 94-99% of domestic violence survivors have also experienced economic abuse. Between 21-60% of victims of domestic violence lose their jobs due to reasons stemming from the abuse. Victims of domestic violence lose a total of 8 million days of paid work each year. Eight million days! Between 2005 and 2006, 130,000 stalking victims were asked to leave their jobs as a result of their victimization. Without jobs, victims can lose their freedom, confidence, and livelihood. So not only are victims losing access to the financial resources they *do* have, they are even further limited because of the loss of *future* income.[4]

Victims are not the only ones struggling to see economic abuse as domestic abuse. There is a clear trend emerging where other countries are more proactive in protecting economic and other forms of domestic abuse by clearly outlining it in their forms. America is falling behind. It is difficult to prove economic abuse, not only to ourselves, but to the legal system. If you are not legally married, you may have more freedom and the ability to get out. Once you are married, there are more legal obligations and challenges associated.

Economic abuse creates a "forced dependency" situation where even when victims are able to get away from their abuser, which is a challenge in itself, they find themselves forced to return because they are unable to care for themselves and/or their children financially. When children are involved, it is nearly impossible, especially for stay-at-home moms who have not been working regularly outside of the home to find employment that can both pay their bills and cover childcare. Without a bank account, credit, or any form of savings, victims are often unable to qualify for loans or even housing.

But it doesn't stop there. Abusers often continue to abuse their victims long after the victim has made a successful escape from the situation. In a marriage, one may not have control over the finances, but will be held legally responsible for the debts occurring at the time of divorce. Even if they escape the marriage without a ton of debt, often incurred by the abuser, victims can accrue extensive debt upon leaving the situation due to attorney fees, ongoing custody battles, and abusers dragging their victims back to court time after time for lengthy legal battles.

An abused mother will do whatever it takes to survive. It is our nature to protect our children at all costs. That often leads us to stay in abusive situations longer than we should because we want to provide for them. Sometimes, it takes abuse toward our children for us to see the impact of the situation on them and thus find the strength to move out. When the abuse is primarily economic, it is often more difficult to see the benefits of leaving. The reality is, it might be more difficult for a while. You may be buying your groceries from the dollar store, your children may not be able to participate in all of the activities they did previously, or you may live on the rough side of town for a while. It *is* a difficult and challenging transition. Even when the abuser is removed, you may still have to live in that state for a while. You may still *feel* abused, because the fallout from the abuse does continue.

Young women are often easy targets of economic abuse, though no woman is immune regardless of age, experience, or education. Abusers do this for a living. They prey on trusting, loving women who want to be loved and cared for. This chapter started with Erika's example of how economic abuse in one  marriage primed her for additional and escalated abuse in her second marriage. Because economic abuse can look so different, it's difficult to look at one situation and know if it is economic abuse or not.

Economic abuse was the highlight of my story. Even so, it took me years to recognize it as such. Married between college and graduate school, we didn't have a lot. Pulling my husband away from his career, family, and daughter to further my education, I wanted to prove my commitment to my marriage and career. I took multiple part-time jobs including cleaning the toilets during sporting events, tutoring athletes in the evenings, teaching classes, and working an assistantship. I also cooked three meals a day, prepped food for my husband for when I worked late, and hosted birthday parties to help him feel connected to our new home.

I was so desperate to prove myself that I did not hold him accountable to his side of the deal. Rather than pushing him to get a job, I encouraged him when he wanted to finish his degree. We took out student loans in my name while he majored in Japanese, hung out at late-night "study groups," and stopped attending classes when it got inconvenient. All of the tuition and bills that weren't covered with my part-time jobs were being charged on my student loans. We maxed out every semester, each time he reminded me that when I got my big, fancy job after graduation, we would be able to pay them back in no time.

He did eventually find a part-time job and he showered me with a new computer and great pictures taken with his new, professional camera equipment. The income he brought in was not enough to cover his new hobbies, so those expenses, in addition to his schooling, were also paid for by my student loans. My program took us to another city for a year before we moved across the country. Each time, finding work was "too difficult" or "not worth it" since we would just move again. Meanwhile, I was studying for my doctorate, working forty hours at one job, eight hours at another, and three days at the university where I spent the night on a cot in my office two nights a week.

When I pulled in front of a "help wanted" sign in a liquor store window and handed him the application, he figured he could be a wine and scotch connoisseur. He did get the job at the liquor store and was very good at it. I was happy to meet his request to sit with him every time he was working because I thought he just wanted to be near me. I would work in the back office during his shift any time I was able. I also happily supported his new hobby of filling our liquor cabinet because "at least he was working," and "it helped him serve the customers to know what it tasted like."

Unfortunately, this professional development was not supported by his part-time job. Again, the extra bills and expenses were covered by my student loans. When I was stressed or upset, he would buy me something special (and expensive) because "I deserved it." Of course, those gifts were all covered by my paycheck while our living expenses were covered by my student loans.

Two moves and four years later, I was working a full-time job, remodeling our new home in the evening, and cleaning up after an unemployed husband who slept all day and watched movies, played computer games, and drank all night. Any time I suggested he get a job, it was "beneath him," he was "too good" for that job. When he did find employment, he would quit a week later because "the manager was a jerk" or "they didn't give him the day off he asked for." We had $25,000 of credit card debt, two car payments, and $85,000 of student loan debt, all in my name because he had no income and no credit.

The most common economic abuse looks like victims having no assets in their name. This creates a sense of isolation and the inability to leave. In my case, I had all the assets in my name. This created an environment where I had to work more hours just to cover it. He was left living a lifestyle of freedom from responsibility. I had worked multiple jobs through my undergraduate degree and never took out a single loan. When we got married, I had one credit card that was completely empty, a car that was paid off, zero student loan debt, and $3,000 in savings. I was used to working hard, I just wasn't used to having so little to show for it. I was used to being alone, but I wasn't used to being so lonely. I definitely never expected to be so lonely in my marriage.

When I left, I gave him anything and everything he wanted, including the car I had paid off. I took on all the debt and just begged for him to let me walk away. Despite how much I wanted out, I didn't want him to be burdened with debt forever. I knew I had the means to get out of it eventually, but I knew he couldn't. Now, 10 years later, I still have $45,000 of student loan debt gaining over $2,000 of interest every single year. It continues to haunt me and is a constant reminder of *the poor choices and painful memories of my past. At times, I feel completely hopeless, like there's no way it will ever go down. It feels like the last connection to my past, and it is a burden I have carried with me into my new marriage. It is a burden that steals from my children and my overall happiness.*

Some men never leave the adolescent phase. When they find an achievement-oriented woman, they prey on her loneliness and exploit her supportive nature.

Early on, I had to quit my job when we moved. He did not allow me to work outside after that, though that's not how it started. At first he was supportive, even helping every once in a while with my children so I could interview. As soon as he thought of a situation in which it would be inconvenient for me to work, whether or not it was a real possibility, he would talk me out of the job. I remember thinking that if I was going to bring in an income, I was going to have to do it in a way so as to not interfere with his life.

Six years in, when I asked for a divorce, he removed all the funds from our joint account. He eventually made it so volatile that I couldn't continue the child care business that I had started to try to "contribute" as he demanded. He hid mail, stole deposit slips from my account before taking all of the money, and removed clothing, jewelry, and perfume from my room, hid them, then told me I was crazy. The more I resisted his control, the more he would exert his will to dominate.

Christian women often find themselves easy targets for economic abuse because we are raised with the understanding that, along with every other part of your life, you and your husband become one in the area of finances. We join our accounts and keep nothing from each other. We think we are being "good wives" by giving up all financial independence. In healthy, loving relationships, this is a wonderful way of showing trust and dependency on each other. In unhealthy relationships, this can set the stage for economic abuse where the victim is held prisoner in her own home, unable to care for herself financially.

Furthermore, the workplace is a prime setting for economic abuse. Not only are women still making an average of 81 cents for every dollar men make, we are often taking the greatest career hits when starting. This "motherhood penalty" ultimately results in a $900,000 loss of income over a 40-year career.[5] Additionally, in times of crisis such as the recent pandemic, women in the workforce are often impacted more significantly than men. Women occupy hourly, service positions at a higher rate than men, and these positions are generally among the first reduced during times of economic downturn. Again, referencing the recent pandemic, women were more commonly called upon to address the increased childcare and schooling responsibilities as offerings began to shut down. Even as schools and daycares open back up, women carry the additional burden of virtual schooling, juggling ongoing shutdowns, and monitoring new requirements, further decreasing their ability to focus on work and career.

Not all women are designed to or interested in staying at home with their young children, yet it is often the woman's paycheck that must be justified when having this discussion. We have heard multiple times that it's not worth it for a woman to go back to work because she doesn't make more than childcare would cost. That is a great decision point if the primary reason the woman wants or needs to work is to help support the family. In many cases, though, the woman enjoys her career and wants to work. It isn't about making money, but about doing something she loves outside of the home. Yet it is her paycheck that must cover child care expenses to make it "worth it" for her to work.

This is even more prevalent in relationships where the partners adhere to more gender-based roles of supporting the family versus supporting the home. The woman is often assumed to be the one to stay home without discussion or debate, setting her career back many years, sometimes to the point where it is non-recoverable. The woman is then left with no means to support herself and is often put in a position of financial dependence on her partner. In unhealthy relationships, this allows her partner to exert not only financial control, but further confine, isolate, and limit her. Furthermore, if the relationship comes to an end, she is now less able to support herself and her family due to her career set-back and diminished career potential. If she couldn't make enough to cover childcare *within* her relationship, after several years out of the workforce, she certainly isn't in a better position to cover childcare and work now.

Maybe you can't relate to any of these examples. If that's the case, we are so happy! We would, though, still encourage you to review the following tips on how to keep yourself protected. These tips are applicable to many situations, not just economic abuse.

Why it matters:

- Victims are often forced to return due to economic abuse.
- Can't afford to get out; can't afford to stay out.
- Continued financial fallout for the rest of your life or as long as your kids are in the home, including debt, bad credit, stalled-out career, etc.
- Continued attorney bills, relocation costs, medical and therapy bills, etc.

Economic abuse is one of those areas where there is not always a clear line between healthy behaviors and unhealthy ones. Fiscal responsibility can look like controlling behavior. Financial flexibility can look like irresponsibility. It can be hard to tell. That's why this is one area where it is important to play close attention to red flags, gut feelings, and patterns.

We recognize that there is a line, and similar behaviors in two different relationships can be classified very differently. It is important for women to know where that line is for them and which side of that line they are on. As in all behaviors, there should be mutual agreement and understanding. You should never feel dominated or coerced into a decision you don't fully agree with. Are you both in agreement with the goals and how you will get there? If not, it sets the stage for struggle, difficulty, and bitterness.

> *I have a young friend who is very financially mature and savvy. He has spreadsheets indicating where his money is going each month, and he saves more than he spends. He is frugal and lives debt-free. His wife enjoys shopping and having nice things. Before she married him, she saw his spreadsheets and knew that she would be expected to live within certain means and save more than she spent. We were visiting one day, and she mentioned that she couldn't go to her favorite store much because it was too expensive. She then laughed and said that it didn't fit within her allowance. My antenna immediately went up. I questioned her a bit to make sure she was comfortable with it and was in agreement with the decisions, and ultimately, she was. Still, I'm glad I checked, and now she knows she can come to me if she ever starts to feel uncomfortable with the arrangement.*

These types of conversations are critical to have early and often. Make sure you understand and agree with the life you are getting into. Thinking that you can bring and maintain your own spending habits into a relationship with someone whose habits are rigid and inflexible is a recipe for disaster. If you see a potential red flag or challenge, have those conversations right away and fully explore the implications of moving forward in the relationship.

Economic abuse can still exist in healthy relationships where one partner is oblivious to or removed from the finances. If one partner passes, for example, and steps have not been taken to protect the surviving partner, then they can be severely economically damaged due to the lack of preparation. Engaging in some of these steps will not only help protect yourself in potentially abusive relationships, but even those healthy relationships.

. . .

So, what do you do if you are in an economically abusive situation? Below are some tips, in progressing order, that will help you (re) establish financial independence or help put you in a plan where you will not be completely devastated financially if / when you choose to leave your situation but will also put you in a better place if you choose to stay. Our goal is to help shift the power back; to help you regain your power in the relationship. Not to lord over your partner, but to feel like and be the equal partner you deserve to be. As a society, we need to normalize financial independence and security rather than demonizing it. Financial independence creates options, and options lead to healthy futures.

- Emergency evacuation box including originals (or at least copies) of birth certificates, marriage license, passports, other important papers, phone numbers, cash, and an available credit card in a safe place or even at a friend's house
- Bank account in your name and a credit card - even if nothing is in it.
- Extra copies of car and house keys you can access easily.
- Emergency phone numbers (general tip) - don't be "locked" to your phone, something that can be taken away or left behind.
- Keep track of things you purchase with your own money, especially when cohabitating. Keep your receipts.
- Track gifts and note items inherited from your family or pre-existing to the relationship. Write it down.

SEXUAL ABUSE

Sexual assault and abuse were a large factor in my story. From the beginning of our relationship he exploited my vulnerabilities, infected me with an incurable disease, and exerted his sexual dominance.

I don't remember a time when I didn't feel scared to say no or even talk about concerns. Sexual assault and misconduct were rampant. Sexual abuse has been part of my story since the age of five or six, to "losing my virginity" to an unwanted person and in an unwanted circumstance. Sex became flippant to me. I didn't care anymore. Why should I? Nobody else cared about me. The abuse of my past became a tool to be exploited by the next abuser.

Sexual abuse and assault are intense subjects. Like so many other areas of abuse, it is deeply personal, and many women are embarrassed or uncomfortable even talking about it. That lack of discussion often leaves women feeling alone in their experiences or like what they are experiencing isn't abuse because we don't openly discuss it within intimate relationships. Just because we don't openly and frequently discuss this type of abuse does not mean it is any less real or occurs any less frequently. In this chapter, we hope to break the stigma and silence around sexual abuse within intimate relationships.

Sexual abuse involves acts covering a wide range of unwanted sexual behavior and tactics used to assert power and control. The formal definition of sexual abuse is coercing or attempting to coerce any sexual contact or behavior without consent.[1] In short, it is using sex in an exploitative fashion or forcing sex on another person. Having consented to sexual activity in the past, or anticipating consenting to sexual activity in the future, does not in itself indicate current consent. As we discussed in the section **Defining The Language We Use**, it is important to really know the definition and application of consent. In her book *Enough: Breaking the cycle of Emotional Abuse in Romantic Relationships*, Dr. Adrienne Maclain laid out a great foundation for consent called the IDEAL model of consent: in order for someone to give true consent, the agreement must be: Informed, Direct, Engaged, Aligned and Lucid.[2]

Sexual abuse includes, but is certainly not limited to:

- marital rape (also includes unwanted sex (a.k.a., rape) of unmarried partners).
- attacks on sexual parts of the body.
- forcing sex after physical violence has occurred (or when physical violence has NOT occurred).
- treating one in a sexually demeaning manner.

Sexual abuse may involve both verbal and/or physical behavior. It is a highly debated and controversial topic in the United States especially in recent years and social movements. In order to completely grasp this broad category it is important to use words that adequately describe these horrific situations.

The Tactics of Sexual Abuse

Infidelity

Sexual abuse may involve the abuser having affairs or openly flirting with other people in front of the victim, potentially even using that information to taunt the victim. Cheating exposes the partner to physical risks without their awareness or consent. Although infidelity in any form is abusive, blatant, in-your-face infidelity is a tactic for maintaining control.

Callous Disregard

Callous disregard is demanding sex at times when sex is not desired or conceivable:

- during or due to an illness
- after having a new baby
- after a very trying day
- when there is a full house of company
- after an abusive tirade

"But instead of yielding and caring for the whole being of his wife, a common characteristic of an entitled husband is to disregard his wife's circumstances and expect or demand that sex proceed as usual."[3]

Coercion

Coercion is the use of force, guilt, or manipulation, or not considering the victim's desire to have sex.[4] This may include making the victim have sex with others, have unwanted sexual experiences, or be involuntarily involved in prostitution. Coercion may include:

- Implying or stating that he will get violent.
- Threatening to leave.
- Forcing the victim to find "another" woman.
- Exposing the victim in some form.
- Punishing the victim or her children.

Coercive sexual abuse can be very confusing because after being "persuaded" (a.k.a. bullied), consent was technically granted. The victimized wife is left wondering, "Was I sexually assaulted or did I agree to it?" Whatever form of coercion is used, be it physical, financial, or emotional, any sexual act which is not based on mutual consent constitutes sexual violation. It leaves a wife feeling confused, dirty, betrayed, and assaulted.[5]

Exploitation

Exploitation is engaging in sexual activity with a victim who is unable to make an informed decision about their involvement in sexual activity because of being asleep, intoxicated, drugged, disabled, too young, too old, or dependent upon or afraid of the perpetrator. Exploitation is easy to see within the workforce when someone feels as if they do not have a choice but to engage in unwanted sexual acts due to their hierarchical relationship with the abuser. Many organizations have put a stop to supervisor/subordinate relationships because it is very difficult to determine the true extent of consent versus exploitation.

Yes, one always has the "option" to say no in a given situation, but that "choice" also often comes with consequences. Although it is technically against the law, retaliation is very real and often hard to pinpoint. A victim who turns down advances from her supervisor may not be invited to key meetings, be turned down for promotions or advancement, not have opportunities to travel to desirable locations, or even be fired during a "restructure." Even uncomfortable work environments, often referred to as hostile work environments, can make it so difficult that victims ultimately leave the team or organization, thus resulting in economic challenges related to abuse.

Insulting

Laughing or making fun of another's sexuality or body, making offensive statements, insulting, harsh judgment, or name-calling in relation to the victim's sexual preferences/behavior.

Pornography

Many men fall into the addictive trap of pornography. It may feel like an innocent act, but consumption of pornography by a partner can be painful for many women. Opening the door to pornography individually or even within the relationship is a dangerous slippery slope. Intentional or not, it often makes women feel insecure and unworthy of love.

In the hands of an abuser, pornography can be a powerful tool to make women comply with their wishes or even make the victim feel like it's her fault that he's addicted. We are not saying all pornography use is wrong and bad or trying to shame anyone who enjoys it, we have simply lived the pain and regret of allowing pornography into our relationships and have watched the destruction and ultimate breakdown of ourselves and our relationships that resulted. Please be cautious when considering pushing beyond this boundary. Some dangerous phrases or ideas include:

- I have to look at porn because you won't have sex with me.
- I'm just learning how to please you better.
- It will be good for us to watch together; spice things up
- You should watch this; you could learn a few things.
- See how much she's enjoying that? Maybe you would, too...
- At least I'm not cheating on you.
- You are okay with watching a threesome, so you should be okay with having one.

Unrelenting Pressure/Harassment

Pleading or demanding of sex in such manner that the pressure of it never lets up. In such situations, it feels easier to give in than to deal with the alternative.

Examples include:

- Being lectured, sometimes for hours.
- Being degraded.

- Threatening of withholding of affection unless it culminates in sex.
- Told they are the cause or made to feel responsible for their husband's use of pornography, flirtation with others, infidelity, etc..
- Sex on demand is an expectation or "right" within the marriage.

I was explicitly forbidden to use the word "no." I was only allowed to say, "Yes, if..."

Unwanted Acts

If the victim has expressed that they are uncomfortable with or uninterested in a sexual act, the abuser may behave as entitled, insisting, and completely disregarding what the victim has expressed.

Examples include:

- Expressing that something hurts, but they don't stop.

My first husband told me outright that he couldn't get off unless I was crying.

- Relentlessly being told or asked to perform, or having to hear about, a specific sex act you've already declined.
- Undesired sexting or demands of it.
- Being recorded while engaging in sexual activity without consent.

"It is possible that the abuse is so severe that a wife is too frightened to even give a voice to her preferences."[6]

Violation

This is typically in the escalation phase, the worst being rape; however that is not the only form of violation.

Other forms include:

- Actions performed while someone is sleeping or intoxicated.
- Unwanted sexual touch.
- Being forced to engage in unwanted acts to avoid another form of abuse.
- Ignoring or enjoying tears or other expressions of discomfort.

Withholding Sex

As we discussed in the verbal abuse section where the "silent treatment" is a form of abuse and isolation, withholding sex from the victim can also be used by an abuser as a control mechanism. This can be extra triggering and shame-inducing for women, raised as we are to believe that desire for intimate contact is bad, wrong, unfeminine, unnatural, etc. Overtly desiring or asking for sex from a man can be emotionally challenging, all on its own. Layer on behavior such as deliberate withholding, mocking, rejection, and shaming from a spouse, and you have a perfect storm of mortification.

――――――

 These stories are so hard to tell; to put onto paper. As with each of the tactics, we could write pages and pages of our story, but especially within this category. In all honesty, there are many memories that have been buried deep because they are just too hard to speak of with others. This is a vulnerable topic for us, and probably for you too. If at any point you need to pause, please don't hesitate to do so.

> *I was raised to not talk about sex. We didn't discuss it, we didn't make jokes about it, we didn't look at it. We were completely sheltered regarding anything sexual or body-related and just didn't discuss it at all. We talked about it more in church when we participated in "True Love Waits," an*

*international Christian organization promoting sexual absti-
nence until marriage, within our youth group. Even then, it
felt awkward and uncomfortable. I never dated in high school,
so the "sex talk" never really came up. I remember being so
uncomfortable dating that I made a pact with God. I would
marry the person that I was finally comfortable enough to date
if He would just make me comfortable enough to date someone.*

*When I finally did start dating in college, I never mentioned
my sex life to my parents and let them go on believing whatever
they wanted regarding what may or may not have been
happening. That's not entirely fair: I definitely encouraged
their belief that I was completely innocent and flawless when it
came to morals. I began to struggle with the pact I made with
God and felt like He was letting me off the hook. My relationship wasn't great; we argued a lot and I didn't feel that it was
the relationship I had always imagined. It wasn't bad; it just
wasn't good. I couldn't put my finger on exactly what it was.*

*When I did try to break up with him, he told me that since we
had sex, we were already married in God's eyes and it would be
basically like a divorce if we didn't get married. Of course, I
had never heard it put that way before, but his dad was a
preacher, so if anyone understood what God was really saying,
it would be him. Divorce was another taboo topic that would
later haunt me, but in that moment, it was enough to make me
feel completely trapped. I vowed to give my relationship 100%
of myself since I had already made a commitment. It would be
2 1/2 more years before we were actually married, but in my
mind, I was already pinned down.*

*Sex continued to be a sticking point and a place I began to feel
truly victimized in our marriage. When you grow up thinking
it's "bad" and a "secret," something you don't talk about, then
it's hard to make the transition to sex suddenly okay and even
good within your marriage. I remember the day after our
wedding, everyone was having brunch in the lobby of our hotel.
They had gifts for us and wanted to see us off, but I was so*

embarrassed, knowing that they all knew what we did up there. So much so, we literally snuck out of the hotel with our bags. I was flat against the brick wall, sliding past so that no one would see us. I didn't call our family until we were half-way to the airport for our honeymoon. I just couldn't bear to face the knowing eyes.

Six months into our marriage, my husband cheated on me with a good friend of mine, a bridesmaid at our wedding. We were at my parents' house, and she came over to watch a movie. At some point, I fell asleep. They betrayed my trust while I slept not three feet away. It was three months later that word spread around, and one of my other friends confronted them about it. She said that if they didn't tell me, she would. I was in the middle of writing a 40-page mid-term paper when he drove up to my office at school to tell me. To this day, I still move my fingers, as if typing the words on a keyboard when I am feeling anxious.

He said he did it because he was certain we would have a three-some one day anyway, so he didn't think I would mind or that it mattered much. Yes, he had been talking about a threesome since we got married, or even before. Since I didn't shut him down, I guess he took that as a sign of approval or acceptance.

For years, I put up with questionable behaviors. I heard someone say, "You can be raped by your husband just like you can be raped by a stranger." I remember blowing that off thinking how ridiculous it was. Once you get married, you are one. You don't have any say anymore, right? I just thought that's the way it was. Those words slowly began to sink in and I realized that I really didn't have a say. He was always pushing me to go farther than I wanted to go, using my previous acceptance of a "little bit more" as justification for pushing just a little bit beyond that.

I thought I was being a "prude" or letting my past doubts interfere. I wanted a good, healthy marriage, and I understood this was an important part of it. I was doing everything in my power to be a good, supportive, loving wife, why would I stop here? From doing things beyond my comfort zone and pain tolerance to opening our bedroom to others, each time he would justify that he was doing it to try and satisfy me, yet I was the one left feeling vulnerable, broken, and so far from anything I was comfortable with. I didn't even recognize myself or our relationship anymore.

But how do you tell anyone that this is happening in your marriage? I can control what happens to my body, right? If I really didn't want to do it, couldn't I just say no? The reality was, I did say no, over and over. But it came out more as a whisper, coming up with excuses, or trying to talk him out of it. If I did say no, it wasn't loud enough or strong enough, but when you're dealing with a narcissist, it never really is.

As with other types of abuse, victims range in their responses to sexual abuse. Although you may not find someone willing to discuss their experiences openly, we assure you that any and all responses are normal and okay. We don't get to choose the way we react to abuse. It takes time to learn new coping mechanisms and time to heal the wounds created by an abusive  environment. Over time, we encourage you to seek help and develop healthier ways of responding to the abuse, but that does not mean that there is anything wrong or broken with the way you initially respond.

In addition to degrading the victim's self-worth, how would she even begin to tell anyone about what she is experiencing? Like having a splinter in your backside, there is an added layer of embarrassment when it comes to telling others what happened. Already vulnerable, this type of abuse often pushes the victim into deeper levels of isolation.

Examples of withholding include:

- Emotional and physical stonewalling: withdrawing all affectionate contact for purposes of control.
- Banning the victim from the marital bed, forcing her to sleep on the floor, couch, or elsewhere.
- Mocking, belittling, and shaming her for her sexual desires or proclivities.
- Deliberately making her feel undesirable, unattractive, not worthy of sexual contact.
- Making her beg for sex, or demanding a quid pro quo, i.e. making her perform a certain sex act before he will show her physical affection or allow her any pleasure.

Since this subject is not as openly talked about, we want to take an extra moment to discuss the many myths surrounding sexual abuse within romantic relationships and help clarify exactly what constitutes it.

Debunking Common Myths of Sexual Abuse within intimate relationships

Myth #1 Sexual abuse must involve unwanted sex with the abuser:

Although rape is a prominent aspect of sexual abuse, many sexual behaviors outside of intercourse fall within this category. We want to draw your attention to the line regarding abusers engaging in affairs. In this vein, flirting with others could fall within the category of sexual abuse. Although the intent of this behavior is not always to hurt or control the victim, the behavior itself can be abusive when it is hurtful to the victim, particularly when that hurt is made known. Many people are naturally flirtatious. Many people have affairs because they are lonely or extremely sexually charged, or even because they lack respect for their relationship. Not all flirting or affairs are categorized specifically as sexual abuse, and it doesn't have to be. Some of us need to quantify it as "bad enough" to leave, and not having the label of abuse makes it hard to cross that line. Although this book is focused on abuse, we want

192 ERIKA SHALENE HULL & DR. CHERYL LEJEWELL JACKSON

victims to understand that behaviors do not have to be classified as abuse, and their partners do not have to be classified as abusers for the behaviors to be painful and unhealthy. This way of thinking kept us and continues to keep many others in unhealthy, unsafe relationships for far too long.

> *Thinking it was cute or flattering (I don't know), he would hit on other women right in front of me. I would laugh and jokingly roll my eyes, but it wasn't funny to me. It made me feel dirty and unworthy, like everyone knew I wasn't good enough.*

So, what makes flirting, affairs, harassment, making fun of the victim's sexuality, unwanted touching, or even withholding sex from the victim sexual abuse? Because this abuse is sexual in nature, we opted to group this type of behavior under the same category. We recognize that many people are uncomfortable with this topic in particular, and we did not want to have it randomly "pop up" in other sections.

> *I caught him cheating with a woman while I was giving birth to our daughter, which wasn't the first time by far. Caught is probably the wrong word, because that implies that he was trying to hide it. At times he would bring other women into our relationship. Sometimes it stayed virtually but there were many times I would entertain, feed, and make sure she was comfortable in my own home while he tried to sleep with them. This was never something I honestly wanted to participate in, especially in these circumstances. However, by this time in our relationship, I had become so demoralized, degraded, and honestly, thankful at times, that at least he wasn't touching me.*
>
> *He frequently wanted me to invite other women to come to bed with us and make the arrangements. He even provided details around the height and size of the women he wanted me to find. He asked daily for updates; how it was going. I had to provide proof that I was looking and making the invites. It wasn't just*

women either. I had to seek out men as well, anything to fulfill his fantasies right in front of me.

His depravity was one of the major contributing factors of me finding the strength to leave.

Myth #2 It isn't rape if you agreed to it in the past

This argument makes its way into many relationships, even non-romantic ones. Many abusers *and* victims hold this belief that rape is not possible once consent has been given. Or if they feel they have been violated in a specific instance that it isn't valid because they have agreed to it in the past. This faulty belief holds many victims prisoner in their own previous decisions, shame, and embarrassment. The reality is, each and every sexual act must be agreed and consented to, and either partner has the right to change their mind and withdraw from the activity at any point. Each decision involves a unique set of circumstances. Joining a relationship, agreeing once, or signing a marriage license is *not* a blanket agreement to all future sexual encounters with someone. We must change our *own* thinking around this as we work to change the mindset of others.

Although this myth is not unique to marital relationships, it is quite prevalent and rarely discussed. For that reason, we will spend the majority of our time in this section discussing the topic from that angle. Even if you are not currently in this situation, please take the time to read this section as the majority still will be relevant to other relationships where consent may have previously been given or future consent is anticipated.

We are taught that marriage is a beautiful partnership where the hearts and bodies of two individuals are united as one. Sex in relation to marriage is the coming together of this emotional and spiritual bond. When this is what we have based our foundation on it is hard to imagine the possibility that sexual abuse or violence can occur in a marriage. In reality, the frequency in which sexual abuse occurs in a marriage is much higher than what is reported. Sexual abuse in a marriage is a terrifying reality for many and one that is typically endured in silence and isolation.

Abusers who abuse within a marriage or any romantic relationship often have a sense of entitlement, believing their spouses exist solely for their satisfaction and to meet their personal needs. This way of thinking is instilled into society norms, generational thinking and reinforced by examples they see. This includes sexual needs and desires. When the wife does not comply or respond in a manner they want, the results are a pattern of coercive and punishing behaviors designed to force their compliance. The intimate part of the relationship is not about attaining equal pleasure, or an openness to talk about needs and/or desires. There can be an unwillingness to consider the victim's feelings or desires without judgment as part of the abuse as well.

So, what does this look like in a relationship? In all relationships, there is a need to come together to work out mutual balance between one's own personal needs and desires and those of the other person. This is healthy in a relationship.

Many psychologists have also acknowledged that in most cases, the husband is typically disengaged in other areas such as household management, parenting, and connecting relationally to others.[7]

It is not uncommon for women to be raped early in the relationship or on the honeymoon, so that the conditioning began early for them to be compliant or be terrorized. This starts to make more sense in our minds when we stop thinking of the "typical" rape scene we see in the media.

In situations of rape by a romantic partner, including a spouse, it is common for people to wonder how women do not realize what is happening to them. This can be hard to understand but in order to break down the confusion we must try to understand the pressures that bring it about. The following are six of the most common psychological pressures and coercions that bring about some of the confusion.

Pervasiveness of religious fundamentalist teaching about sex in marriage. These teachings have placed the responsibility for a man's purity on his wife's ability to provide unlimited sex. It is not a wife's job to keep her husband from sin. Yet we are taught over and over that:

- Men need sex.
- Withholding sex is always a sin.
- Your spouse has rights to your body any time and in any way.

In these situations, the spiritual plan for a healthy, willing mutuality is ignored. By encouraging this mentality, victims experience unnecessary guilt. Additionally, it portrays a God who is indifferent to and even sanctions a victim's suffering, creating a wedge in a wife's spiritual relationship. Sex was created to be an expression of relational and spiritual intimacy, not merely an act or need. Abuse damages that relationship and corrupts the associated physical expression of intimacy.[8]

Manipulative tactics - the desire is for the wives to be off balance and disoriented. If the wife believes she is responsible for the issues or is made to feel sorry for her husband (abuser), then she becomes easier to dominate.

Expression of remorse - this is used typically after an attack or during calm sessions. They are not intended with any truth or willingness to change, instead the intent is to reset the power and control dynamic. The main focus is still on what they want and getting his world back to compliance. True remorse is only when someone is truly horrified with their behavior and seeks help to stop immediately. Possibly they do it again even after expressing a dislike to it. Abusers may attempt to show remorse through gifts, tenderness, apologizing or giving attention that feel kind or even 'normal'.

The abuse is not constant - As in other types of abuse, sexual abuse is not necessarily a constant. There may be days of kindness or calmness and the abuser may even participate in household activities, creating a feeling of partnership. This inconsistency create confusion for the victim. She may begin doubting and questioning her own feelings and memory.

In the lighter moments, the victim often feels badly for not having loving thoughts toward her husband, wondering if she is exaggerating things and making a big deal out of nothing. Although peaceful periods make it more difficult to recall the darker moments, the cold feelings remain, creating additional confusion, because no matter what, emotions remember the experiences. During the positive times, she may even want to be intimate with her husband and even enjoy sex. This creates the confusion of "How can I be abused if I desire or enjoy sex?

Utilizing coercion to get consent and generating additional confusion. As we discussed earlier in this section, coercion is the use of force, guilt, manipulation or disregard for the victim's desires. The following paragraph so beautifully outlines the impact of coercion on the victim's future judgment, we decided to include it in full.

"For example, if a husband asks for sex repeatedly and his wife knows that if she does not comply that he will lecture her for hours and be frighteningly harsh with her children, she might give in to the demand so as to avoid an escalating punishment. What is confusing about coercion is that if she acquiesces, she believes: "I agreed to it." It is then very difficult to have clarity about what happened prior. So, she might feel defiled but thinks that it is unreasonable to feel this way. We need to combat this by helping these women to identify coercive tactics and by making sense of the emotions that they are feeling."[9]

Making the victim feel sorry for them - Abusers are the ultimate blame-shifters and become masters at finding excuses to avoid taking responsibility for their actions. These characteristics can typically be found elsewhere in their life such as on the job, extended family and others. Abusers will blame a stressful job, alcohol, the temptations of the sexual world, their jealousy or own insecurities, but no matter the additional excuses, blame is directed toward the victim. For example:

- You are a prude; sex is no fun for me. I have to push your limits.
- You never want to have sex with me. I cannot bear the constant rejection. I have no choice but to force you into it.

- Since you have let yourself "go," I am tempted all day by beautiful, put-together women. You could at least watch porn with me to help me get aroused and keep me faithful.
- You have no idea what it is like for me to be married to the only woman on the planet who doesn't desire me.
- You just spent all afternoon nagging me. How about showing me that you don't hate me?

It is important to remember that marriage does not:

- Equal consent.
- Obligate spouses to participate in any sexual act at any time.
- Equal sex-on-demand.
- It is not "wifely duty."

If he came to bed naked, I knew he expected sex no matter what. I wasn't allowed to go to sleep before him. He would roll me over and say, "I told you not to go to sleep before me." If I said no even in the nicest way possible, the withdrawal and deliberate removal of any affection would ensue. He would remind me at times of how awful he could be if he wanted to but I had the ability to prevent the behavior. It was my choice, but it wasn't really.

Choosing between two bad options is not a choice, it is survival.

Marriage does not equal consent to unlimited sex or unlimited types of sexual acts. Period!

Myth #3 Men need sex

We touched on this in the previous section, but there is a prevalent idea that men need sex, that they are unable to function properly and effectively without regular sex. It is the woman's responsibility to fill that need whenever and however it occurs, and if she does not, he has the right to take it or fulfill that need elsewhere.

Abraham Maslow, an early pioneer in modern psychology and the father of Maslow's Hierarchy of Needs, outlined the human needs at each level until achieving self-actualization. Not only is sex not mentioned within the first run of basic, physiological needs that include food, water, warmth, and rest, but he does not mention sex at all in his hierarchy. He does, though, include intimate relationships along with the need for friends at the third level of the hierarchy under the needs of belonging-ness and love.

Not only is sex not a physiological need for men or anyone else, but to believe that it is the *woman's duty* to provide such needs, even if it *was* a necessity, is ludicrous. It is outrageous to think that, yet that way of thinking has made it into our cultural norm. Perhaps we don't think about it that way and certainly would never *say* it that way, but you can hear it in the way we talk about it, the jokes we make, or the things we tell ourselves. We experience it in the way we respond to rape within the confines of an intimate relationship or how we justify inappropriate behavior because "a man has needs" or "that's just how men are."

Sexual abuse in a marriage is whole-body, devastating trauma. It has been proven over and over that it is more difficult to reveal and experi-ence sexual abuse by an intimate partner than by a stranger. What is even more devastating is that many wives continue living with the husbands who violated them, or if they do escape, they are required to have contact due to sharing children. We do not have the expectation of sexual assault victims to have any contact with their rapist, much less share living space, a home, and a bed. Most of us have a scene come to mind when we think of rape. A violator in a dark alley awaiting his prey. A hand reaching out and snatching a jogger, covering her mouth with a dirty hand. Fighting, terror, blood, tousling, and force. We can clearly see it and almost experience the horror ourselves. When this is the image we have of rape, it is difficult to imagine a wife being raped in her king-sized bed atop a white comforter in the suburbs and then sending her husband off with a sack lunch the next day as he drives to work in his Ford Fusion.

There is certainly a diversion that is hard to wrap our heads around. Even as victims, we struggle to see ourselves on the same level as a victim of date rape or of random assault. And to be fair, the violation and the terror that accompanies an attack by a stranger is extreme and incredibly traumatic. Yes, those characteristics often accompany rape, but they do not *define* the rape. Just as we have read with the previous types and examples of abuse, we must begin breaking the stigma of what abuse looks like and therefore is.

Even as victims, we struggle to break the stigma around wife rape. We ourselves often come to believe the stigma, that we made a choice to marry him and so somehow deserve to be in this situation. That this is just "part of the deal." We had a choice, whereas victims in non-marital rape didn't. If this is you, we encourage you to ask yourself:

- Did I really have a choice? Could I have said no?
- Have I said no in the past? If so, what was the result?
- What would have happened if I had said no?

By the way, him pouting and carrying on about you not wanting to have sex with him is a form of abuse. It is childish and not physically abusive, sure, but it is manipulation and coercion in an attempt to get you to do something you do not want to do. You may feel that you don't have a choice because it is easier to simply say yes and "get it over with" then listen to his pouting.

Despite previous choices, actions, or what was considered acceptable, you always have the right to change your mind. Women are often the butt of the joke when it comes to how frequently we change our minds, but it is absolutely our right to make decisions based on how we feel in that moment, especially when it comes to our own bodies. Establishing boundaries for yourself is a positive first step toward knowing when you are being pushed beyond what feels comfortable. Make those boundaries known to your partner, and don't be afraid to stand up for them. Whether or not he respects those boundaries will give you a good idea of the integrity of your partner and the health of your relationship.

Sexual abuse within a marriage or any romantic relationship is often the last thing we are going to talk about. Not only do we often not recognize it as abuse at all, but it is embarrassing. While everyone else is talking (truthfully or not) about how juicy and thrilling their relationships are, the last thing we want to do is bring up awkward things happening at home. We have to start having the hard, uncomfortable conversations so that they stop being so hard and uncomfortable. Sexual abuse is a hard subject to talk about openly, because of shame, stigma and confusion. *All* of these contribute to the most self-destructive behavior of all: SILENCE.

Wow, that was heavy. Let's take a pause to breathe for just a moment. Maybe you need to reread a section that feels blurry or familiar. If you feel the need, it's okay to cry, scream, or just stare into space. We imagine that at some point in your life you have felt something that we have mentioned. Feeling oppressed, especially in an intimate relationship is not rare, but because we so rarely talk about it, it certainly can feel that way.

When we have released even the smallest parts of shame ourselves, it has fueled us to be not only more aware, but more vigilant to stand strong in knowing that our bodies are our own and belong to no one, not even our spouses. We are not property; no human is. What happens with and to your body should be 100% your decision without manipulation or coercion.

If you or someone you know is experiencing sexual abuse, below are some tips you can begin implementing immediately to protect yourself:

- Trust your instincts and your personal boundaries. It is a good idea to make sure that, no matter what situation or relationship you are in, you are comfortable with what is happening or being asked of you.

- Protect yourself from unwanted pregnancy through your own birth control. Do not depend on the abuser using protection.
- Protect yourself from sexually transmitted diseases and do not just take someone's word for it that they are not infected.
- Put immediate physical distance between yourself and your abuser.
- Establish boundaries for yourself regarding what you are comfortable with and how far you are willing to go. Make those boundaries known to your partner and establish your right to exit the situation if your boundaries are being trampled..

PHYSICAL ABUSE

I look down and I can see it. When I am washing my face or the dishes, I can see it. When I am typing this book, I can see it. It isn't large or vast. It isn't gruesome or eye-catching for a stranger. It is a small scar on the top of my right hand that follows the path of nerves and ligaments, about three shades different from the rest of my skin. But as insignificant as it is in the grand scheme of life, it is my reminder that although I survived, the scars will always be with me. Outwardly there may only be a few but internally it is a war field of bodies left to suffer, die and scream alone in the pain. These scars cause real pain and trauma on a body, more so than outward scars.

In general, the public population still thinks about domestic violence in terms of physical assault that results in visible injuries. I was partially guilty of that. I remember times where I would fight back and say, "Why don't you just hit me? It would be so much easier." In my mind, I wasn't a battered woman until there was a physical sign, but this is just one type of abuse. The more I researched and learned, the more my eyes welled up with tears as it became very clear, "This is me."

I know that there were times when I would think about how wrong things were, how horrible it felt, but I still didn't leave. How can I, when the physical signs are what people want to see in order to believe or help out? Flash forward to when I did get away, and even then, the attorney advised me to not pursue any of it. "Keep it simple and calm. Let's just get this wrapped up as easily as possible and move on." Aren't they supposed to do what is best for the client? Shouldn't an attorney want to protect? Domestic violence and the associated abusive behaviors have devastating consequences. Though life-threatening abuse puts the victim at a higher immediate risk, the long-term destruction of an individual that accompanies the other forms of abuse is extremely significant and cannot be minimized. These forms of abuse can be even more devastating and present lifelong challenges to overcome.

P hysical abuse is one of the main types of abuse most people think of, usually in the most dramatic of ways. Television shows and movies portray battered women with puffy eyes and bloody lips. When celebrity abuse makes it to the nightly news, it is because an athlete or movie star has punched his wife in an elevator or she is seen hiding behind big, designer glasses.

We don't tend to take notice until there is evidence of physical abuse. Only then do we categorize it as "abuse" and begin questioning why the victim doesn't leave and perhaps still stands behind their abuser. There is no doubt to the observers that abuse has now officially taken place because we, as a society, recognize that it is "never okay to hit a woman." As a result, even abused women themselves often don't consider themselves abused or recognize the gravity of the abuse until it becomes physical and visible.

I struggled to see my relationship as "bad enough" or the abuse as "real" because he didn't punch me. It's like my abuse didn't qualify unless his hand hit my face with a closed fist.

Physical abuse can happen in many forms and amounts. It is not uncommon for even small amounts of actual physical contact to be enough in a domestic violence situation to maintain the power and control dynamic. The threat of physical abuse, use of "accidents," or blaming the "clumsiness" of the victim is prevalent in many, maybe most situations.

Physical abuse and violence are also escalating actions. Abuse often starts fairly slowly, enabling the abuser to gain control over the victim through verbal and psychological abuse. If an abuser began by slapping or punching his victim, it would likely set off instant alerts and, unless physically restrained or otherwise threatened, the victim would likely begin looking for a way out. She would most likely not willingly stay in such a situation. Like a virus that kills its host, this would not bode well for the ongoing success of the abuser. Although it may start off slowly, physical abuse often makes its way into abusive relationships, even if infrequently.

> *Holding up his hand he said, "Remember, this side is discipline, this side is abuse."*

As suggested in the opening of this chapter, victims often beg for physical abuse so they would have a "reason" or "excuse" to leave.

> *I have heard countless women say, "I just prayed he would hit me," or "I yelled at him just to hit me so we would finally have a reason to leave." Whether intimate partner, abusive parents, or any type of relationship, physical abuse has become the gold standard or tipping point for abuse.*

Sadly, by the time the physical abuse begins, they are unable or unwilling to leave. Either they lack the financial ability to escape, the psychological and social damage is too great, or they are too afraid of their abuser to risk it. One of the biggest factors in the inability to leave is having one's social support network annihilated by the abuser.

In the course of these abuse circumstances we are sharing, some experienced varying degrees of each one of the forms of physical abuse listed below. Sometimes a lot at once, sometimes less frequent but everything was explained, blamed, or joked away. How impactful it is to list these all at once and see the picture that for so long was hard to really see, much less speak up against.

Physical abuse is a broad category that includes so much more than being thrown around and punched. Victims may experience intense physical abuse without ever having a bruise or scar to show for it. Many of the examples listed above have been covered in previous sections, particularly psychological and sexual. Like verbal, physical is often the "vehicle" for inflicting psychological abuse or control through fear, isolation, and confinement. According to the AMEND Workbook for Ending Violent Behavior,[1] physical abuse is any physically aggressive behavior, withholding of physical needs, indirect physically harmful behavior, or threat of physical abuse. This may include, but is not limited to:

- Hitting, kicking, biting, slapping, shaking, pushing, pulling, punching, choking, beating, scratching, pinching, pulling hair, stabbing, grabbing, shooting, drowning, burning, pushing into or hitting with an object, threatening with a weapon (gun, knife, hands, feet, fire, etc.), or threatening to physically assault.
- Forcing alcohol and/or drug use.
- Withholding of physical needs including interruption of sleep or meals, denying money, food, transportation, or help if sick or injured, locking victims into or out of the house, refusing to give or rationing necessities.
- Abusing, injuring, or threatening to injure others like children, pets, or special property.
- Forcible physical restraint against their will, being trapped in a room or having the exit blocked, being held down (related to confinement).

- The abuser hitting or kicking walls, doors, or other inanimate objects during an argument, throwing things in anger, destruction of property.
- Holding the victim hostage.
- Reckless driving.
- Self-harm intended to induce feelings of pity, guilt, or fear in the victim to manipulate their behavior.
- Provoking, taunting, pushing, or otherwise coercing the victim into violence such as pushing the abuser away or smacking away a threatening hand, so as to justify "retaliation" and use it against them in future arguments. "See? You're the violent one!"
- Anything that hurts or threatens to hurt the victim or anyone/thing they care about.
- Forced sex (rape) or other sexual activities would also fall under physical abuse, but is pulled out separately.

In my marriage, physical abuse did not start immediately. I was a few years into our marriage before I recall abuse that I considered physical. Perhaps that was because, even now, I struggle to recognize some of the early signs of physical abuse. It was small things, like shoving past me, knocking me into a chair or the corner of the wall. "Accidentally" stepping on my toe or closing the door on my hand. Sometimes it was knocking something out of my grasp. Over time, I was indoctrinated into the physical abuse that was going on, but still looking for the black eye and bloody lip so that I "had proof." I didn't recognize it at the time. I didn't like it, but I wouldn't have labeled it "physical abuse." When I was pregnant with my fourth, he got angry about something and threw a cell phone toward my stomach from 30 feet away. At one point, he took a dirty diaper and threw it at me. He threw the diaper with such force and power, enough that it actually busted my lip.

Despite the fact that I finally had the bloody lip to show for it, many would still struggle to see it as physical abuse because it doesn't fit into the lines of that category. "Well, he probably wasn't aiming for your face (stomach, arm, back...)" "Well, we all throw things when we get angry. I'm sure he didn't mean it." "Are you really upset about that mark? Wuss." It's easy to justify.

Is that what we think we deserve? Is that what we think others deserve?

This type of thinking must stop now.

Abusers are fueled by physical dominance and the power it gives them. It isn't always about physically hurting the victim, though that is often what happens, but about creating an environment of fear and control. Physical abuse is simply the vehicle some abusers choose to get to that destination.

Let's pause for just a moment before digging into this further. We have mentioned several times that many, most, potentially even *all* of us have abusive tendencies from time to time. You may be thinking, "Well, I have slapped my husband for being a jerk, but I'm not abusive." Sure, many of us have lashed out in anger or frustration. We want to be very clear that punching, hitting, kicking, or any other physical action that hurts another person *is* abusive behavior.

My husband and I were watching a movie together on the couch recently. He said something a little short. Without thinking, I reached over, punched him in the shoulder, and said, "Shut the fuck up."

When we spank children, we do it in a controlled fashion and call it discipline. That said, there is a fine line between discipline and abuse. Although you may not be an abuser, per se, you need to be aware of how easily your behaviors can move from loving to joking to abuse. When it hurts another person, whether intended or not, it is abusive behavior. That does not always mean the person is abusive. Sometimes, abusive behaviors, especially verbal and physical, are a result of an abuser's inability to appropriately express their emotions.

Many of us don't learn how to properly respond to anger or frustration, so we react by lashing out, verbally or physically. We yell, hit, slap, or even throw things. Again, we cannot reiterate enough that this is not okay, but it can be stopped and reversed. You, the victim, don't need to sit around in an abusive relationship and wait for the change to take place, but in a safe environment when there is recognition, an apology, and a true attempt to change, an abuser may be able to stop the abusive pattern. In many cases, counseling or learning more appropriate ways to manage stress and anger will be required to fully move past the abusive tendencies and learn new ways to handle their emotions.

Before I had children, I had a little dog that I loved like my own child. We did everything together. After a difficult day at work, I came home to him needing a walk, to be fed, and wanting to play. I was getting more and more agitated when I asked him to do something, and he didn't respond immediately. I grabbed a rolled up newspaper and hit him harder than I meant to. I was sick about it for days. How could I have been so out of control that I hurt another living being, one that I loved so much? What if that had been a child?

When my husband and I started a family, I told him that I wasn't opposed to spanking if it was deemed necessary, but we must have a process in place to do it calmly and without crossing that line. I also took spanking or slapping of any kind off the table for myself. I know tempers run in my family, and my first reaction is often to reach out and hit, punch, or slap, even if just on the leg or hand. I had to set that boundary for myself. Until I'm ready to address it and get to the root of my struggle. Until I can demonstrate calm discipline in other areas, I cannot allow myself to even approach that line for fear of crossing it and hurting my child, spouse, or someone else.

As we have advanced, this type of behavior has become largely unacceptable... in public settings. There are still groups who believe that the line between discipline and abuse is a lot closer to the discipline side. There are plenty of people who believe speaking calmly to an angry, tantruming child is ineffective and all they need is "a good spanking." To begin understanding the responses of others, you must first understand your own. Acknowledging your natural tendencies is the first step in learning to address it.

When my boys are acting up or even doing something silly, my mother-in-law's go-to response is, "They're your boys," or "He's your husband." Before she even finishes, I can feel my blood begin to boil. My heart races and my blood pressure rises. My face gets hot and my mind begins racing with all the snappy, hurtful responses I could spew. It takes everything I have to not snap back. I usually settle for an eye roll and leave the room. It bothers me for hours afterwards. I can't focus on my work and I certainly can't write something inspiring when I feel like such a hateful person. It wasn't until we were building out the section below where we discuss the words people use that I suddenly realized why this bothered me so much.

In my first marriage others would regularly say, "He's your husband," or "You married him" as if I was somehow deserving of the way he was acting or it was my fault because I married him. As if I needed to be reminded of my choices. It felt like such a slap in the face; like they were throwing their hands up and saying, "You made the bed, now lie in it.. They kept emphasizing how it was all my fault because I made the first decision to marry him, and therefore I deserved whatever negative consequence came my way. It's going to take a while to unpack all of that and get to where it doesn't make me want to serve her head for dinner, but recognizing where my reaction comes from is the first step to changing my response and also for not feeling like such a terrible person for having the reaction in the first place.

It's not only up to the one displaying the abusive behavior to recognize it and change it. The victim plays a major role in this as well. We must value ourselves enough to use our voice to stop abusive behavior before it becomes a pattern. When we value ourselves, our relationships, and others, it is a gift to raise the concern so it can be addressed.

Discussions or arguments, under no circumstance, should ever become physical. Some people are prone to more physical responses to anger, and arguments are a common place for those to come out. Despite their life experiences or personality that may give them a greater propensity to respond that way, it is not healthy, and never okay. Regardless of how much they were provoked or whether the victim "brought in on themselves," physical violence toward another person during an argument or any other time is never okay, acceptable, or the victim's fault.

Whether we are engaging in abusive behaviors ourselves or see them in others, we must use our voice to stop these behaviors. We cannot sit back and let them continue, hoping they recognize it in themselves. It is our responsibility to stand firm for ourselves, our relationships, and the ones we love.

Although the thought of physical abuse often conjures up images of bruises and black eyes, there are many other forms of physical abuse, legally recognized physical abuse, that often go unnoticed. It is important that you understand them because they do have legal implications and can be a lever you can pull to get the help you need.

Destruction of Property

Destruction of property is pretty self-explanatory. It is the destruction of or damage to property including property of the victim, abuser, shared property, or even property unrelated to either. Whether the abuser is throwing property, using their own body, or using a weapon is irrelevant. Additionally, whether or not the abuser is throwing it *at* the victim with the intention to harm is also irrelevant.

Individuals may destroy property for a number of reasons. Starting at the lowest end of the spectrum, they destroy objects as an expression of anger or frustration. Throwing dishes or stabbing pillows is often portrayed in the media as a means of releasing anger. There are even businesses that have started opening up, providing patrons the opportunity to break dishes or throw knives at targets. Destroying things is often a go-to when it comes to stress release and may not be directly intended to have an immediate impact on the victim. Regardless of intent, it is difficult to not be affected by someone damaging property. It is often a sign that the individual is somewhat out-of-control, which leaves the victim feeling helpless and at the mercy of their emotional state.

We were arguing about something. When I sat down at my desk, a framed picture of his daughter fell forward and landed face-down. When he came back into the room and saw the picture down, he thought I was angry and turned it over. He stormed downstairs, fuming. He was drinking a beer and threw the bottle against the wall in the kitchen. Not knowing what happened, I ran downstairs thinking that he had fallen or hurt himself. When I saw the glass everywhere, I was so grateful he was okay and afraid of what else he might throw that I began apologizing for the fight, the picture, and anything else I could think of to try and calm the situation. Rather than continuing the discussion later to actually resolve the argument, I just dropped it. It was easier to stuff it down than to risk him getting angry or hurt and damaging anything else.

Destruction of property can also be a form of psychological abuse, particularly when the property being destroyed or threatened belongs to the victim. It's bad enough to throw a plate at the wall, but when it's your wedding china or passed down from your Great-Great Grandmother, it transcends categories of abuse.

Kidnapping

One type of physical abuse that we have not thoroughly discussed is kidnapping. Under psychological abuse, we discuss confinement at length. Although similar, kidnapping and confinement are different. Confinement is defined as restricting one's freedom of movement primarily based on psychological factors. Kidnapping is focused on restricting movement or even moving a person based on physical force.

Though the legal definition of kidnapping can vary from state to state, for general purposes, we will clarify the base definition we are working from. Kidnapping is defined as holding someone against his or her will, without legal authority, through force, threats, abduction, or imprisonment. In the state of Texas, "unlawful restraint" is defined as "intentionally or knowingly restricting a person's movements, without consent, so as to substantially interfere with the person's liberty, by moving the person from one place to another or by confining the person.[2]" By this definition, the confinement we discuss later under psychological abuse is a form of kidnapping and may be charged that way. The challenging part is proving it to be the case. Please use your state's legal definition to better understand where your specific situation falls. Regardless, undesired or unwanted restraint is abuse, whether physical or psychological. One is not "worse" than the other.

The term "kidnapping" can be misleading. It is important to understand that no child has to be involved in the situation in order for charges to stick. The fact of the matter is there are several scenarios where domestic violence between adults evolves into a kidnapping situation.

In adult romantic relationships, kidnapping can appear in a number of different ways:

- He has threatened suicide before. Tonight, while drinking too much, he threatens to kill himself, waving a gun around or having it visible, if you try to leave.
- A spouse blocks the other in the bedroom during a fight and refuses to let them leave the room or use the phone despite

repeated requests to leave. When they try, they are physically shoved back into the room or prevented from leaving.

- He threatens to follow you if you try to leave the house to go to work.
- He holds you down or physically restrains you "until you calm down" during an argument.
- He threatens physical harm against you or someone else if you try to leave, go to a forbidden place, or talk to an outsider about your private life..

When someone attempts to restrain someone against their will, whether a romantic partner or stranger, that behavior is a felony, and they may be charged as such.

When angry, he would puff up and storm after me to prevent me from leaving the house. Many times, he would yank the car door from my hand when I was trying to get away from him. When I was able to get in the car, he would frequently put his foot behind the tire so I couldn't pull out of the driveway.

As we mentioned previously, categorization is only relevant as it relates to legal filing of charges. There is no "hierarchy" of abuse or a certain level that must be achieved to trigger abuse. You may be experiencing abuse that is very physical to you, but we failed to include that example here. That does not mean it is not physical abuse. We simply chose an organizational method that was both supported by research and also met our purposes of creating awareness.

If you or someone you know is experiencing physical abuse, here are some tips:

- Be prepared to reach out for help. Sometimes we need to prepare ourselves mentally to make a call for help, and that is ok. Have a cell phone charged at all times, contact numbers saved in

other places and possibly memorize a
few close numbers.

- Create your own private code word to use with your children
  or support network.
- Lean on a support network and if you don't have one, please
  keep in mind that there are services available, and this is what
  they are for.
- Always have a prepared "excuse or reason." Having several
  plausible reasons for leaving your dwelling at different times or
  for exiting situations that might become dangerous.
- Put physical space between you and your abuser as quickly as
  possible.
- No matter what you do, stay safe! You deserve to be and feel
  safe at all times!

SOCIAL ABUSE

I wanted to share pictures of the good times. I also wanted to keep up the image that things were great. I wanted to look normal, to feel normal, to be normal. I knew, though, that he would dissect the picture, analyze the comment, and critique my post. If the caption wasn't "just right" he would put me down. He may make me remove it, make me change it, or comment in a way to suggest that I was incapable of even getting this right. Heaven forbid I post a picture of myself. One time when I did, he left a sweet comment for everyone to see. Afterwards, he sent me a string of texts putting me down, shaming me and making me feel guilty/bad about the photo, asking me whose attention I was trying to get.

Within this new age of technology, social abuse has become a new form of abuse. Although it could easily be tucked under psychological or even verbal abuse with a bit of a stretch, we felt it worthwhile to pull it out and discuss it separately.

Social abuse is a new term and is generally defined as the coercion of an individual in a public setting or the collective abuse by a group of people toward an individual.[1] For our purposes, we are focusing on social abuse within the age of technology and social media. We define social abuse as using technology, including social media, to manipulate, harass (related to cyberstalking), control, isolate, or create fear within the victim. Technology and social media in particular are powerful resources for connecting people, building community, and sharing information.

Although it has advanced quickly, changing the way we live our daily lives, it is still a fairly new development. We are seeing more and more cases of the damaging effects of online bullying and cyberstalking, but many people still lack the appropriate respect for social media and how it can be used as a powerful tool in the hands of an abuser. As we will discuss in this section, like any other social tool, it can be used as a healthy support system, but it can also be used as a means of abuse. There is a constant tradeoff between the potential harm and benefits. Every interaction has the potential to go one way or another, even between individuals in healthy relationships whether friends, family, colleagues, or even acquaintances.

Many victims are caught between the pressures of posting about their lives, putting on a happy face for everyone to see, and dealing with fear of the repercussions from their abuser. In a world where we should be able to reach out socially, we can feel more closed off than ever, not really knowing that what we are experiencing is wrong. Additionally, not understanding what technology can do and what abusers are actually capable of can create a ramming hammer of confusion and fear.

In addition to making engaging on social media a challenge for their victims, withholding access to social media or online interactions is also a form of abuse. It is a form of control and isolation resulting in the victim feeling disconnected from their network and the world around them. It effectively keeps their victim "on a shorter leash."

It is easy to create an online persona that hides your true identity. Using a different account with a different name, abusers can track or follow their victims, often acting in an attempt to "catch" their victims in doing something wrong: liking certain pictures, posting certain things, checking in at certain places, commenting on someone's post. Even after the victim leaves the relationship, this type of social abuse or cyber-stalking can be used to continue the attacks on the victim.

Abusers don't always spy on the victim themselves either. They may enlist the help of friends, family, or even their new partners to monitor the victim's activities and/or make comments. It is simply impossible to completely get away from the possibility of being attacked online. Putting up one barrier only leads abusers to seek out others.

> *When he remarried, I noticed his new wife following me online, commenting on my posts, and posting things on her page in direct reference to something I had just posted. In most of these cases, other people, mutual friends, were pointing out her posts to me. Even when we don't seek it out, negative comments are often still brought to our attention making it even more difficult to avoid. In preparation for promoting this book, I began sharing articles and posts and also shining a bit of light on my own past experiences. She would immediately make a post discrediting my experiences saying something like, "I don't know why people try to bring things up years after. If you didn't have a problem with it then, why would you have a problem with it now?" She would also send me long messages, attacking my parenting style, justifying her relationship, or telling me what a terrible wife I was. Of course, that is in addition to the multitude of conversations where she would confide in me or ask how I dealt with his behaviors. I would see her happy posts and know that she is simply putting up the same façade I was for so many years.*

Some say the answer is "well don't be on social media" or "change your phone number." This type of response perpetuates the notion that the victim is responsible for their abuse and responsible for stopping it. It takes all responsibility off of the abuser. Social media is a very real, very big part of connection in our society today. Grandparents can see regular pictures of their grandkids, high school friends reconnect after 20 years, and former colleagues stay in touch. It is a powerful tool for building and maintaining relationships as well as critical networking relationships that open the doors for opportunities later on.

Additionally, many victims conduct business through social media via pages, groups, and advertising. Many of these businesses operate outside of their personal image, but many more are closely connected to their personal profiles, building community with connection to their lives as a whole. Taken a step further, children and other family members of victims often serve as the connection point between the two, if they are not being harassed and attacked themselves. Social media is simply one vehicle for abuse. If that is taken away, abusers will simply find another vehicle. Asking victims to refrain from social media in order to appease an abuser or stop the abuse is absurd and unfair.

That said, there are situations where refraining from social media, changing phone numbers, changing locks, or even moving house are exactly what a victim needs to do in order to stay safe. In those cases, victims absolutely should take every precaution necessary to reduce their proximity to the abuser as well as cut off their access. We are not trying to suggest that is never the case. There are also situations where abusers walk away and never try to make contact with their victims again.

 The pendulum swings both ways and the experience is different for everyone. Discussion of the extremes is by far more interesting than the middle ground. It is easy to lose sight of that middle ground where the abuse isn't "that bad." We aren't even sure what "that bad" means, so we often default to it being okay or not discussing it at all. These middle ground topics are a huge part of better understanding the abuse we experience. We often remain silent because it doesn't seem "important" enough to discuss or we think it is too different to talk about. We think we are the only ones experiencing it and don't want to upset the dynamic of the room, the friendship, or society as a whole. We must continue to have these middle ground conversations, recognizing that there is a wide range of experiences that still constitute abuse.

Talking to my college-aged daughter and hearing her friends, social abuse is a big issue. She mentioned that her boyfriend was keeping track and would get mad if she didn't respond on Snapchat according to his timeline. Her friends chimed in and said they were also mad because she let their "snap streak" die down. Snap streaks are a great example of accepting "mandatory contact," whether by girlfriends or a romantic partner.

Domestic abuse is about control, and digital media offers many options to effectively control others through what Stark coined as "coercive control".[2] Stark utilized the coercive control model in his efforts to shift perspective away from violence against women being just acts of physical violence to all the forms of violence and abuse in his book.

In a new digital age, traditional forms of abuse have taken on a more contemporary form, like stalking, verbal abuse, and the accessibility and immediacy of any digital technology can result in a greater risk to not only be abused but for abuse to extend to those forms. Abuse can now continue on even in the physical absence of the abuser. It can increase their control in their victim's lives, because it can now be a constant. Frequent calling or texting, expecting an instant pick-up keeps the victim on constant alert.

He would cycle through times of constant texting and calling expecting immediate response, with the implication that I had nothing better to do than to wait for his contact. During these times I don't recall having much more than an hour with no contact. I was so thankful for times or jobs that prevented him from having constant access to his phone. Since the beginning of our relationship he used social networking, media, apps, past contacts, email, basically anything he could to flirt and try to lure someone into exchanging it back with him. The intentional opposite side of the cycle was for him to completely ignore me even when it was a simple home management type of question. He stayed in control of our communication: when it happened, how it happened and what it was about. It's hard looking back and seeing how much control he took.

Just as abusers use constant attention and contact to keep their victim isolated and confined, they also use complete silence to keep their victim guessing. The abuser may go dark for hours, not contacting the victim and not responding to texts or calls. This silence may be topped off by coming home later than usual, extending the periods of silence. Knowing that they could have responded but chose not to is yet another way the abuser maintains control in the relationship.

What about images? Yeah, the pictures they have on their phones, the ones they took without your permission or even the one you sent him per his demand/request, images rooted in sexual abuse. There is a constant anxiety that develops in a victim about who has seen an image, what they've done with it, and what will come of it if they try to defend themselves. Cyber communications and records are a type of abuse that causes victims to constantly worry about their abuser's database of images. Digital images remain with the abuser long after the relationship has ended. What will come of those images can leave the victim filled with fear and shame.

Social media, instant messenger, or other websites, applications, and programs that allow people to see when others were "last active" may be used to check-up on or stalk their victims. Many of these tools are intended to help friends connect and stay connected with each other. In the hands of an abuser, it is another method to track and monitor their victim. Clearly, these enhancements were added to programs for a reason, and that is because even healthy individuals want to know when their friends are active and online or when they were last. It isn't that unusual and isn't always a sign of abusive behavior. At first, this behavior can actually feel kind of nice. It feels like he is really interested, and it can feel good to know that someone is a little jealous of you. It is easy to become deconditioned to that behavior and it can quickly become more controlling. Knowing when behavior turns from non-dangerous to controlling can only be understood within the context of each relationship. Some red flags to consider when your activity is being monitored:

- Your behavior is being regularly monitored. Most people are not continuously monitoring each other's activity. If they are curious, they may look, but it is not a constant thing.
- Online activity is a frequent conversation topic, and his comments are often aggressive or accusatory.
- He tries to limit your movement or activity, using the tracking tool as a threat or reminder that he can see you.
- His comments and behavior make you anxious, concerned, worried, or even uneasy.

Let's remember that you are your own person and deserve respect and privacy. You don't owe anyone an explanation. Defending only perpetuates their insistence that you are doing something wrong. If what you are doing is decent, kind, respectful toward the relationship, there is nothing to defend. You are online. Period, end of story. No explanation required to anyone.

> *After my divorce, I was slightly infatuated with different men quite regularly. Having married young and never really dating before, much less in the age of social media, I was like a kid in a candy store with a twenty dollar bill. I didn't quite know what to do with myself. I would check on them throughout the day through LinkedIn, Instant Messenger, or whatever tool we were both connected on. I would daydream about what they were doing, where they were, if they were away, or imagine that somehow, we were only a few feet apart staring at each other through the computer. If there was a profile picture involved, I would use that as an opportunity to stare at their face multiple times throughout the day. When I was interested in someone on a dating app, I would see when they were on last to get an idea of whether or not they were looking for other women out of pure curiosity.*

I had been seeing one guy for a couple of weeks when I flew across the country to visit a friend of mine. There was a three-hour time difference. I was up late one night scrolling through the profiles, winding down from a busy day. The next morning, he called early and berated me for 45 minutes about how I was cheating on him by looking at other profiles. He said I was clearly not interested in him because I wasn't being faithful since I was "up at three o'clock in the morning looking at other men." In reality, it was only midnight since I was on the opposite coast, but that is irrelevant. Regardless, he ended the call by telling me that he couldn't be with someone who was an untrustworthy cheater.

Yes, I was, in a very real sense, stalking my love interests. Although it was psychotic and unhealthy for myself, it wasn't harmful to them. I wasn't doing it to be intimidating. In fact, years later I found out that you could actually see how many times someone looked at your profile, and I was mortified. If I had even imagined that he would know, I never would have done it. This man, on the other hand, intentionally sought my activity out to monitor and use against me.

After separation, abusers may still utilize social media to attack, threaten, and track. Other family members and friends may be drawn in. With the access and availability, "leaving" doesn't necessarily sever the ties to your abuser completely. Communication is not limited to phone calls anymore. We have texts, email, social apps, networking and more. There are endless possibilities for abusers to stay connected to not only the victim but their entire social network. In many cases, social media allows you to remove followers, friends, or contacts and even block them from seeing your content. We highly encourage you to do that when possible and do not seek them out on these platforms. It can be tempting to see what they have been up to, but this only opens the door for them to continue hurting you with their words or actions.

During our separation, he contacted many of my family members and friends through social media. He gave them his side of the story and asked that they pray for us. He used this opportunity to defame me, trying to get their support in our relationship.

It is not our intent to create a guidebook for abusers or give them ideas they hadn't thought of before. Abusers don't need help. They are more likely to come up with these ideas on their own because that is how their minds work. Victims, on the other hand, don't often think of these things. "He would never do that." Maybe he wouldn't, but it is our goal to equip victims with information to turn the tables and create more balance. Only by creating awareness through knowledge can we better prepare and take our power back.

The door of possibility is so much wider in this day and age of technology. Victims may find it hard to participate in the social and fun parts of the internet because someone is always watching them, waiting to attack. They may live in constant fear of payback that will come from speaking their truth. Rather than engaging fully and freely, they may monitor every action, always considering, weighing the potential risk. Oppression is the inability to freely express yourself. Victims facing social abuse suffer from this oppression. Not only do they miss out on interaction with others, but others miss out on engagement with them. Oppression is what keeps the cycle of silence going strong.

There is a greater feeling of uncertainty and safety when an abuser has the ability to intrude on their victims, no matter their location. The boundaries extend past the physical realm. In some cases, such as mine, it made me close off the outside world. I always felt like I was being watched and I was overly cautious to not do anything that would cause fallout. Interesting enough, it never really mattered because there was no pattern. A post today was okay; a similar post tomorrow could be bad.

Tips to prevent social abuse:

- Adjust privacy settings on social media accounts. Make sure only friends can see posts.
- Adjust settings so that you must approve posts or comments.
- Block your abuser and any of his friends or family.
- Turn off any settings that report your address, location, or phone number.

PSYCHOLOGICAL ABUSE

"Psychological abuse is the death of who you were."

I stopped to grab a bite to eat after a doctor's appointment. A dear woman had offered to watch the babies, while the older ones were at school and had insisted that I take the time after my postpartum follow up to get some food without children. For me, this was unheard of.

I decided to try a local place where I had never been. The only available parking was across the street at a different shopping center. There was a used book store, a Chinese restaurant, an attorney's office, a local pub, and an ophthalmologist office. I only have this information ingrained into my mind because of the events that followed when I returned home that afternoon with him waiting for me.

I later found out that he called the attorney's office located there the next day, to see if I had gone to see them. I didn't know how he always tracked me; he always knew where I had been, or made me believe he knew. That was the thing, the truth was never really the truth with him. He even hired a private eye to follow and track me when I went to visit family. When I asked him about it, the story was so convoluted that I didn't even know what I knew. It's hard to explain unless you are experiencing it. Ultimately, I just dropped the subject because it would only make it worse for me and it didn't really matter because he had wasted time and money to have someone watch me take care of our infant and spend time with an aunt I had just met. Looking back, I guess that was a win for me; I just didn't know it.

Psychological or emotional abuse is very closely tied to verbal abuse because the intention of verbal abuse is to harm the victim psychologically, meaning mentally and/or emotionally. Where verbal is the vehicle, physical is the destination, psychological is the fuel. Abuse in general is very psychological in nature. Even physical abuse impacts the victim psychologically and over time, wears the victim down to a point where they accept the abuse.

Even in our research, many of the same examples are provided for verbal, psychological, emotional, and mental abuse, making it very difficult to clearly differentiate between them. Because the intent and result of most abuse is psychological damage, this category is by-far the largest. For the sake of categorization, we will attempt to focus primarily on the 'non-verbal' or 'less verbal' forms of psychological abuse in this section.

Psychological abuse is rampant in our society. Because there are often no physical signs, it is sneaky and hard to detect. Even though it flies under the radar, it's very serious. Sometimes it's relentless and ongoing; sometimes a precursor to physical abuse. The goal is to undermine another person's feelings of self-worth and independence. Mental control, over time, can be extremely damaging to a victim's mental wellness. It creates fear, confusion and doubt for the victim. Undermining their self-esteem can be detrimental to the victim's identity, dignity, and self-worth, sometimes leading to anxiety, depression, and PTSD. Psychological abuse can also manifest itself physically through physiological responses such as fear and have direct physical impact on health.

According to the AMEND Workbook for Ending Violent Behavior, psychological abuse is any behavior that exploits another's vulnerability, insecurity, or character. Such behaviors include continuous degradation, intimidation, manipulation, brainwashing, or control of another to the detriment of the individual.[1] Does that sound familiar? It should. Many of the forms of verbal abuse we mentioned are also psychologically abusive, not just because no one deserves to be yelled at or spoken to in a hurtful and disrespectful way, but because of the psychological damage inflicted by those words. Constant criticism, name-calling, or attacks on character are damaging to one's self-worth. Over time, this type of abuse degrades a victim's ability to and desire to get out of the situation.

We hear the term 'brainwashing' or 'brainwashed' thrown about, sometimes flippantly. At times it may even conjure drastic pictures in our head based on what we have seen in a movie. Brainwashing is a serious aspect of psychological abuse and at times is only considered in the most dire of circumstances. However, brainwashing occurs when what one thinks is altered or changed in order to comply with the dominator.

Psychological abuse refers to *consistent and persistent* actions and behaviors intended to psychologically manipulate someone else, such as making someone feel shame or guilt over and over again. Because it can be hard to pinpoint, it is important to look for patterns of behaviors that could indicate abuse. Ultimately, most abuse is psychological abuse because the intent is psychological pain, torment, or control. Psychological abuse involves the abuser "playing mental games" or tormenting the mind of the victim through words or actions.

It is important to point out that more than any other type of abuse one must look at patterned behaviors to get a concise view and understanding of what is happening. Legally, this has been identified as "pattern of behavior" and defined as behavior by one party in an intimate relationship that is used to establish power and control over the other person in the relationship through fear and intimidation.[2] We must acknowledge that it exists in order to understand it fully.

Fear: Through Threats and Intimidation

Threatening in emotionally abusive relationships often happens two ways: threatening physical harm and threatening by telling you to do something you do not want to do, with implied emotional fallout or other consequences if you do not comply.

We touched on threats in verbal abuse because they tend to be verbal in nature. Remember verbal abuse is the tactic or mechanism of delivery of psychological abuse. Fear can be a powerful motivator. Many of the decisions we make, good and bad, are based in fear. We buckle our children into their car seats despite their protests and tears because we fear what might happen if we get into an accident and they aren't properly buckled in. We follow laws and rules for fear that we will be living in chaos if everyone makes them up as they go. We don't always need to experience the outcome firsthand to make decisions based on avoiding that given situation.

Fear is the basis of power and control, making it an effective technique in the hands of an abuser. This type of abuse of power can be found not only in romantic relationships, but in churches, government, organizations, schools, friendships, and anywhere people are involved. Fear is such a powerful motivator that when a power-hungry, insecure group or individual has the opportunity to use fear as a mechanism for control, it is often too tempting to resist. By creating enough fear in the potential outcome, abusers don't even have to put much effort into controlling their victims. The mere mention of the feared end is enough to manipulate the victim into doing exactly what they desire. Putting a little effort into creating an environment of fear pays out huge dividends in the end.

> *I was being asked to make some ethically questionable decisions on a project. When I pushed back, my boss reminded me that there was some reorganization going on and every team would probably be asked to make some cuts. He didn't have to make any direct threats; I could read between the lines to get the message he was spelling out.*

Additionally, threats are not always verbal. Non-verbal threats can be and are often used to inflict fear. A look, a gesture, or the abuser moving toward the victim can be an effective threat. In this section, we want to dig into the threats and related psychological implications associated with stalking and the destruction of pets.

We know this sounds really heavy and maybe even a bit of a logic leap, but stick with us and you will be able to see how these pieces fit together.

Fear: Stalking

> *After my divorce, I dated a guy whose mother had been a vegetable for a decade or more, and doctors couldn't figure out what was wrong. I knew he loved his mom. He always went home to visit her and took her little gifts. He would often drive by my house on his way home from work or throughout the day, even though it was out of the way. I would be in my living room and see his truck drive by at all hours of the day and night. In the mornings or after work, I would find cigarette butts on my front porch outside of my bedroom window and even woke up to footprints in the snow. He wasn't even trying to hide it. One day, he came over while my housekeeper was cleaning. He said he left something, so she let him in. He looked around for a while, digging through my drawers and looking for any sign that someone else had been there. As he was leaving, he told her, "If she's not careful, she'll end up like my mom." I don't know why, but she didn't tell me that story until after we had broken up.*

Stalking in the simplest form is the unwanted pursuit of another person. A person commits stalking if they intentionally or knowingly engage in a course of conduct that is directed toward another and if that conduct would either cause a reasonable person to fear for their safety or the safety of their immediate family member.[3] Under this definition, stalking is actually a class 5 felony. If the behavior would cause a reasonable person to fear physical injury or death of themselves or their immediate family member, then it could even be a class 3 felony. Within this definition, "course of conduct" means maintaining visual or physical proximity to a specific person or directing verbal, written, or other threats, whether expressed or implied, to a specific person on two or more occasions over a period of time, however short, but does not include constitutionally protected activity. "Immediate family member" means a spouse, parent, child or sibling or any other person who regularly resides in a person's household or resided in a person's household within the past six months.

Agh, that is a lot of words right? We know it feels heavy. This all does, but as women who have experienced so many varying degrees of stalking, we didn't know or understand our rights. We share this to increase your awareness, make sure you know your rights, and what behaviors are not just scary and hurtful but *illegal*! By knowing your rights and understanding various behaviors employed by abusers, you are better able to take actions to protect yourself when the opportunity arises.

Stalking is a continuous behavior that is typically connected with other actions such as repeated harassment or threatening behavior toward the other person, no matter if the recipient is a total stranger, acquaintance, current or former intimate partner, or anyone else. It can be very physical, emotional, psychological, and even economical. As we discussed in the economic section, stalking often leads to the victim's loss of employment or reduction in wages, which further limits their economic independence and freedom.

Stalking behaviors are common tactics used to create a sense of fear and intimidation and/or to control someone who may fear for their safety or the safety of those close to them. It is a terrorizing crime that is hard to identify in the beginning and feels like there is no end. When one behavior is found out, the stalker often switches to another behavior, making it difficult to identify. Stalking behaviors of any kind can include *any* behaviors if they have no reasonable legitimate purpose depending on the context in which they are done. These behaviors are only limited by the stalker's creativity, access and resources.

The reason stalking is a psychological abuse is due to the fact that it can cause tremendous amounts of fear without the slightest physical injury, though it does have a high correlation to physical and sexual violence and can be lethal. It is extremely effective as a tactic of control for domestic violence abusers.

When I began the discussion of getting a divorce, he confined me to the upstairs guest bedroom. One day while I was out, he hid an old baby monitor under a dresser and covered the light with a sock. He kept the receiver in his room so he could listen in on my conversations with my children and any phone calls I made from that room. During those months, time seemed to be a distant thing. I found the monitor by chance as the baby was nursing one night; the sock must have slipped because a small glow of light was sneaking out from under the dresser. It took a bit to reach where the light was, short arms and all, but as I pulled and slid my arm back to the open area, my stomach curdled. This was a moment where I knew fear! At other times I was able to excuse or dismiss the fear but not this moment. He wasn't even home, as he was working the midnight shift, but he didn't have to be present for me to curl up in fear. He was intruding on every part of my being, even in my sleep.

The shock lasted what felt like hours but I knew I didn't have a lot of time. It was already 3:30 am and if the baby didn't wake up soon, one of the other children would and he would return shortly after. I gathered enough courage, though my entire body was in pain from shaking in fear. I scoured every place I could think of including what used to be our bedroom. Sometimes I would pause, thinking I was crazy and I didn't really just find what I did, but in the last moments of exhaustion, I looked one last time in the master closet. In a brief second I thought I could hear the baby's muffled moan, I moved a stack of clothes and it was there, listening to my room. He must have forgotten to turn it off when he left at 10:00 p.m. Again, my body responded faster than I could comprehend and froze in fear.

This book started with the story of him calling the attorney's office the moment I stepped through the door. He knew exactly where I was the moment I arrived. Sadly, that behavior didn't stop, even after I left. As is often the case in stalking situations, I never did figure out exactly how he did it. Each time was different. Yet time and time again, he showed up exactly where I was, though he had no reason for being there and no way of knowing I would be there outside of stalking.

Although stalking is typically seen when intimate partners have broken up or when the victim and the abuser were never together, victims can be and are often currently in romantic relationships with their stalker during the stalking, even married to them. In cases of stalkers who are currently or formerly in relationships with their victims, research shows results can be even more detrimental than in cases where victims were never romantically connected with their stalkers.

Stalking during a relationship or after it has ended is high-risk behavior. It is typically defined as the willful, malicious and repeated following or harassing of another person, accompanied by a credible threat of violence. It has been increasingly recognized as a serious crime in the United States. Safety precautions must be taken if it is occurring to you or someone you love. And remember, in most states, these behaviors are also against the law resulting in a felony charge if convicted.

Why do we remind you about this? Because you have rights, even when you feel like you have no control or choices.

A Stalker...

- has extensive and intimate knowledge of the victim and their routines (history, social or family contacts, daily routines, employer, co-workers, neighbors, children, pets).
- is aware of the victim's hopes and fears (so as to exploit them).
- can provide "legitimate" reasons for the behavior.
- has the opportunity for regular contact with their victim through children's activities, court dates, family, mutual friends, work, school, etc.

- is a greater danger when they have direct access to weapons.
- statistically has been linked to an increased risk of kidnapping children.

When stalking is identified, it is generally true that:

- The more established the relationship that existed prior to the stalking, including spouses or intimate partners, the more likely the stalkers are choosing to use their behaviors in order to gain (or regain) power and control over their victims.
- The great majority are male perpetrators targeting female victims.
- The less of a relationship between stalker and target that occurred prior to the stalking, the more delusional and/or mentally disturbed the stalker.

I had met a man through a mutual friend and had one date where we met at the location. He didn't have my address or know where I lived, as far as I know. At least I never gave it to him. Before our next date, he showed up at my house with a flower. He said, "I couldn't wait another minute." A few days later, he left a flower on my car.

As in most abuse, stalking behaviors come in many different forms. Not all abusers follow their victims through dark streets or watch as they come and go from their homes. There are many ways stalkers pursue and haunt their victims. Plenty of these behaviors cross over into other areas of abuse that we have discussed.

This is the nature of abuse; it rarely fits into a single category. Sometimes abusive behavior/tactics fit into more than one category because it serves as a vehicle in one form, a fuel in another and a result or outcome in the other. In this case, behaviors may fit in this category because of the intent, which is to inflict fear and intimidation in the form of control through being "ever present," demonstrating that they have free, unhindered access to the victim.

He never let me out of his reach, really. Texts, calls, required attendance to his location despite what needs existed. In the beginning it seemed sweet and attentive. It was comforting to know someone wanted to talk with me. The problem became that he was the only person I was "allowed" to talk to. Allowed in the sense that he was in contact with me so much that there was no time for anyone else. At times, it was hard to keep it up, especially when the babies were young, but he didn't seem to care or want to understand that my lack of communication with him was not a slight and it definitely didn't mean I was chatting with someone else. He would look over my shoulder, ask or insist I tell him everything. It was like I didn't really exist and I was just an extension of him. There was constant confusion of what was right, wrong, truth and a lie. There were days that my mind would hurt and honestly it was just easier to give in, go along or just give up all together.

Additional examples of stalking behaviors include:

- Mailing cards or other cryptic messages - nowadays this looks like texts, snaps, DMs, comments and more.
- Breaking windows or vandalizing a partner's home.
- Taking the partner's mail.
- Leaving notes, gifts, or other objects on doorstep, car, or at work.
- Watching a partner from a distance.
- Following, monitoring, or having surveillance of victim and/or victim's family, friends, co-workers.
- Hang-up calls on the telephone.
- Repeated threatening communications or attempts to communicate, especially after being clearly informed to stop.
- Following the partner with a car or on foot.
- Hiding in bushes or other surveillance of the partner's home.
- Surveillance of the partner at work.
- Kidnapping the victim or children or threatening to do so.
- Other trespassing.

- Vandalizing the partner's property (to show that "I was here and have free access to you.")
- Breaking into the partner's house/car or stealing things to show they were there and have free access to the victim.
- Filing numerous pleadings in court cases.
- Filing for custody of children regardless of their needs.
- Not respecting visitation limitations.
- Harassing telephone calls or notes.
- Violation between restraining orders.

Stalking is one of those categories of abusive behaviors that can start right in the beginning of our interactions with someone. It is also sometimes hard to recognize when you are in the midst of it. It feels innocent at first, showing up at your work, to "just say hi" or attending an event they were previously highly opposed to, both really the disguise to see what you were up to. How about following you to college? This could feel like an amazing commitment to the relationship, but it can also be to keep tabs on someone.

Have you ever experienced someone "watching" or being aware of who becomes friends with you on social media? Even things that initially seem cute or fun can ultimately become useful for stalking. We know that it seems like you have to be hyper aware but in reality once you know the tactics you can  begin to see patterns before they elevate. It is in knowing that helps us acknowledge and keep our own personal power. Vigilance is not weakness and it is not fear.

> *Long after the divorce and custody arrangements have been finalized, he is still taking me to court on a regular basis to try to get out of child support, change arrangements, or to complain about something I am doing. We must then be in contact directly or through our attorneys. I hear his voice, read his name, and see his face more than I want, always stirring up the past. It is constant, and the legal fees are endless. It's a part*

of our society, legally and socially, that has become an accept-
able form of abuse that they can get away with, putting pres-
sure on a victim, hoping they mess up, and the abuser wins.

Another form of stalking is cyberstalking, which simply means stalking, tracking, or watching over a computer or other technology. Cyberstalkers need not be in physical proximity to their targets and are therefore sometimes able to remain anonymous or even enlist others to help them stalk. This form of psychological abuse is frightening because the victim is in constant fear of where the abuser is and when they will appear. It is closely related to social abuse.

As I stood looking at the drawer of the make-shift night stand
in my room, something felt off. I knew I had closed it; I was sure
of it. But you know, maybe not. Ok, what did I come in here
for? Oh yeah, my iPad. I pull it open the rest of the way and I
feel it again. Wait! This is not how I left things. I'm not losing
my mind. But then again, you are sleep deprived and nursing a
baby. Get it together!

Those were not uncommon moments toward the end, but at the
time I couldn't pinpoint anything to a T; at least that's what I
thought. It felt like he was always finding new ways to invade
me. I later found undeniable proof that he had broken into my
personal email, checked my phone records, and stalked me
socially with fake accounts and accessing my locked iPad. These
were being done while we were "separated." I wanted a divorce
and he wouldn't have it. So we separated: by him forcing me to
live upstairs with all of the children and only being able to
come downstairs to eat.

In the United States, stalking is a crime on its own. Even if it's your husband. Fortunately, if you track what is happening to you, it can be one of the easier types of abuse to prove legally. Because of this, it can be a great first step to get them away from you. Stalking *is* serious.

Please be aware that a stalking situation may never be resolved to the victim's satisfaction or to the satisfaction of the suspect. Also, not all the suggestions presented will be appropriate or feasible for all situations — each case is to be analyzed individually, as not any two relationships are the same. There are real actions and thoughts you can put into place to help no matter where you are in the pendulum.

At one point, my oldest daughter called the police because she was afraid for her life and mine. Because there was no physical evidence of current violence, they didn't remove him or offer us any protection. What we didn't realize at the time was that she could have said he was stalking her, shown proof, and they would have arrested him. Unfortunately, we did not know that, and they didn't tell her. Honestly, we didn't have the words to name what he was doing completely and no one was offering to help us understand either, especially those that were called to protect and serve.

What can you do if you know, suspect, or want to protect yourself from future stalking?

- Tell someone you trust.
- Don't use credit cards they can track. Use cash if/when possible.
- Have your car, phone, or any other devices scanned for tracking programs.
- Change your routine. Switching up what you do can help you feel safer, provide a distraction for the stalker or even make it more work than they want.
- Document how you are being stalked. Keep a journal in a safe place and make note of the date, time, and activity. If you have texts, letters, or any physical evidence, keep that in a safe place

and note the date it was sent. This will all serve as critical evidence and can help you get the help you need to get away and safe.

> *During our separation, I didn't answer the phone when he called. When I returned his call, he asked where I had been. Feeling no need to be completely honest, I left out a few stops. He asked where else I had been, to which I answered, "It's really not your business." He then proceeded to tell me about a program you can put on someone's phone to track where they've been. He knew I was so low-tech that I would never have suspected it and never be able to figure it out. To this day, I still don't know if he really tracked my phone or not, but it was enough to make me question every move I was making. Even hundreds of miles away, it always felt like he was right there.*

Ok, before we move on to, in our opinion, another horrific tactic used by some abusers, we just need to pause again. Take a deep breath. If you have ever experienced any of the pendulum swings of stalking, it can be hard. The lasting effects can be a challenge.

> *I still look. To this day I watch. It can be overwhelming some days and others just a few extra glances at what vehicles are on the road around me.*

Fear: Destruction of Pets

> *When I first met him, I remember thinking, Wow, a guy with two cats. To me, that showed the ability to care for something, attention to detail, and more. There is just something romantic and tender about a big, strong man caring for a small, defenseless animal. It gives you warm fuzzies in all the right places.*

It could be that my past experience was the opposite, a complete lack of care or concern for anything else living, so I was entranced by the affection he showed toward his animals. It wasn't long before he surprised me with a cat of my own, something I had mentioned in passing. Since childhood, I had always wanted a cat, but for one reason or another, I never had one. It's funny how his behavior toward animals was one of the first things I loved about him and also one of the first things that truly filled me with fear. As much as I tried to block out some of the images, I can't shake the memory of him throwing the cat because he smelled urine on the furniture. It was the first time I remember feeling a true alarm. Despite other signs, I could always "justify" the action. Once the abuse turned towards the animals, it was becoming increasingly difficult to brush it off or think I was turning it into more than it was.

At the same time that animals were an outlet for abuse, they were also used as a ploy for comfort, compassion, and trust. After relocating to a new home, farther from my family and friends, he bought us a small puppy. It was an effort to make the move more bearable and an attempt to rebuild my trust. It was all part of the roller coaster ride we couldn't get off of, but again, it worked to subside the growing questions and doubt in my mind. To be honest, I was looking for any signs of love and compassion. I so badly wanted to be wrong. I didn't want to be right that I had married into yet another bad situation. I wanted to believe I was being picky and that we did have a healthy, normal marriage. I was eager to hold onto any signs of compassion that I could. Newly pregnant, living in a new town, and caring for his ailing mother who moved in with us, the new puppy was a welcome break from the flags that kept increasing. He kept me weighed down with so much responsibility that at times it was hard to see anything really. Fish tanks, new pregnancy, moving, animals, school for him, some form of income, his mother's care (which was a whole other form of abuse), his life demands and all the rest of life that comes with being a mom.

Abuse toward the dog did not start right away. Just like his early interactions with the cats, there were signs of hope. Through the years, the aggression toward the dog escalated and became more frequent. Disguised as "training" and "showing dominance as the leader of the pack," it soon turned to intentional neglect and punishment. He would tell me I knew nothing about training animals. The dog was left chained up outside, and we weren't allowed to feed him. Although we would sneak him food and water when we had the chance, it was horrible to see the mistreatment of an animal and not be able to do anything about it out of fear of our own safety.

The anguish and sense of desperation I felt having to follow through with his demands was such a violation of my own values. I knew well enough that what was going on wasn't right and I did not want to be a participant in it, my children to be a part of it, or witness the death of a pet by the hands of a human. I can't quite recall the breaking point, but I was scared enough to become a liar in order to survive and devise a plan to get the dog out of our home. My decisions were based on abused-mentality. He was so frail and sickly looking, so I suggested that we take him to the vet. "Maybe he has a stomach worm." The vet I had to use was nowhere close to our home, and it took a lot to coordinate considering I was a nursing mother of three, running an in-home daycare, with no real support. After a long 24-hour period of time, the dog was finally safe and would be taken care of. Of course, to return without the dog required a believable cover story regarding his sudden passing. Not only was I returning without the dog, I was gone all day, and not meeting his every need. Dangerous territory. When I turned the dog into the shelter, I didn't even give them my personal information because I would get in trouble if he ever found out. Going against his authority was the most dangerous territory of all. Fortunately, the sad "truth" of the dog's sudden passing made the day more tolerable and I avoided the consequences that I was afraid of. I now understand that lying can become a survival mechanism, a protection from retaliation or a comfort to ourselves.

The vomit I tasted as he posted on social media for all to see, compassion and heartfelt words of loss, is a taste I will never forget. It became a more frequent taste over the next few years. The things he showed and expressed outwardly for others to see was so completely the opposite of what was going on and who he was. For the rest of us, grieving wasn't a luxury we were given, so this situation was no different. Tears were to be hidden and jokes would be quick off of his tongue as a form of torture. If there was any solace, it was that our beloved pup was now safe, away from the hands of his "pack leader."

Destruction of animals, particularly pets, is the intentional abuse of animals as a method of domestic violence. Abusers often use animal abuse as a means to exploit the close, emotional bond between a pet and its owner to inflict harm on the human victim. They may harm or kill the animal to inflict emotional pain, use threats against the animal to gain compliance or control over the human, and/or use these methods to abuse the human or coerce them to return after leaving the house.

Violence to an animal can be gruesome and extreme, or appear in other ways such as intentional neglect, inducing aggression, or harsh discipline. So what would/could an abuser achieve through the abuse of animals in a domestic abuse environment? Abusers may abuse pets to:

- Demonstrate power
- Teach their victims a lesson
- Serve as a scapegoat for their anger
- Isolate a victim
- Punish
- Perpetuate the constant threat of terror
- Deter or punish attempts to leave the home
- Harm by forcing participation in abuse
- Confirm power by denying the ability to grieve after the harm or death of an animal

Not all of these are achievable solely through the abuse of animals. Other types of abuse may be enhanced or complimented through the use of animal abuse.

The psychological aspects of this type of abuse are numerous. An abuser who tortures or harms an animal, particularly in front of their victim, only further embeds the idea that he has all of the power in the relationship, and that she is helpless to protect the animal. This establishes the groundwork for the fear that she could not protect the animal therefore she would not be able to protect herself if he turned the torture toward her. Remember the balance is off and logical thinking is squashed. Emotional responses are used as currency to the abuser and serve to drive even more confusion.

Why animals? First of all, the physical abuse of an animal is easier to keep under the radar and has a lower risk of detection. Additionally, animals are often used as a means of control over someone, or intimidation. It is a way to show authority or power, revealing signs of what could come your way.

Although abuse of animals is a powerful tool for abusers to use against any victim, women without children may be particularly vulnerable to this type of abuse. Women, especially those without children, often consider pets as comfort, companions, and even family members. These women can often be more susceptible to the psychological influences of abuse toward animals because, in a way, the animal takes the place of children. Similar threats and fears exist as they would if the abuse was directed at one's children.

When we take into consideration that social isolation has most likely already set in, it would be fair to assume a victim would become reliant on an animal for emotional support and companionship. The abuse or killing of an animal would subsequently inflict significant harm on the human victim, psychologically and emotionally, allowing the abuser to establish yet another level of control and compliance of demands.

As you read in the previous story, women with children are not immune to the psychological abuse of witnessing the mistreatment of animals. It is still a very powerful tool for abusers to inflict psychological pain on their victims. Most people do not want to see an animal abused. It is a natural and compassionate reaction to feel physically pained when witnessing abuse of another living thing. That's why this tool is so powerful.

The question becomes, if he can do that to an animal, what will he do to me? And that is exactly the type of fear the abuser wants to inflict on his victim.

When a woman has a pet, especially without children, she is more often reluctant to leave because her options are even more limited or restricted due to the pet. Many shelters will not take pets, forcing the woman to make a choice between getting herself to safety or protecting her animal. Many times, a woman will choose to leave the shelter or even stay in an abusive relationship because she is not willing to give up her pet. Of reporting shelters, 85% report being informed of animal abuse in the woman's home.[4] Yet many still are not equipped with the ability to accept pets.

Violence to an animal is a direct threat to a victim when in an abusive situation. Unfortunately, as a society, we have just recently begun tying it together.

A substantial amount of research has made a connection with the relationship between domestic violence and animal abuse.[5] The collective research has shown over and over that in an abusive household there is often more than one victim, and an abuser is highly likely to harm both an intimate partner and domestic animals in the home. Still, the legal system does not provide a great deal of protection for women in the case of abuse toward animals. In many ways, the pets themselves have more protection than women. If animal abuse is the sum of the provable abuse, prosecutors won't do anything about it in regards to domestic abuse, and the woman is back in the home. Most women won't even report it because if he found out about it, it could be worse. There are, though, efforts taking place to petition for "protection of animals" to be included in civil protection order when it is a co-abuse situation. This would provide additional protection for the animal when a victim is able to attain a civil protection order after proving abuse is taking place.

If you suspect you are experiencing abuse through the destruction of a pet, what can you do?

- Get the pet out of the situation by any means necessary
- Protect the animal
- Stop the abuser from using the animal to abuse you
- Get out of the situation because it is likely to escalate
- Recommend your partner seek help
- Take action to get yourself help

Control

Power dynamics can often play a significant role in relationships. This push and pull for power often leads to abuse within the relationship, and the abuse feeds the imbalance of power, thus creating a stronger cycle of abuse. In a loving, trusting relationship, it shouldn't feel like anyone holds all the power. Rather, there is a healthy balance of power and responsibility between the two parties.

As we have discussed throughout this book, Christian beliefs of the man being the head of the household are often used as justification for a power-hungry husband to run the family with an iron fist. In the biblical context, there is a balance between the head (the husband) and the heart (the wife). Whereas the husband is ultimately responsible for leading the home, he is also responsible for caring for and loving his family, in particular, his wife. It is not fair or appropriate to reference this aspect of scripture without applying it completely. A marriage was intended to be a partnership, not a dictatorship. In healthy, loving relationships, there is an agreed upon balance of responsibility.

> *Growing up, my parents had clear lines of responsibility. My mom made all of the decisions 'within' the home and my dad made all of the decisions 'outside' of the home. When a large purchase was to be made, it was discussed and agreed to.*

Although my father was the clear head of the home, my mother had equal responsibility in her space. Neither overpowered the other. There was mutual respect and love shared across both.

As an adult I expected this respect and care was part of a loving marriage, and he said he loved me.

Abusers often engage in controlling behaviors as a way of limiting the freedom of their victims. This abuse is displayed in many different forms and has a number of outcomes, but the basic premise is that these behaviors are limiting the victim's freedom of movement, or stopping the victim from contacting or building meaningful relationships with other people (such as friends or family). It may also include stopping their victim from doing the things they normally do, such as social activities, sports, school, or work.

He would talk about my family so that I felt like they were butting into our business too much or crossing a line. Eventually, I stopped talking to them because I wanted to "protect" our marriage through our struggles. When I finally left, my family had given up hope that I would ever leave because they had no idea we were struggling at all. I stopped telling them anything and kept it all to myself. I didn't think I could talk to them about it, so I didn't. Friends stopped hanging out because they didn't want to be around him, family stopped coming by because they didn't feel welcome or comfortable. Slowly but surely, it was just the two of us.

I had a new coworker whose wife just had a baby. I thought it would be nice to go for a visit and take her a little gift. They had recently moved and didn't know many people either. I wanted to go by on Saturday morning since the evenings are sometimes difficult with a young family. When I mentioned that, he said, "Saturday is the only day we get to spend together. You are always working. We never get to spend any time together." I never did go see her.

Psychological abusers may control their victim's finances, as we discuss in detail under economic abuse, in an attempt to force them to stay in the abusive relationship. Control of finances often leads to the victim being forced to ask for basic needs to be fulfilled like face wash, shampoo or even things of greater or lesser importance. This creates a sense of hierarchy in which the victim is always at a lower level than the abuser, creating a very unhealthy dominance and forced submission.

> *I was tired and had things to do after putting the kids down for the night. He wanted to play video games together. I said I really didn't want to and had so many things to do. He made me feel bad about not spending time with him, not ever doing what he wanted, and choosing everything else over him, so I played the games. Yet when I wanted to watch a certain movie or do something together, he said it was stupid, a waste of time, or just something he wasn't interested in. When it was something he wanted to do, my interests didn't matter, but when I wanted him to do something with me, he would only do it if it was something he wanted to do.*

Control: Ignoring Requests

The abuser may inflict additional control by disregarding, ignoring, or neglecting the victim's requests and needs. As we discussed under verbal abuse, this can result from the abuser downplaying the need for medical care. In many instances, abusers control the money, use of vehicles, and the ability to move freely, thus making the victim run all requests through him. By denying basic needs of his victim, abusers maintain control of the victim and leave her with a sense of dread and lack of worthiness.

> *He controlled the money, except for what I brought in through my in-home daycare, but even then, he controlled how it was spent. When the children needed new clothes, shoes, food, or school supplies, I would have to ask for money. Many times, he would either refuse to give me money or wouldn't give me enough to meet those needs. He would say, "They don't need any*

new clothes," or "They can wear the shoes they have." Fortunately, I had my extra income that I could use to supplement at times if he wouldn't agree, but it didn't go far, even for required or regular doctor visits. He would say, "There's nothing wrong with you," when I felt that I needed to go.

Sometimes he wouldn't allow me to use the car or give me money for the co-pays or even watch our kids. If I already had a prescription, I could usually get it filled, but many times I wasn't allowed to do that. I am still suffering from the implications of going years without seeing a doctor when I needed to. Many of my current struggles could have been reduced or eliminated if I had been able to get on certain medications earlier.

Control: Religion

Religion can be a very difficult and sensitive topic. Many religions have practices that are borderline or fall squarely in the abuse category. When both parties are supportive of the religious practices, there is little ground for a legal charge of abuse. That said, many "consenting" parties are giving their consent out of distress or due to the repercussions if they don't. Just as we have discussed throughout this book, when a victim gives consent based on the threat of worse punishment if they don't, that is *not* true consent. Anytime one person is being harmed by another, that is abuse, regardless of how the abuser is attempting to justify it.

Not allowing the victim to practice their religious beliefs or isolating them from the religious community are other abusive behaviors that fall under control and religion. Again, this can get tricky because of how intertwined religion is with one's identity, values, and beliefs. When victims are engaging in religious practices that go against the abuser's own beliefs or values, they may attempt to deny them access to that practice in an effort to protect them. In that case, the intent is not to isolate or abuse, but rather to limit exposure to the very real dangers presented by association with the cult.

When an abuser prevents their victim from engaging in their religious practices, they are not only preventing them from engaging with others and controlling their movements, they are also interfering with their salvation and future. Connection with other believers is an important aspect of many belief systems and a critical component of overall well being. Not being able to practice your religion and surround yourself with like-minded believers can begin to erode your deeper, spiritual relationships, having a snowball effect on your life as a whole.

Religious abuse can also take the form of forcing religion on others. This may be a more common practice in cultures where religion and culture are deeply intertwined, and the religious foundation is based on strict laws and rules.

Part of what makes religion so powerful is the personal choice and connection with your belief. Any time religion is forced upon you or you are being mistreated in the name of religion, it is not okay or healthy. Even though we provide some extreme examples of abuse in the name of religion, in many cases, the abuse is not intended to be harmful, but to keep the victim on the "straight and narrow" with the purpose of protecting them and securing their place in the afterlife. As we mentioned earlier, it is an abuse based in fear and control. Even less legalistic religions like Christianity can cross the line between love and abuse when parents, partners, or community members attempt to force their beliefs on others in the name of love and salvation.

Guilt and shame are common forms of religious abuse when used to make someone feel bad for their actions, behaviors, thoughts, words, or lifestyle. In an attempt to "straighten them out," lifelong damage can be done. That guilt impacts future choices and the way victims feel about those choices. Victims may have lasting doubt, insecurity, and bitterness resulting from guilt and shame they experience in the name of religion.

> *Growing up, I knew that sex before marriage was a sin. When I lost my virginity, I kept it a secret from everyone. I knew my family would be so ashamed and disappointed. I thought the only way to make it right was to go ahead and get married. Growing up in a Christian home, divorce was never an option.*

I knew I would not be looked at the same in the church, in my family, or in my community if I "gave up" on my marriage and didn't "give God a chance to fix it." For eight years, I struggled with my sin, my choices, and the fact that I was so unhappy with it all. I felt like I didn't deserve happiness since I was such a terrible sinner. Since sin was the foundation of my marriage, I thought that it was my punishment to live the life I had chosen.

Control: Isolation

Early in our dating relationship, my lease was ending. He was about to be deployed overseas with the military, so he offered to let me move into a townhouse we both could agree on while he was gone. He offered it up as "You help take care of my place and save a little money at the same time." We made plans to chat regularly via video calls. He would always schedule the calls for the evenings. This made it difficult for me to hang out with friends, relax with time to myself, or have any kind of social life at all. Many times, he would schedule a call and then never show up. I would sit around all night, waiting for him to ring. He would sometimes call later and say, "Something came up," or he may not call at all, claiming that he forgot.

When we didn't have video chats scheduled, he would call or text all night; just checking in, seeing what I was up to. If I did happen to hang out with a friend, we were constantly interrupted with his phone calls. If I didn't answer, he would be irate and question what I had been doing that I couldn't answer his call. Eventually, it was just easier to stay home and wait for his calls than to attempt to do anything else. I would tell myself, "it's not a big deal, he likes you a lot and it's just easier than dealing with any fallout. Plus I like staying home."

Many controlling behaviors result in the victim becoming isolated from their network of family and friends and greater community. By limiting their involvement and movement through controlling behaviors, external relationships slowly erode and break down. Although this category is tucked under controlling behaviors, this is not the only way a victim may become isolated from their community. We will go ahead and discuss isolation in full here, though not all behaviors would technically be captured under the category of control.

Isolation is a relatively common "entry point" to abuse. It can start off slowly and appear quite innocent. Many victims don't even realize they are being isolated until they have been completely cut off from their friends, family, and support system.

Relationships are a basic human need. Aside from extreme introverts, most people need some interaction with other people to live healthy lives. That's why solitary confinement is such a severe punishment. We need human interaction. We need to relate to others. Removing that connection from people is psychologically harmful.[6] During isolation, control is garnered by bringing the prey into the predator's world, so much so that they accept it as their own.

> *As I started building relationships with coworkers, I began to realize that I was dealing with more than typical marriage struggles. I watched other couples engage with each other in positive ways. I listened to men talk about their wives using uplifting words. I experienced co-workers treating me better than my own husband did. It put the idea in motion that perhaps my unhappiness was more than just my problem. I started to wonder if there was a chance for me to be happy one day.*

By keeping the victim from other people, activities, and experiences, the abuser is not only isolating the victim from resources (personal, public, and relational) that may help them leave the relationship, but they are also keeping them from experiencing a world that may not reinforce their perceptions and beliefs. The victim may begin to realize that what they are experiencing is *not* healthy or "normal." Additionally, these relationships and activities may serve to rebuild the victim's self-esteem and confidence, which is absolutely not what the abuser wants them to experience.

Isolation itself is not a singular behavior, but the outcome of many kinds of abusive behaviors can take on many different forms. Just like when an abuser's behavior becomes habitual, accepting it becomes the norm. When he wants us to stay home or wait around for his call, we justify by saying things like, "Well, I wasn't doing anything anyway." Well, you were doing something two months ago, before your relationship. Why are you doing nothing now? Were you actually doing nothing, or have isolating behaviors simply created a new norm for your life? In this way, victims promote the abusive behaviors by integrating them into their own beliefs and norms. It is by no means the victim's fault, and we are not suggesting that. We are simply highlighting the way abusers weave their behaviors into their victims' lives in such a way that they can't adequately describe what is wrong or how it happened. It becomes the victim's choice to do, or not do, certain things when the victim doesn't remember actually making those choices to begin with.

Isolation is a large topic. In the next sections, we're going to break it down a bit into smaller chunks to wrap our heads around it a bit better. Before we jump in, take a moment to pause. Grab a cup of coffee and come back.

Abuser-Activated Isolation

In the first, most direct form of isolation, the abuser cuts the victim off from their social network such as friends and family or prevents them from building a social network including friends, colleagues, and even acquaintances. It often begins as an expression of their love for the victim with statements like, "If you really loved me you would want to spend time with me, not your family." As it progresses, the isolation expands, limiting or excluding their contact with anyone but the abuser. Eventually, the victim is left totally alone and without the internal and external resources to change their life.

I started a new job on a fairly new team. My teammates were all fairly young, and close to my age. On occasion, they liked to grab drinks after work. It was a great way to get to know each other. I called to let my husband know that I would be late because I wanted to grab drinks with my team. I would hear the sadness in his voice as he said, "Oh really? I was hoping we could spend some time together tonight." We hadn't spent time together in weeks. I would come home, cook dinner, clean up, read, do some work, and go to bed... all alone. When I asked what he had in mind, "I don't know. There's a movie out I thought you might like. We never spend any time together. I thought it would be nice." I would come home instead of going out with my friends. I would cook and clean then ask about the movie. "Yeah. It's not on tonight," or "You actually wouldn't like it," or it was actually a movie I had no interest in, or "We don't have the right cord for the DVD player." Whatever the reason, there was rarely actually a movie. Just like every other night, we would go to our separate corners or I would sit on the couch and watch him play his game or watch whatever movie he was interested in. Meanwhile, my team had inside jokes I didn't get, shared experiences I missed, and grew together while I became more and more isolated.

It may be easier to think of isolation as a pivotal tactic instead of actual abuse. It is a tactic used by controlling partners to weaken their victims, prevent them from hearing others' perspectives and to bring them into line with their beliefs and requirements. Abusers create a dependency on them. Over time, the victim has no one else to talk to, no one to share with, and the abuser is the only person the victim can connect with. It is a way of keeping the victim right where he wants her, otherwise known as a "keep" tactic.

It is not uncommon for possessiveness and jealousy to be large factors of motivation to isolate someone from social contact with friends and family. Another motivator for isolation is to forcibly make the victim extremely if not solely dependent on their controlling partner.

The tactics used are very similar in a lot of circumstances and it is easy to find these themes when talking to past victims.

A. Guilting her into spending time together or creating scenarios in avoidance of spending time with others

- Manufacturing situations aimed specifically to isolate her.

  I asked if I could meet a friend. He immediately responded that we had plans that he forgot to tell me about. When I asked about the plans later, they were canceled or he had the wrong date.

- Makes her feel bad or guilty for trying to make connections. An abuser may only allow things that are acceptable to him or justified. For example, if joining a book club infringes on his time, he will have stipulations or outright refusal.
- Not allowing time alone to really see what is happening is also a form of isolation in a relationship. This happens within many parts of the relationship. From the abuser dictating how his victim spends her time, to when they talk and about what, to not letting them have any solitude even in the home, and many other ways.

  I was rarely allotted alone time in ways that I thought would be normal every once in a while. Like staying up to watch a show on my own, you know the type that most men scrunch their nose to. But that wasn't the case. I was conditioned fairly early on that he wanted, insisted, that we go to bed at the same time. If he was up late then so was I, but if he wanted to go to bed, I had better be there as well. Same with the morning. He would expect me to rise at the same time as him, and if I didn't, it would be clear by how loud he was that I better wake up. It just always felt like a state of unrest.

  In times that seemed like a true miracle, where all kids were quiet and the baby was asleep, where I might get to read or go to the bathroom, he would be there demanding attention in some form.

- Insisting that you care more for friends, family, children, and pets then they do for them.
- Claiming that you never spend any time with them, that they miss you, and just want to spend time with you.

We had a vegetable garden that was overflowing. I bagged up some extras and was going to run them to a friend down the street, a friend he introduced me to and "allowed." As I was trying to leave, he said, "Don't stay very long. You always stay too long when you go over there. Don't leave me here with these kids." I decided to take the kids so he didn't have to "deal" with them. The last thing he said was "I can't believe you are going over there instead of spending time with me." Even the amount of time to drop off, say hi, and insist that I couldn't stay was too long for him.

- Their plans are always or more often fulfilled than yours are.

I was tired and had things to do after putting the kids down for the night. He wanted to play video games together. I said I really didn't want to and had so many things to do. He made me feel bad about not spending time with him, not ever doing what he wanted, and choosing everything else over him, so I played the games. Yet when I wanted to watch a certain movie or do something together, he said it was stupid, a waste of time, or just something he wasn't interested in. When it was something he wanted to do, my interests didn't matter, but when I wanted him to do something with me, he would only do it if it was something he wanted.

B. Enforcing that he is the only one who understands her or loves her.

- Attempts to isolate the two of you as a couple, professing that the two of you can handle anything together especially when told that your family or friends don't like him very much, or that you would be happier without so and so giving their two cents.
- Demands loyalty to him, as opposed to others and typically in a very short time period of meeting, loyalty that is not adequately earned breaks healthy boundaries quickly.
- Putting the victim in the position of choosing him over children or other family members and friends.

I was enjoying online dating for a while after my divorce. I was surprised by how many men asked if I was seeing anyone else and would get angry, sometimes even dropping me if I said I was going on dates with other men or even talking to them through the website. Sometimes, they would have this reaction even before we met for the first time.

- Attempts to get the victim to choose him exclusively by accusing others of not liking him or being jealous of your relationship.
- Does whatever he can do to provoke jealousies and/or rivalries, creating division in relationships or connections. He may mention that someone said something about her or accused her of something or even confided in him about her, really any stories or lies they can manipulate will be used to get the victim to cut ties.

We had only dated for a short time, maybe a couple of months at this point. I had expressed information to him in regards to a few friends. Really just giving some background so that he felt a bit more comfortable with them. One of my friends was having a hard time in her marriage and just needed the support of her girlfriends. He would criticize her behavior or the things she would say. Eventually getting irritated when I would spend time with her. Accusing that because she was behaving in a particular way, then I must be too.

- Demands that relationship issues be kept between just the two of you, insisting that it is nobody else's business. He may claim that what is between the two of you is special and unlike anything else, so no one will understand. There may be an environment established of "keeping up appearances" and "we don't talk about the bad things so people don't judge" in order to create the appearance of perfect marriage so that if anyone hears something a little off they wouldn't believe it, creating shock and disbelief towards the victim if she does say something. This is a new level of privacy that is based on secrets and false illusions.

C. Blatantly limiting access to information and/or others, typically without a real pattern or logic to it.

- Controlling incoming information: What she reads or views, potential connections, punishing her if she spends time with those that are not approved, purposefully moving towns or even countries.
- Controls the money to prevent use of the car without permission, limiting access to others that would counteract what he was saying or doing. Changes in this would be inconsistent to make the victim feel invalidated when showing concern.
- Prevents you from leaving or punishes you when trying to return by restricting access like locking doors or changing garage codes.
- Tells you that what you are doing makes him jealous and insists you not do it. It could be chatting with past friends, old acquaintances, the waiter at a restaurant, anything to eliminate your contact. They can express their fears based on past

relationships to insist they were afraid of you running around on them. After having a child is a prime time for this type of isolation tactic that can have a lasting benefit to the abuser.

- Tells you that you are not allowed to see specific people. This is typically seen in restrictions of any communication with all people of the opposite sex without any exceptions.
- Dismissive of invitations to participate in activities with friends or family. This isn't an instant thing and is typically very subtle, from refusing to go visit family, making the victim choose between leaving him all alone or visiting with family "that you can see anytime." This tactic can also look like the abuser removing themselves from hanging out when friends or family are visiting, shutting themselves off in other rooms.
- Puts limits on visits with others or outings such as how long you can be at the gym, or what an acceptable amount of time would be to spend with friends.

Early in our marriage, he moved us back to his hometown in another state. At first, I thought it was a much-needed fresh start. We moved away from my job, my network, and my other children's father. The only person we knew in our new community was his mom who moved in with us. Eventually, I made a friend. She was a friend of his, so he allowed it. I was not allowed to really work or participate in activities unless it suited him, so there was no way for me to even make any other friends. All of my time was spent at home with my children and taking care of his mother. With all of my responsibilities, I'm not sure I would have had the time or energy to make friends, even if I had the opportunity. Even when I would go see my "approved" friend, he would stop me from hanging out too long. "You had better be back in 30 minutes." Errands started to even feel like they were timed. It was difficult to have any time to myself or time to spend with others.

D. Creating an uncomfortable environment for others:

- His behavior causes friends and family to choose to stay away. It is not uncommon for the abuser to behave decently enough some of the time and then be blatantly rude or argumentative enough to cause others to not particularly want to be around them. When someone is unwelcoming and unfriendly, people naturally tend to shy away.
- Victims may find themselves overcompensating by being extra agreeable, talkative, or friendly, even laughing about or explaining away behavior to portray a sense of normalcy.

He was so obnoxious and annoying to be around. At first, it was fun. Everyone seemed to love him. They laughed and joked, but they soon realized that's all it was. He couldn't be serious or laid back. He was always 100% amped up. He would joke about and be disrespectful toward me. He always had to be the center of attention. He rarely gave me the chance to visit with anyone without him taking control of the conversation. I thought everyone was having a good time but me. Apparently, people started getting tired of it. They never said anything, but they would slowly stop inviting us over or coming over when invited. My friends stopped inviting me because it always involved him coming along.

Years after my divorce, I would bump into former colleagues at conferences. When they heard the news, they would all tell me how happy they were for me. They would tell me how uncomfortable it was and how they wished we had a chance to get to know each other better. My field is small and networking is crucial. Colleagues from other programs lean heavily on and are still very connected with their graduate cohort. I didn't have a chance to develop those connections because they were smothered before they had a chance to grow. I still suffer from that loss today.

Self-Isolation

When living in an ongoing abusive environment, it is not uncommon for a victim to self-withdraw from friends and family, a majority of her close relationships, in order to save face or because of feelings of being misunderstood, shamed, judged, stigmatized or otherwise unsupported. In these cases, victims isolate themselves from existing resources and support systems because of the shame of bruises or other injuries, the perpetrator's behavior in public, or the perpetrator's treatment of friends or family. Self-isolation may also develop from fear of public humiliation or from fear of harm to themselves or others. The victim may also feel guilty for the abuser's behavior, the condition of the relationship, or a myriad of other reasons, depending on the messages received from the abuser. This type of isolation results in the same loss of access in abuser-activated isolation.

> *I knew my parents would ask how things were going, and it got harder and harder to lie. I wanted to avoid all conversations, knowing that I would have to pretend everything was okay. I stopped encouraging them to come for a visit. I was embarrassed for them to see what he did all day, and all night. I didn't want them seeing how he treated me. He didn't hit me or call me names, but he was disrespectful, made inappropriate jokes, and was inconsiderate. I didn't want them seeing that he didn't help cook or clean, that he drank all night, that he slept all day, and I didn't want to have to defend any of it. As close as I am with my parents, they didn't visit me once during a three-year period. It was too uncomfortable for me to have them come.*

If a victim didn't have a strong support system initially then complete seclusion can become a defense mechanism. If relationships around them are also dysfunctional, there might be a feeling of not being able to speak up because that was "normal." Secrecy can become more about not feeling embarrassed and less about being coerced into silence.

Victims may begin to feel like they are the crazy ones because no one else sees the abusive behavior. Other people see a completely different side of him, making the victim feel like they must be overreacting or blowing it out of proportion. If they do bring it up, they may hear, "I can't see him behaving like that," or "that's not like him." Unless the abuser slips up, most connections never see or hear the abusive behavior. The victim may withdraw from others because they just can't handle feeling like they are living in a world that doesn't make any sense.

A victim can self-isolate out of fear of consequences real or perceived. When an abuser gets irate for certain behaviors or actions of their victims, the victim will naturally stop out of fear of the fight, or yelling, or anything else. Victims will start to reduce social activities of their choosing because it is just easier to do what the abuser wants and they don't want others to see how the abuser behaves. A victim will stop going places because of an abuser's behavior when they return such as refusal to speak to them, sulking, excessive demands of attention or other acts, trigger statements that incite fear or shame. A victim will start to feel dread or impossibility to feel joy with things that they would normally look forward to.

Social Isolation

Social isolation is the third type of isolation where the victim is left feeling "different" or not having a "normal" relationship and therefore feels she can't relate to others. In this case, she may or may not physically separate from others, but she feels distant, which prevents her from making close connections with others. Others may actually cut her off because she is "too much" or seems to be constantly surrounded by a cloud of drama. Social-isolation is the final step to feeling isolated in every aspect of your life. Not only are you physically isolated from others and necessary resources, but you are emotionally isolated from sharing life with someone else. True connection with other human beings is essential for navigating and understanding the world. Sharing stories with, getting opinions from, and bouncing ideas off of others is how we develop and understand how our lives fit into the bigger picture around us.

He had a high need to be liked and accepted by others, and prided himself on being young and hip. Never really getting to experience college when he was enrolled the first time, he was really taking advantage of the opportunity this time around. He joined "study groups" where he and his college-aged coworkers would sit around smoking weed until the early morning hours. I rarely knew where he was and just prayed that he would come home. Eventually, I started to not care if he came home, for which I felt incredibly guilty. He asked me to go with him once to meet his friends. Trying not to be a party pooper, I went. Before long, they were all sitting in a circle passing a joint around. Everyone was having a great time, and I was completely left out. I am such an introvert; I hate parties and strangers anyway. Watching them all get high while I sat in the corner sent my anxiety through the roof. They all asked me to join several times. They were all nice people and none were "potheads" as I always imagined or saw on TV, what could a single puff hurt? I had never smoked a cigarette, so they had to teach me how to smoke. After a few unsuccessful tries, I finally got the hang of it. It was horrible, but I did start to feel more comfortable. Maybe I was just a big party pooper like he always said, and I just needed to relax a little. Still, I just knew the police would barge through the door any minute and haul us all off to jail. I couldn't believe I could be so careless with my career.

As I graduated and we started our "adult" lives, I thought he would grow up and move on from this behavior. He knew I didn't like it and was against drugs of any kind. I didn't even take the recommended dose of Advil when I needed it. During his liquor store employment period, we experienced a spike in the drinking and "hanging out." He met a gal who invited us over for dinner. By the end of the night, she was chopping up crystal meth. My heart was racing and I needed to get out. They jokingly battered me throughout the night, convincing me that it wouldn't hurt me, it wouldn't show up on a drug test, and I could just relax. I continued to drink wine, trying to calm my anxiety and just "enjoy" the situation and stop being such a "prude." At three in the morning, they were wired. They were having so much fun and I was on the verge of toppling over. I finally gave in and tried a line they had separated out for me. I still don't know if I did it right or if I actually got any up my nose, but I still find myself rubbing my nose sometimes, trying to get it out.

Isolation is sneaky and, like most forms of abuse, can come in many different packages. It is critical to have a strong support network, even in perfectly happy, healthy relationships. There are seasons where friends and family fall to the background as you get settled in a new relationship, start a family, or hit a busy season with work. That said, if you notice that you are regularly being restricted from spending time with others, being made to feel guilty about being with others, or are not being included in activities that you otherwise should be included in, you may be experiencing psychological abuse in the form of isolation.

What can you do if you suspect you are being abused through isolation?

- As always, we recommend you begin by having a conversation with your partner about what you are experiencing. It could very well be that your partner is incredibly needy or truly misses spending time with you during a particularly busy season. Having a conversation will help draw your attention to how these issues should be addressed.
- Identify ways to spend time with others, even if over the phone, through quick chats, or while shopping together for groceries.
- Remember we were never meant to be an island. Isolation abuse wins by making you not only feel but think you are alone. You are not alone.
- Find community groups, school activities, and volunteer services.

Control: Confinement

At one point, he said he was "testing the waters" on a separa-tion and would say he was showing me how he could take care of the kids. During these times, he would make me go upstairs to my room where I could feel the emotional pull of wanting my babies. It was torturous.

Confinement is often used synonymously and in conjunction with isolation because they do share similar qualities and confinement often leads to isolation. That said, there are differences. As we mentioned, isolation is a common entry point to abuse. It starts off slow and involves the process of detachment or separation. Confinement, on the other hand, is the act of confining or being confined, restrained, or phys-ically or psychologically held. With that definition, confinement and kidnapping also begin to sound similar. For our purposes, confinement is the psychological restraint where kidnapping is the physical restraint or physical movement from one place to another, which we talked about in previous sections.

He would call me in the middle of the afternoon while I was in class or at night while I was working late and say he was about to walk to the bar or start walking to my office. I could tell he had been drinking. I knew he would do it, and then be at risk for getting arrested, getting hit by a car, or passing out on the side of the road. If I didn't drop everything and go get him, babysitting him the rest of the night to keep him from doing something harmful to himself, then it would be my fault that he got hurt.

Whereas kidnapping is a little easier to clearly recognize as abuse, confinement is restraint based on psychological influences or threats, which is more challenging to recognize. The fact that the victim *could* leave any time, they aren't being physically restrained, gives the impres-sion that the victim is willfully staying in a given location or in the rela-tionship as a whole.

When an act is based in fear, it is never consensual. A victim of abuse is not making an active choice to stay in a relationship over leaving the relationship. Rather, they are making a choice to stay in the relationship over whatever threat or fear they expect to experience as a result of leaving. This fear is holding them in the relationship against what they would generally have wanted in the first place.

"If you leave, I'll kill myself." This was regularly mentioned when I would suggest that we would be better apart. Although drinking was often a part of it, as is the case when your partner is an alcoholic, it doesn't have to be. In this case, the psychological implication is that if you leave, he would harm himself or someone else. If you are so selfish to want to leave, then you can live with the fact that you caused harm to someone else. Most decent people don't want to inflict harm on someone, even if they don't want to be with them anymore.

I was able to finally leave when I got to the point where I thought, "I hope he does. He doesn't add any value to the world or anyone else." I knew when I got to that point that it was over for us. I hated myself for even thinking about it. I hated who I had become, and thought I was a terrible person. Terrible for thinking it, terrible for moving forward, just an overall terrible excuse for a human being. Long after the divorce was in process and even finalized, I wondered if I was even worthy of living because of the person I had become, all because I finally stood up to the psychological restraint he had me under for years. For finally calling his bluff and saying that my happiness was important too.

No, I didn't want him to die, but I had lost touch with my own judgment. I didn't even know who I was anymore. That's a form of psychological abuse because you feel terrible about yourself and a form of psychological confinement because it can leave you feeling like you have no choice but to stay in the relationship. It weighs you down. Am I that selfish that I'm actually considering it?

Confinement doesn't have to be as blatant and obvious as this. An abuser can create an environment of confinement by keeping the victim in a state of unrest or uncertainty, constantly having to be available to care for or serve her abuser. She is unable to make plans, spend time on important tasks/activities, or stay focused on her job because he is constantly reaching out or needing support.

In these situations, abusers will demonstrate tendencies to under-value their own lives, leaving the victim to overcompensate, trading their own value for their abuser's.

> *I was traveling for several days for work. I left him food to eat, afraid he would not eat and starve if I didn't, or that he would try driving to a restaurant after he had been drinking too much. One night we were talking and he said he hadn't eaten. "You knew I wouldn't eat that salad." By the end of the call, I had ordered him a pizza to be delivered so that he would eat something and not have to leave the house to do it.*

Victims often feel confined by the sense of responsibility they feel for their abuser. If I don't come home when he needs me, if I'm not here when he calls, if I don't make myself available to him, he will do something to hurt himself, someone else, or something, and it will be my fault.

The Ben Franklin Effect says that people will like you more when they do something nice for you. Most people believe the opposite. If I do enough for them, they will eventually like me.

Victims are constantly putting the abuser's needs above their own. The harder she tries to gain his love and affection, the more it creates division in his mind. His pedestal rises higher while hers gets lower. Even she begins to see the divide as his love becomes less attainable and more desirable.

As we have mentioned, confinement is one of those types of abuse that straddles two categories: physical and psychological. Most people recognize the physical side of confinement, often referred to as kidnapping:

physical, unlawful restraint. When picturing confinement, we often conjure up images of someone chained in a closet, stuffed in a car, or physically held down. This level of kidnapping is clearly extreme, incredibly traumatic, and more easily identifiable. Once kidnapping has reached this point, the victim generally recognizes that she is in an extremely volatile and abusive relationship, but at the same time is made painfully aware of the difficulty of leaving that relationship unscathed.

Fortunately, this level of physical abuse associated with kidnapping is less common than the psychological side. However, psychological abuse related to confinement is no less dangerous. In fact, because it is generally not considered "as extreme" as the physical, victims may look past it. They justify and therefore tend to stay in the relationship longer than they should because they don't perceive the intensity of the threat from their partner.

Confinement may involve confinement to a physical space or simply to the relationship.

> *He released air out of my tires so that I would be late or not be able to drive anywhere. I know the air was released because my pressure indicators were always spot on and had not shown signs of pressure loss. Once aired up, they had no problem keeping air... until the pressure was released again another time. It was just another way to prevent me from leaving.*

Related to the discussion on self-esteem, when a victim feels they have no control over their situation or ability to leave, they eventually stop trying to escape. This concept, learned helplessness, has been used to explain the victim's role in continued abuse. Peterson and Park define learned helplessness as "the physiological state of being where previous experiences can cause disruption in motivation, cognitive thinking, and emotions, which can result in passiveness, depression, and having feelings of hopelessness." [7]

This concept was first discovered when researchers were studying dogs in confinement. Dogs were placed in a cage with a partition separating two sides. Researchers would then send small electric shocks to one side of the floor, and the dogs would jump over to the other side. The dogs learned to simply jump to the other side to escape the shock. At that point, the researchers sent the electric shock to both sides. The dogs jumped from one side to the other. When they learned, over time, that they could not escape the shock, they eventually gave up, lying down and simply taking the shock. Even when the shock was removed from the other side of the partition, the dogs stopped trying to escape.

Victims in abusive relationships find themselves in this state of survival mode. Over time, they stop trying to leave. Instead, they learn to adapt to the situation. Related to learned helplessness is Stockholm or Hostage Syndrome. In this case, hostages begin to develop an attachment to or psychological alliance with their captors. It is a protective mechanism and survival technique to change the way we view the situation.

Women in abusive situations involving confinement or kidnapping often take on these same characteristics. They learn to adjust to the situation, learning to be happy with what they *do have*, learning to see the positives, and being grateful for the good times. This response is so strong, they can begin to believe they are actually in a positive relationship when focusing on the good.

This is where the line gets blurry when it comes to laws and prosecution regarding kidnapping or confinement, especially in romantic relationships. When the victim takes on these responses, they often appear to be supportive or "okay" with the situation. The reality is, that agreement is based on survival. They are not a willing participant in their situation but have simply learned to adapt and make the best of it. Would we say the dog in the early studies was a willing participant? Would we say the dog was okay with being shocked because he simply gave up? Absolutely not, yet that is what we do to victims in these situations.

What to do if you are being confined:

- Keep an extra set of car and house keys in a safe place where you can access when needed, like if they take the car keys and you are stuck or if they lock you out of the house
- Keep emergency phone numbers where you can access them even if you don't have your phone. Never be "locked" to or dependent on your phone.
- Talk to someone you trust.

Confusion and Insecurity

"What did I do wrong? I don't know what I did wrong."

Not much more than a week after having my fourth child, we drove to my sister's wedding. He made me drive most of the way, taking only a few breaks to feed the baby, since it was my sister's wedding and he "didn't want to go anyway." During the small window when he was at the wheel, he looked at my phone and saw a message exchange with an old friend. He immediately pulled over and kicked me out on the side of the highway. He pulled up several yards and made me walk back to the car. I didn't even know why he was so angry. What did I do? I didn't do anything. After driving all that way, we were two hours late for the shower because he would make us stop and refuse to continue on. I remember standing in a fast food parking lot begging for him to let me back in the car with my children and newborn baby.

While getting ready for the wedding the next day, he left me in the hotel room with the children. We were supposed to attend, but there was no childcare provided and he refused to "babysit" so that I could see my sister get married. I couldn't leave them, and he was nowhere to be found. I completely missed the cere-

mony but made it to the reception because he decided to grace me with that. My eyes were puffy and bloodshot, but we made it. He then insisted on standing in every picture while making it completely miserable, eyeing me with anger or a balled up fist when he could, but he put on such a great show, asking me to dance in order to keep up appearance while intentionally stepping on my feet to remind me that his power was still very much there. My family knew something was wrong but didn't want to talk about it. "It's okay. We can talk about this later. This is your sister's wedding."

Using reality-distorting statements or behaving inconsistently, abusers create confusion and insecurity in the victim. Saying one thing and doing another, stating falsehoods as facts, and neglecting to follow through on stated intentions creates an environment where the victim isn't sure what to believe or what is going to happen. This can even include denying the abuse occurred and/or telling the victim they're making it up. It might also include crazy-making behaviors like hiding the victim's keys and berating them for losing them. This often catches victims completely off guard and can result in the victim blaming themselves for doing something wrong to cause the inconsistency or confusing behavior.

Reality-distorting statements aren't just used by abusers either. When suffering from psychological abuse, victims begin experiencing what we call deferred reality. This is when victims convince themselves that what they are experiencing "isn't that bad." This mentality is akin to the idea of positive  thinking in which the victim focuses on the positive things in their life, the positive aspects of their relationship rather than the bad. Like "looking for the silver lining," they opt to see things as better than they actually are.

. . .

We all do this from time to time, and it can be a very beautiful way of living. In cases of domestic abuse, though, this positive outlook or deferred reality can be dangerous and unhealthy. Just like positive thinking can actually rewire your brain to see things as better than they may actually be, scanning the environment for the positive, deferred thinking can result in victims overlooking behaviors that should indeed be red flags.

> *We came home after having a really nice time out. Suddenly, he was angry. What just happened? What did I say? What did I do wrong?*

This type of behavior can make you doubt basic logic, because you are dealing with someone for whom basic logic doesn't exist. The only logic is his logic. There is no logic within that. You can't argue with it or understand it.

> *My logical thinking was destroyed because I was told I was wrong over and over again.*

> *We would be out and the kids would start acting up. "See, I told you they were shit heads, always acting up." Later when they would do something and I would get onto them, he would chastise me with, "What's the big deal? They're just being kids."*

The truth is this part can still happen even after leaving. In order to stop your abuser you must become more knowledgeable on the tactics they use. When you acknowledge and then accurately recognize the behavior then the patterns can be found. Even an inconsistent pattern is still a pattern.

What to do if you believe you are experiencing this type of abuse:

- Keep a journal of incidents. Record them if possible. This can assist in helping disorientations, lifting guilt and confusion.

- Asking for clarification in situations in the moment can help determine how and what tactics are being used in the moment. This can help reduce future confusion and insecurity.
- Talk to a trusted person or therapist to gain perspective.

Wow! Talk about a heavy section. If you feel like we do, you are probably wiped out. Perhaps your eyes have been opened to things you would rather not have known. Researching for this book was not easy. We regularly had to take breaks to digest the information but also just to get away from the ugliness and horror of the world. As difficult as this may have been to read, it is critical to your understanding of exactly what constitutes abuse. Without this base knowledge, the rest of this book would be irrelevant. Without this basic understanding of the abuse you may have experienced, trying to understand when it's time to leave would be difficult.

Leave what? That was a tough one for us. Based on our upbringing, leaving an 'uncomfortable' situation wasn't appropriate or right. We felt we needed to 'push through' and 'lie in the bed we made'. Had we just had the knowledge and vocabulary to name our experiences, it would have been easier to see that what we were experiencing wasn't simply 'uncomfortable'. And without the understanding that what you experienced was in every definition of the word, abuse, you may struggle with why you are still experiencing such trauma and difficulty coping with your new life.

Understanding the categories and types of abuse is foundational for every step that happens next from recognizing it within your own relationship, relationships of others, or even how *you* treat other people. That is why we spent so much time, half of the book, diving into those difficult categories. We commend you for making it this far and thank you for taking the time to dig deep and invest in yourself. It would have been easy to skip through all of the dirty, painful, and difficult realities.

In the next section, we will address the question of "what now?" Now that you recognize various behaviors, what are you supposed to do about it? Beating yourself or others up for being in an abusive situation is never the answer. We encourage you to approach yourself and those you love with compassion and understanding. When you are ready, please continue the journey with us.

Part Three
Break the Cycle

WHEN IT'S TIME TO LEAVE

As the years passed, I found myself doing more and more things that weren't in alignment with my beliefs, morals, and personal standards. What was initially justified as compromise or "figuring things out" turned into consistent patterns of misalignment. More frequently, I found myself questioning why I was agreeing to do something that I wasn't comfortable with. The strong, moral, independent woman was quickly fading and being replaced with someone I didn't even recognize. There were parts of my life I couldn't talk to anyone about and would have been devastated if anyone ever found out. I felt like a fraud. I struggled to face my friends and family. I didn't like who I was becoming, and I couldn't see things changing any time soon.

Several times over the previous few years, I had the revelation that the idea of divorce didn't scare me anymore. Before then, it had never been an option. The word "divorce" wasn't in my vocabulary; I wouldn't even allow the thought to cross my mind. He would agree to change or work on a number of things. We would hug and I stuffed those feelings back down, believing each time that he loved me or cared enough to

276 ERIKA SHALENE HULL & DR. CHERYL LEJEWELL JACKSON

sincerely try to change. It wouldn't take long for things to get back to normal. The loneliness rose quickly, and I would begin to slip back into the feelings of despair and depression.

Through work, I had met someone who lived in a neighboring community. Being in the same field, we had a lot in common and quickly built a friendship. As divorce became more of an option to me, we became closer. Even as friends, he treated me so much better than my husband ever did. He listened to me when I spoke; he talked to me and showed interest in my interests. We did things together. We laughed together. He had a good job and had a team of people who liked and respected him. He wrote me sweet cards and made me care packages when I had far to drive. He sent me sweet texts just to let me know he was thinking of me.

To be fair, when you are in a broken, damaged relationship, it doesn't take much to be impressed, which is why it is so easy to fall back into another abusive relationship. You are looking to be treated well; you want to believe you are worthy of love and affection. For me, I was finally being treated the way I imagined someone worthy of love would be treated, and I began to believe that I was indeed that person.

I found myself being more open about our friendship, almost willing my husband to question our relationship. I started being less supportive of his behaviors and withdrawing from him. I stopped trying so hard to limp our relationship along. It was like I wanted my husband to just give up on me. I struggled to find enough of a reason to leave the relationship, so I tried to give him enough reasons to not want me anymore. Perhaps if I showed him how undeserving and unworthy I really was, he would see that I wasn't worth keeping around. Unfortunately, this way of thinking often backfires.

When a new job opportunity arose in another state, I jumped on the chance to make a clean break. One thousand miles away from family or any support, I couldn't leave him stranded, but packing up and both going our separate ways? Now that felt more reasonable. It was the perfect getaway. I don't know that I would have had the courage and strength to do it, though, if my friend had not shown me what a healthy relationship could look like. He showed me that I was valuable and worthy of love, affection, and attention. Broken as I was, I certainly did not treat him the way he deserved, but he never changed who he was. I began to realize what grown, adult men looked like and how they acted and treated others. For the first time, I felt a flicker of hope that my life could be different, better. It wasn't about him; he was just the spark that lit an entirely different way of thinking. Through his kindness, he completely changed my life.

Regardless of how bad a relationship is, it can be difficult to leave. It's the same with leaving a job, a home, or school. Closing a chapter, no matter how bad, is often hard. There is such a sense of finality, it aches. When you have been isolated from your established communities, psychologically downtrodden, financially insecure and/or physically threatened–the ability to leave is nothing near simple, normal, or easy. Even thinking about leaving can bring about feelings of confusion, uncertainty, fear and even distorted perspective. At times you still feel hope that the situation will change or try to convince yourself that it isn't that bad. You may feel too weak to leave or even embarrassed that you stayed so long.

It is particularly difficult for empaths, those who deeply sense the feelings and emotions of others. As empaths are trying to leave, we deeply sense the pain of the other. In addition to addressing our own trauma, we are now feeling theirs. This creates a greater struggle and makes it even harder to follow through. As much as victims may want out of a relationship, they don't want to *hurt* the other person. Even in an obviously abusive situation, oftentimes victims feel regret or struggle with inflicting pain on someone else. Sometimes it is simply hard to admit that the relationship is over, regardless of the circumstances. It is important to remember that just because it's hard doesn't mean it's wrong.

Almost every relationship I have ever had has been difficult to end. Once it was finally done, it was a relief, but doing it was hard. I felt bad for making them sad and struggled to go through with it, even though I knew it was the right thing to do. Even when I was miserable in the relationship, it was hard to let it go. Regardless of how sensitive I tried to be to their feelings and explain how it was better for both of us, it never made it any easier for either one of us. Only when they got aggressive, saying hurtful things and sometimes being abusive did I finally feel like I could slam the door and walk away. It felt like there had to be something that was bad enough to end it when the fact that I was unhappy would have been reason enough. Sometimes, how they handled the breakup was what finally gave me comfort.

It is easy, especially for women, to confuse feelings of compassion and empathy with the idea that you are making the wrong decision. Many women get in and stay in bad relationships because they confuse these emotions. Closing a chapter is hard, regardless of how good or bad that chapter was. It is a natural response to finality. It sounds crass, but the easiest way for both of you is to simply pull the band-aid in one tug. Dragging it out leaves the impression of hope, in which the other person may try to change your mind even harder, bringing up happier times or playing off of your emotions.

You can love the abuser, but not his behaviors. The key is to love and care for yourself first and foremost.

When we were separating, I was trying to make it as easy as possible. I wanted him to be set up and not financially ruined. I wanted him to be as comfortable as possible and be left with as much of his self-worth intact as possible. I would listen to his concerns and fears, and tried to remain his friend until he could regain his network and start a new life.

In the midst of trying to convince me that we could make it work, he would often say, "How can you care about me this much and not love me?" Or "If you care about me this much, we should be able to make it work." It was confusing, even to me. How could I want the best for him and not want to be with him?

Most people don't want to hurt others. We truly do want the best for others, even those who hurt us. That does not mean I wanted to be with him. Eventually I had to stop treating him kindly because it was confusing both of us. As hard as it was to not take his calls, cut him off, or put my foot down, I had to do it. I had to convince myself that I didn't care about him just to be able to live with myself. When I finally made that switch, we were both able to accept the impending divorce and begin to move on.

We *want* to help them, and sometimes believe we can. Maybe you think you are the only person who really understands them, or that it falls under your responsibility to fix them. The truth is this, no matter how hard to hear, by staying and enduring, accepting the behaviors, we reinforce and enable the problems to continue. Some people refer to this as enabling or perpetuating the problem.

Women are often viewed as cold, bitter, or heartless when leaving a relationship. This can be because we must give off that impression in order to have the strength to leave. Publicly we must appear confident and heartless. At home, we cry into our pillows. This is where it is critical to have a trusted friend or family member who can serve as a strong council during this time. Someone who will support you, hear you, and remind you why you need out. It is very easy to cave at this point, but we need people in our lives who will continue to push us in the right direction, regardless of how much we may cry. Crying is not a sign of weakness and should not cast doubt. It is a natural reaction to pain and change.

- Ending a relationship can be sad, that doesn't mean it's wrong.
- Pull the band-aid off in one tug.
- Empaths feel more strongly. This should not be taken as a sign that you aren't doing the right thing. Keep moving forward.

For some, it finally gets bad or dangerous enough that the dangers of staying outweigh the risk of leaving. Other times, victims get tired of the life they are leading and decide they want to give another life a try. Maybe their children have graduated high school or they have simply grown weary of living in an abusive, destructive marriage. It may also involve experiencing something better from someone else, or seeing your own worth and what life could be like in a healthier relationship. This can come from a friend or romantic relationship outside of the abusive one. It isn't often enough just for family to tell the victim how worthy they are. Many times, we have to experience it for ourselves.

Before moving on, we would like to take a pause and note that in both of our stories, what finally gave us the strength and confidence to leave our abusive relationships was the recognition of our worth by a man. Granted, we were both on the edge of the cliff, ready to jump, but it wasn't until a man voiced our value that we believed in ourselves. Although we were increasingly isolated, we both had loving parents and a few friends who loved and encouraged us. Why do we place so much value and credibility in what men think? Why did it take a man saying it before we believed it? Why do we need men to see our value before we see it in ourselves? More importantly, how do we begin to change this cycle?

Like abuse, it begins with the acknowledgement of the pattern, and the intention to make a new choice. You can choose to recognize your own worth, regardless of what the men in your life have to say about it, and we hope you will. Not just for you, but for the other women out there waiting for permission to love themselves without a permission slip from a man.

Other factors that could help get a person to the point of leaving:

- Facing reality and choosing better. In many cases, the victim doesn't realize what is happening is abuse. They give up hope that the abuser will change, or see through the lies and realize the abuse is not their fault.
- Accepting Support. Support comes in different forms when a victim finally reaches out. It can be hard to understand, but what matters is that when someone is so isolated when they reach out, it can be difficult to accept help. Accepting that help can be a significant changing point for victims in their journey forward.
- Protection of children. Protecting children from further abuse, learning abusive behaviors, and stopping the cycle are major reasons victims leave abusive relationships.
- Fear and exhaustion. When pain, fear, and emotional exhaustion hit a point that it becomes simply overwhelming, it can be a lightbulb moment for victims, realizing that living in fear is not normal or okay.

Whether or not to leave an abusive relationship is never an easy decision. Ultimately, we encourage you to make your decision based on who they are now, not the person you hope they will eventually become, because there is no guarantee that someone will change. There are many cases that show where an abuser and victim have been removed from each other's lives while receiving the specific help and assistance they both needed. They made the choice to come back together after proving their ability to have a healthy relationship and the willingness to continuously work on keeping it that way.

Many times, it is the fear of the unknown that keeps us in an abusive relationship. Leaving brings on so many more unknowns than we can even possibly foresee. Fear of what your partner will do, what threats they will fulfill, wondering where to go, how to get there, who to trust, how to accomplish all of it which is a lot, especially when we have children. Fear has dictated our actions for way too long, keeping us in dangerous and/or unhealthy environments. Fear should never be a part of any relationship dynamic.

Safety Plans

Even if you aren't facing abuse, there are always things you can do to keep yourself safe and protected. Whether you are ready to leave or not, it's essential to plan for a safe exit. Safety tips vary from scenario to scenario and person to person, so please do what is best for you and your situation.

- **Know your abuser's warning signs and triggers**. You know your situation better than anyone else. Pay attention to the signs or clues of an abusive outburst and be prepared to engage your safety plans.
- **Have several real and believable reasons to leave the house**. This can help to physically remove yourself from the tension, giving the situation time to de-escalate.
- **Establish (a) safe area(s) in your house** where you can go if your abuser is being aggressive or an argument starts. Avoid small, enclosed spaces without exits, or rooms with weapons. Ensure the room has an external door or window and a phone, or bring one with you.
- **Establish a code-word, phrase, or signal** to use to let your support system know that you are in danger without tipping off your abuser. For example, "Can I get that recipe for your strawberry cake?" or "I'm craving iced coffee."

In the midst of my situation, safety was never in the forefront of my mind to think about because no one had ever told me that. Many times, I would try to escape by going to our bedroom or bathroom, both areas I would have never considered a "safe zone."

Escape Plan

As you begin to think through the potential of leaving your relationship, especially if you are married, it is important to know the laws in your state. Some states require a separation period, while others do not. In a physically abusive and dangerous situation, these laws should absolutely not stop you from getting out of that situation, but knowing the unique requirements of your state can help you develop a plan of action.

- Have the car fueled, parked facing the exit, driver door unlocked, hide a spare key, emergency cash stash, clothing, important numbers and documents (stashed elsewhere if you can).
- Practice the plan - when under pressure our minds will have a hard time holding on to bravery. Practice, rehearse. Get yourself prepared.
- Memorize critical phone numbers and information in case you lose access to your phone.

Protecting your privacy

It is not uncommon for an abuser to try and successfully monitor their victim's activities, from tracking on phones, computers, vehicles and internet use, privacy can be a challenge these days. There are precautions that can be taken if you find yourself in the position of fearing this behavior or retaliation. When seeking out help, either externally or internally with yourself, sometimes it can be a time of uncertainty.. The truth is no one knows how someone is going to react fully to anything. So safer is better than hurt.

Tips for protecting yourself and your privacy:

- Call for help from someone else's phone, or a public phone such as a payphone (emergency calls are always free) or a phone at a public institution such as a library or school, or even a grocery store or gas station.

- If you can do so safely, add in ways to secure your privacy.
- Check your smartphone settings - apps exist where someone can listen in on calls, read texts messages, monitor internet and app usage and track locations. Make sure your privacy settings are as high as you can crank them, and don't be afraid to enlist help from an expert. If in doubt, leave your phone behind when leaving the house, especially when seeking help.
- Prepaid cell phones are a good option for a backup or emergency phone. You can use this plan to make calls for help or support, research information without being traced, or just have the security that you have a safety net available.
  Remember: phone calls are listed on all bills and in most cases the victims are not listed on the bills or utilities so access is not always available.
- Use computers at work, school, the library, or a friend's house to avoid having search history tracked.

We recognize that leaving an abusive relationship is not a viable or realistic option for everyone. Furthermore, we recognize that not everyone actually *needs* to leave a relationship, especially if the abuser shows a willingness and ability to make significant changes. Only you can decide what's right for you. Just remember that *you* deserve to be happy too.

Our top priority in this book is to increase awareness around abusive behaviors, help women identify potentially abusive behaviors within their partners, and provide tools and resources to help victims adapt within their existing relationships or make their way out. We want to empower victims to live their best life, whatever that looks like.

If you choose to stay coping mechanisms and protection to consider:

- Contact a domestic violence or sexual assault program in your area - even if you don't leave, they can provide emotional support, peer counseling, access to resources if you decide to leave, information and more services to support you in your decision.

- Do everything in your power and ability to start to rebuild and establish a support system around you and your circumstances. Get involved with people, activities and events outside of your home, as well as children, when and where you can as your partner will allow.
- Be kind to yourself by speaking encouragement to yourself. It can also be powerful to continue to grow through personal development and continuous learning in areas that interest you or build your skills in professional areas.
- Develop ways to instill a better way of looking at and talking to yourself. Affirmations, or what we like to refer to as "retemories" (re-tem-ories) can be used to counter negative thoughts and comments. The term is a combination of retention and memory, meaning to retain in one's memory. We don't just read these affirmations, we feel them, believe them, and commit them to memory. When we do this, they become a part of us, and we begin believing the positive things about ourselves.
- Build up your inner voice! The conversation that goes on inside of you is so important.
- Keep a gratitude journal. This will help direct your attention to the things you do have to be joyful and grateful for, reminding you of the hope and strength that is still inside of you.

The most important things to try to keep at the forefront of the mind:

- Your safety comes first.
- You are not to blame for battery or mistreatment.
- You are not the cause of abusive behavior and you cannot control or cure it.
- You deserve to be treated with respect and decency.
- Safety and happiness are real and available.

- Children deserve safe, happy lives.

When a woman has reached the point where she can't take the manipulation and abuse anymore, she will usually leave the relationship. This is an incredibly difficult and brave thing to do because she must fight not only his psychological tactics of fear and intimidation, but also her inner shame voice which has been reinforced and strengthened by him over the span of the relationship. It is as much a victory over self as it is over the abuser. For many women, recovery from the abuse is halting and suffers the setbacks of self-doubt, self-anger, and fear of retaliation. It isn't easy to throw off the chains created by years of psychological harm, but please believe that it can be done.

When it was time for us to leave our relationships, there were some things that made it a little easier. **There are also some tips that we did not implement but looking back, sure wish we had.**

- Put physical distance between you and your abuser.
- Get rid of, disconnect or change any joint plans or accounts in which his name can't be removed (i.e., email accounts, phone plans, bank accounts).
- Change all passwords to social media, email, and bank accounts, websites, or any other pages or programs that house your information.
- Don't answer their phone calls or engage with them directly in any way.
- If you have to communicate with them, doing it through a third party is available.
- Set boundaries for how and when you will interact.
- Eliminate the effect of them in your life (e.g., get a different car, get rid of pictures, replace furniture).
- Connect with new and old friends; rebuild your social network.
- Know the laws in your state.

Get help

- DomesticShelters.org: Educational information, hotline, and searchable database of programs and services near you.
- Love Is Respect (National Dating Abuse Hotline): Offers young people a chance to chat online, call, or text with advocates.
- National Domestic Abuse Hotline (800-799-7233): 24/7 hotline with access to service providers and shelters across the United States.

During our separation, he would call me multiple times a day while I was at work, in the evening, late at night. Rather than ignoring the call, I would take it, thinking we could just talk. Many times, I would be crying at my desk as he begged and pleaded, telling me I was a horrible person, and outlining all the ways he had changed. I never hung up the phone, I never turned it off. Looking back now, I wonder, Why did I do that? Why did I engage him? As soon as I answered, I gave him control.

It is important to recognize that you may not always be making "the right" decisions during this time of change, but you are making the best decision you can for the time, given the circumstances. It is important that you give yourself grace, recognize that you are only human, and try to make a better decision next time.

Leaving a relationship can be a long, difficult process. Although our situations were almost opposite in so many ways, including state requirements, the process from the moment of separation to the divorce being final was around two years. This does not account for the year of discussing divorce before the official separation or the years of recovery following the divorce. In one situation, there were no assets to divide or children to dispute while both were involved with the other. We have heard stories of easy, quick divorces. Where that is possible, it is often not the reality. It is best not to go into a divorce with the expectation that it will be quick, easy, cheap, or painless. Even in the best-case scenarios, which is unlikely if you are reading this book. Divorce is messy, painful, and takes a great deal of time. Just be prepared for it, and don't let it catch you off guard or make you think you're doing something wrong. Hold tight, push through, and keep your eye on the finish line. It won't be perfect, but life is better on the other side. We promise!

As you are pushing through and reminding yourself that you are on the right path, we encourage you to remember why you are doing this. There will be times you doubt whether or not you are making the right decision. It will be difficult. We continue to seek justification, proof that we are making the right decision.

> *Throughout the separation and divorce, I hoped and even encouraged him to start dating someone. I wanted to know that he was going to be okay and that I wasn't ruining his life by leaving him. For a long time after the divorce, I would think about him, hoping he had found someone new, wondering if he was enjoying his job, praying that he would get the promotion. Somehow, knowing he was doing well would justify the divorce. See, he's happy now; it was the right decision. I finally realized that it didn't matter if it was the complete wrong decision for him; it was the right decision for me.*

Phew! You made it through another tough section. Just when we think a topic will be a little easier and offer some relief, it turns out to be just as hard-hitting as the one before. We won't make any promises about the next section, but there is a light at the end of the tunnel. If you stay with us, we promise that we will get you there. When you are ready, go ahead and take the next step with us!

THE AFTERMATH

Recognition of the abuse is only the first step in a whole new way of living. Even leaving the relationship is rarely the end of the story. Rather, it often marks the beginning of an entirely new set of struggles and challenges. It is the start of new financial difficulties, addressing a different type of anxiety, depression, and/or fears, and uncovering scars that have remained hidden or locked away for years.

Yikes! That sounds depressing. Although there are many positives associated with leaving abusive relationships, there are also many challenges. We want to take a moment to discuss these challenges to prepare victims and their allies for what happens after they make the leap. So many think that the battle is won when the victim leaves. Sadly, the battle has only begun.

Victimization

For many victims, the abuse and suffering doesn't end when they leave the relationship. In addition to ongoing fallout from the abuse they've already suffered, many victims experience new waves of abuse at the hands not only of their abuser, but of the legal system that is ostensibly there to protect them. Victims who have children or other forms of permanent connection with their abuser such as a joint business or property may experience continued victimization through that constant contact. They are unable to completely sever ties to begin the healing process and are regularly faced with their abuser who often has free contact with them through phone, text, email, social media, or their children. Many abusers will continue to abuse their victims psychologically, mentally, or verbally through constant attacks, exhibiting controlling behaviors, stalking, financial drain, legal action, making threats, or otherwise influencing them through fear or control.

> *I have two children with my abuser, who still have some form of visitation with him. Just seeing his name pop up on my phone can send me into a momentary panic or be enough to spark a memory that haunts me for hours. I am in a constant mode of having to counteract the damage he has done and is doing. The reality of having to constantly interact with them makes it difficult to heal completely. When I get a text from him, I have an instant reaction. I battle with how to respond and spend energy debating, thinking about, and often regretting what I sent. I write and delete. It's such an energy drain. I am not in control of his response or when he contacts me. I am also not in control of the response my body feels when I see a message or even his name. He still has so much control, and I hate it. That is my biggest battle.*

Worst of all, we often continue to victimize ourselves long after our abusers have lost their grip on us. Our thoughts and actions keep us imprisoned through doubt, questioning, and rehashing.

Denial is one way we keep ourselves locked in this victimization cycle. Whether for ourselves or to make it more palatable for others, we begin thinking maybe it wasn't that bad. Perhaps we reduce it to make it more socially acceptable for those around us. As time moves on and memories begin to morph and fade, we begin to doubt our own experiences.

Maybe I was partially to blame.

I could have responded differently or tried harder.

Maybe I gave up too soon.

Could it really have happened that way? That seems so far-fetched.

We discussed attribution theories in a previous section. If you recall, this is the attempt to assign cause to behaviors and experiences. In general, women often blame themselves for things that go wrong, while blaming external factors for the mistakes or failures of others. Sadly, this behavior of justifying the abuser's behavior while blaming ourselves does not end after the relationship ends, or even after we recognize the behavior as abusive and understand that the abuser is making a conscious choice to engage in those behaviors. We continue to doubt, question, and wonder if things could have been different *if we had just...* This is a dangerous and unhealthy pattern that keeps victims trapped long after the abuse itself ends.

> *I am still constantly doubting whether or not I gave up too soon. I relive my marriage, trying to fit the abuse in a box to see if it really happened that way. Maybe I was just over stressed and didn't handle things well. Maybe I made him think it was okay because I allowed certain behaviors early in our marriage. I didn't tell him not to do that; why wouldn't he think it's okay? I keep myself in that cycle of doubt, denial, and living in the past. Sometimes I try to relive the experiences and emotions in an attempt to re-examine them with new eyes. Did I overreact? Was I really as sad and lonely as I thought? Was it all actually my fault? Every time I think about it, I go through a list of 100 things that I did wrong and how I messed up. I internalize my mistakes and downplay all of the things he did wrong. Somehow, I am still trying to protect him and beating myself up.*

Another way we keep ourselves trapped in this circle is by downplaying our own responses to the trauma as if we should be responding in a different way or like we should have "gotten over it" by now. Some women say things like: "I shouldn't 'have' to engage in [coping behavior] to get through this." But sometimes, you *do* need to take the edge off so you can address the trauma in an unemotional, more healthy way. Like taking an anti-inflammatory so your muscles can release and let your vertebrae fall into place, certain medications or techniques can give the victim enough relief to begin uncovering the trauma enough to heal.

> *I suffer from knee damage and scoliosis. When I work too long or don't take care of my body, the inflammation creates a significant amount of pain. My husband gets on me for not taking pain medication or anti-inflammatories. I struggle with artificially covering up the pain and feel like I need to suffer through it to remind myself to slow down. But as I have been told by my husband, physical therapist, and chiropractor, the medication serves to reduce the inflammation so that my bones and tendons can actually begin to heal. The inflammation and tension in my muscles is actually making it worse. As much as I don't want to, I need to take the medication so I can get beyond the surface tension and begin to address the deeper causes.*

Perhaps this thought of not wanting to alter your mental state comes from our religious background of giving something else control, of not trying to give into those things. We feel damaged or not leaning solely on Christ by taking the edge off. Yes, there is some truth to this, and we certainly are not encouraging over indulgence or constant self-medicating, but there is certainly a benefit to quieting the mind and taming the emotions so they can better be addressed at a lower volume, especially early in the process. Over time, you will likely learn to deal with them without assistance from something else, but it is unrealistic to think we can learn to do that when emotions are at their highest.

Take children for instance. When a child is at the height of a tantrum, that is not the time to teach them deep breathing techniques to calm them down. It is also not the time to start talking to them about their emotions. Their emotions are out of control, and their minds can't process the new information enough to grab hold. Instead, you begin introducing calm, deep breathing techniques before bed as you are tucking them in at night. Or perhaps before a meal, we all take a deep, calming breath to get our minds and bodies ready to relax and enjoy the food. You calmly walk them through what to do and how it should feel. You talk about how it makes them feel more relaxed. When they are excited and run to you while cooking dinner, eager to tell you about the lizard they caught outside, you can slow them down by practicing the deep breathing techniques. When they are getting into a fight with their sibling, and you catch them mid-throw, you can walk them both through the deep breathing technique. Over time, they will have built the neural pathways around using deep breathing to calm the body and mind. Eventually, when they are in the throes of a foot-flying tantrum, you can say the words "breathe in," and their bodies will more likely begin to calm down in preparation for the deep breathing techniques. It won't happen right away, but over time, they will begin to pull themselves out of those feelings through the implementation of deep breathing exercises.

The same is true for anyone feeling the onset of emotions caused by trauma. It is unrealistic to think that you can address the strong emotions before calming the emotions just a bit. Although deep breathing would probably be a good tactic for victims to engage in when these emotions begin to surface, it may help to take the edge off a bit while developing those techniques. When the mind is quieted and calm, *that* is the time to begin breaking down and dissecting the emotions in an effort to gain control over them.

As discussed previously in this book, I used to have a strong physiological response to even seeing his name appear on my phone. My heart would race, I could feel the anxiety surging through my body, and I felt physical pain for hours or even days after an interaction. Over the past several months, I have been consciously implementing some of the practices we have discussed in this book. I use mantras, journaling, and estab-

lishing boundaries to reset my emotional state. I recently faced a challenging episode with my children's father without a negative emotional response. I have never felt more at peace and free, not because of circumstances, but due to the fact, I am finally back in control of my life

So, what can you do to begin to break the victimization cycle? First of all, if you are still involved with your abuser, it is much more difficult because you are constantly reminded of the tactics, feelings, and emotions. They are constantly in your face figuratively and sometimes physically.

Breaking the victimization cycle:

- Eliminate contact or reduce as much as possible with your abuser. If you can, direct all communications through email instead of phone/text so you only see it when you are ready, that would reduce the control they have by popping in and out of your life at will.
- Turn off notifications. Let it be your choice when you are ready and prepared to not only respond but what state you are in.
- Only communicate through a third-party mediator, or if you can, an attorney.
- Learn to start telling yourself "real" things that you can hold on to and/or repeat. Replacing the fear or negative rhetoric with real, concrete truths such as, he cannot hurt me, I am in control of my emotions and responses, and his response does not dictate mine.
- Recognize the tactics, acknowledge the situation and then do your best to allow the trauma response emotions to subside so that you can think, respond and behave in manners you actively choose.

- Emotionally remove yourself from the conversation or situation. Don't read into the texts, what he says, or try to understand why he's acting a certain way. His reasons are not your problem; they are his. Don't enter his world by trying to figure him out.
- Create satisfactory alternatives that are in your control. How do you want to interact? When will you engage? What boundaries is he not allowed to cross?

Whether you are still in contact with your abuser or not, we highly encourage everyone who has been through trauma or abuse to work with a therapist. Therapists or counselors help individuals process their feelings and emotions by listening, giving them an opportunity to say their thoughts and feelings out loud. Therapists often ask a question to start the conversation, then they simply ask a few follow-up questions to guide them through the process. By simply talking it out, we can often see things more clearly and even solve our own problems.

Many of us have had the experience of reading a question or a paragraph that just didn't make sense. We read it fast and slow. We analyze each individual word, but it doesn't make sense. You finally decide to run it past someone else, and almost before you're even done reading it, it suddenly makes sense or before you're done asking the question, you have the answer. The mere act of saying it out loud taps into a different part of the brain.[1] Hearing it is a different process, which allows you to experience it from a different angle. Talking to a therapist isn't so much about getting the answers, but about processing your own thoughts and experiences. Voicing them, hearing them, and experiencing them from the outside rather than bouncing it around only on the inside allows you to see it from a different angle. When you actually hear what you are telling yourself or hear yourself describe what you've gone through, you gain a sense of clarity.

Therapists can also serve to help individuals normalize and understand their responses to their environment. They can serve to validate that what they are feeling is an understandable reaction. Furthermore, therapists can help name the emotion for the individual. It is difficult for us to process our experiences because we don't have the language to describe it, or due to our life experiences we are failing to accurately define or assign what is happening. Providing this language brings about significant clarity.

The logistics of this though can present many obstacles and we recognize this. Therapy costs! Financially, time and energy are all expenses of this. So many times we don't even know where to begin or look. This is why time and time again we want to encourage you to know what is available, to look around your community and know the resources provided. Even if it is not for yourself, to have the knowledge in the event you can provide for someone else.

> *There was so much going on that needed my attention, my personal breakdown was not an option. With four children, two under the age of three, my life was full and everything at the time seemed impossible. I needed to be brave and strong for them. I needed to put a smile on my face so they couldn't see the pain. I needed to cook the meals, start the baths, do the laundry, find change to buy diapers, clean... the list kept going. Therapy was not an option. Let's be frank.*
>
> *Therapy costs a lot of money. Or does it???*

In this day and time, the resources available to anyone are so numerous it would be impossible to list them all here. What is lacking is the encouragement to seek out what is available, the stigma, either self-inflicted or external, that utilizing free or reduced cost services makes you less of a person. We live in a beautiful day where we have access not just to physical services but to information, knowledge and empowerment right at our fingertips. We have to make wanting to be better a good thing. Not everything out there is for everyone. However, there is a lot of proof scientifically and personally, that talking to trained professionals has great healing benefits. So, as you go through your own personal process, remember that while the internet can be a great place to start, your girlfriends can provide great conversation, and blogs have their place, talking to a trained professional will provide customized care for your unique circumstances, personality, and needs.

We often hear that therapy is like talking to a good friend. If that's the case, why can't I save some money and just talk to a friend? If you have a friend who can and will listen without judgment, this is a solid option, definitely better than keeping everything inside and not being able to process it. Unfortunately, finding this type of friend can be challenging. What makes therapists unique is that they are trained professionals who know how to ask questions to get you talking, how to encourage you and hold space for you without trying to "fix" anything, and how to guide you into healthier thought patterns without forcing you.

Additionally, therapists are impartial. They aren't your mom or best friend. Yes, you are a client, but they don't come into the conversation with opinions about you, your partner, or your relationship. You don't have to worry about influencing their relationship or creating a negative image about that individual for all eternity. The therapist has no "skin in the game" when it comes to the other person. Their number one concern is helping you process your experiences in a healthy way. As much as your abuser impacted your life, when it comes to therapy, it's all about you.

In addition, they are better able to set aside their work at the end of the day. Friends and family are less able to turn it off and more likely to carry your pain around with them. As willing as friends may be to do that, it is an unfair burden to heap on them. Therapy is a process and can take time to fully work through your challenges. Friends may want to support you, but it isn't fair to ask them to do that for a prolonged period of time. Brief venting sessions or struggling through a specific issue is one thing. Supporting you through processing and recovering from trauma is best suited for a professional.

In the midst of this discussion, we would like to pause for a moment to discuss the difference between *therapy* and seeing a *therapist*. You may very well engage in therapy without ever seeing a therapist. A therapist's role is to walk you through particular aspects of therapy, whereas therapy can consist of practices themselves.

Writing this book has been therapeutic for me; it has been a form of therapy. For years, I brushed my past under the rug. I didn't want to talk about it or even acknowledge it. I knew what I experienced wasn't right or okay, but I didn't have the vocabulary to really put into words what I was feeling, and I certainly didn't understand why. By talking through my experience, hearing about similar experiences and emotions from others, and researching domestic abuse, I was better able to understand not only my experiences but the impact those experiences had on me. I began to uncover layers of my past that I didn't even want to think about or talk about, much less share with complete strangers in a book. Working through those realities and knowing that my experiences may help other women in similar situations gave me the courage to relive many of those events. I had to analyze my own actions and responses, dig into current behaviors that I am still engaging in, and decide how I wanted to live moving forward. I learned how to be gentle and loving with myself, taking responsibility for my role in my past and my future, but freeing myself of all the blame. Fortunately, I was able to learn from someone else, my co-author, who has learned various techniques from her experiences and work with a therapist. I know there is still significant work to be done, but the therapy provided by the writing of this book has certainly been a huge step forward.

We certainly would never want to leave anyone hanging without some concrete actions to take, things you can do right away which could help. We say this because they have helped us and many others time and time again. There is a reason sayings, quotes and other encouraging words become cliche. They work, but only when you are willing to do the work.

Tips on breaking the victimization cycle

- Choose to learn and establish who you are and want to be. Self - awareness is understanding your behaviors, thoughts and feelings.

- Identifying patterns and triggers of your behavior and then acknowledging what you would like to experience instead. This helps you establish a realistic connection between your thoughts and actions.

- Gaining perspective. Even in the times of "normal" life and high stress, the most functioning individual will lose perspective on issues. As individuals the greater our perspective, the greater our capacity to not only receive grace but give it.

- Change your patterns. If something is not working, but you keep doing the same thing over and over expecting different results... isn't that the definition of insanity? Take real time for yourself. We could spend a huge amount of time discussing the benefits of having uninterrupted time to just focus on you but rest assured that every human needs time to just be.

- Engage in self-help practices. Physical and mental rituals such as yoga, meditation, breathing exercises, walking through nature, drawing, writing, and journaling are great practices for clearing the mind and resettling.

- Unplug. Taking the time to really look at how you are spending your time provides the needed perspective to align our actions up with what our priorities are, what might be unnecessary or maybe even an unhealthy distraction.

- Get out of your head! Being in our own minds continuously is not healthy. Prioritize activities that get you out of your head and into your body and heart-space instead.

- Cultivate connection. When we have connections outside of our immediate surroundings, we start to realize and recognize that we are not alone.

- Start practicing the art of transparency. Find and use your authentic voice. Fear is a power that prevents us from being ourselves, it prevents our growth. Lean into what scares you: everything you want is on the other side of your fear!

- Begin to establish better boundaries and firm non-negotiables. Isn't the saying if you don't stand for something then you stand for nothing? But the fact remains you are still just standing there, but you are flimsy, lacking a center of gravity. It is ok to stop compromising your needs, to want to not feel lost or stagnant because as humans when we do, we lose sight of ourselves.
- Start focusing more on the bright spots (a.k.a. gratitude), rather than on all the things you can't control. Even if you are going through a tough time, you can still enjoy small moments of joy. The more we do this, the more our brain begins to train itself to notice what's going right instead of what's going wrong.
- Share your story. We learn more from other people's stories than we do our own. As you share your story, you gain an opportunity to listen to someone else's and that can provide an immense amount of healing.

Congratulations, you made it through some mighty heavy territory! So many women leave their abusive relationships and never look back: never look back at the relationship, and never address the resulting trauma. When we do that, we allow the abuse to continue by impacting our future thoughts, actions and responses.

You are doing great. However, we aren't quite done with the heavy stuff. In the next section, we will dig into the power and impact of trauma. We don't want to depress you, but we do want to show you how important it is to address, and not pretend that it doesn't exist. Most of us are suffering from some form of trauma, whether we realize it or not; abuse is certainly not the only form. Take a deep breath, and let's keep this journey of freedom going strong.

THE POWER OF
TRAUMA

I can still vividly remember the first few weeks after he was removed from our home. I just moved around my home in a state of shock. I went through the motions to take care of my kids, but something was missing. I was paralyzed for weeks. With no yelling, tracking, constant messages, without him, I didn't know what to do with myself. My days were oddly peaceful and strange. My body craved the yelling, the control over my every move, the very one who was hurting me. It took everything I had just to keep my kids alive, and that was enough. It took weeks to settle into a new way of living. As much as I wanted out, life on the outside was an entirely different experience, and I had forgotten what it felt like. I kept waiting for the calls, the text messages, or the door to fly open and him standing there.

People think it's about getting them out of the house, but it's so much more than that. In a way, he was still there, he is still here now, and forever will be. You don't just go back to life before abuse. You may not ever go back to the person you were before.

T hough we are not trauma experts, we can't talk about the effects of abuse without bringing up trauma. Abuse of any kind is traumatic to the victim. Whether a single incident or continuous, abuse can have a significant and lasting effect on the victim. Although we are focusing specifically on abuse-related trauma, the brain does not differentiate between causes. These same principles and processes will be useful and applicable to those suffering from any type of experience-based trauma.

Effects of Trauma

Scientists are beginning to delve into the world of trauma in an attempt to better understand the significant, physical impact it has on the victim's brain. These researchers are finding that trauma is not simply a moment in time as once believed. Rather, it has lasting effects on the receiver resulting in an altered state of being. Additionally, traumatic events across someone's life actually stack, one on top of the other, like layers of soil. With the addition of each layer of trauma, the brain actually changes. These changes aren't simply in the moments surrounding trauma but are long-term changes. These changes include the inability to regulate norepinephrine and cortisol systems impacting one's ability to appropriately respond to stress. Trauma has also been shown to negatively alter cognition and brain structure, resulting in memory deficits.[1]

Although all abusive situations are different, there is a fairly consistent set of feelings and emotions victims experience. Some common responses to trauma that victims experience are:

- **Shock and denial** - You might think, 'Did this really happen to me?' or 'Why me?' And feel unable to accept that it actually happened.
- **Fear** - You might experience fear of the offender, of being alone, or of not being believed.

- **Silence** - You might find that you're unable to talk about the assault, or to describe what it feels like to have been assaulted, out of fear of being judged.
- **Anxiety** - You might feel unsafe or unable to relax. Continuous, intense stress, anxiety, hyper-vigilance, and/or all-consuming fear.
- **Depression** - You might feel sad or depressed.
- **Guilt, blame, and shame** - You might ask yourself, 'Why did I go there/allow it/not fight back?' Continual feeling of being vulnerable and out of control.
- **Low self-esteem** - You might lose self-confidence, and feel 'unworthy', ashamed or 'dirty.'
- **Isolation** - You might want to be alone and to isolate yourself from family and friends.
- **Somatic responses** - You might experience nightmares, flashbacks, disrupted sleep, or develop eating disorders.
- **Mood swings** - You might find that your mood changes quickly from anger and rage, to tears and despair, and back again.
- **Loss of confidence** - You might worry about your ability to do your work or study, or lack confidence with friends or your partner.
- **Loss of trust** - You might find it hard to trust people in your social circle, family, and even the criminal justice system.
- **Inability to concentrate or focus** - You may find yourself distracted easily or even experiencing short-term memory loss, potentially resulting in a loss of productivity.
- **Disruption of routine** - You may find yourself changing your everyday living routine by self-isolating, moving to a new home or work location, changing phone number and/or other contact information, or even changing identity.

These responses impact the choices they make in the moment as well as in the future. Sadly, even if and when the abuse ends, the impact is often felt forever.

Still today, I won't go to practices or some games to watch the kids like I used to. I know he may be there and I can't handle being around him that long. I watched the kids in a play at school. He was about three people from me, against the only exit. He may not have even noticed, but I did. I felt trapped, like I couldn't get out without passing him. It was hard to focus on the play. My mind was racing. I started telling myself things to calm down: You can go home after this, there are plenty of people around, he can't hurt you anymore. It's taking away from my current life because I am distracted and filled with fear much of the time.

These moments may not feel much different than the actual abuse. The same feelings and emotions rush in, the same fears take over, the same strategies are implemented. We must recognize where these decisions and responses are coming from to understand the impact of trauma on our lives.

It is important to remember that everyone experiences trauma differently, and not all trauma is the same. Although we all experience trauma on one level or another, whether we are experiencing "normal," infrequent trauma or significant, consistent trauma will have a very different effect on the victim's brain.

Stacked Trauma

We mentioned stacked trauma briefly. In stacked trauma, the victim is experiencing one trauma after another. This can be within or outside of an abusive situation. Someone experiencing the death of multiple family members in short sequence, multiple illnesses, a job lay-off, losing a house, and a difficult break up may experience significant trauma. Had these same events happened over a longer time period, or had only a few of these events happened, though still traumatic, they could have had a very different lasting effect on the brain.

When it comes to abusive situations, we often try to compare one situation to another. Someone whose partner cheated on them once will certainly experience trauma, but the impact of that trauma and their response to it is difficult to directly compare to someone whose partner has been unfaithful for many years. The compounding trauma stacks and becomes dense, compact layers of scar tissue that can often be difficult to begin breaking down.

We talk throughout this book about there being only one real category of abuse. We do not label one type as being worse than another. We believe all women (and all human beings) deserve happy, healthy, safe relationships, and we are not suggesting that one incident of abuse is any less significant than years of abuse. We hope that has been clear throughout this book.

Now, back to comparison. It is often tempting to try relating to someone who has experienced trauma by sharing your own experiences, or similar experiences of others. When we share how someone we know stayed with their husband after learning of an affair or even a bout of physical abuse and are stronger now than ever, we are trying to provide encouragement and hope. That is positive. Someone who has experienced years of trauma at the hands of an abuser or unfaithful partner may be in a very different place. You simply cannot compare two different experiences. When we do this, as well-meaning as it is, it can cause more damage to the victim by making them think they should be feeling differently or are somehow broken because they can't even imagine themselves in that place. We must recognize that trauma affects everyone differently, and it is impossible to fully understand what someone else has experienced.

"You can't assume that someone didn't experience something because of the way they are acting right now. We all respond to trauma differently."

(Law & Order: Special Victims Unit)

Along these same lines, victims often feel that they are overreacting to a given situation because "she was cheated on and they're still together." They begin to think that their responses are somehow wrong because others would have handled it differently. It doesn't matter how someone else would have handled a situation, especially someone who has not experienced the same level of trauma. They are working with a different set of experiences, history, and brain pathways. We are physically, mentally, emotionally, and spiritually different. It is okay and expected that we respond differently. Trauma extends beyond the abuse. The mind and body have involuntary responses that last for years.

We were running around the house preparing for my son's birthday party. Suddenly, the door opened, and my daughter was standing in the doorway. She was supposed to be at her dad's starting yesterday, what is she doing here? Right now? With no warning, no phone call, no text, he just showed up and allowed a young child to walk unannounced into a home where no one was expecting her. When I went to talk to him about it, he rolled the window down barely enough to hear me. As I was talking, he cut me off saying, "have a good day" as he rolled up the window and backed out of the driveway. Just like that, he shows up in my life and disappears. I have no say and no control over when it happens or how my body responds.

For the rest of the day, my body was still reacting. It isn't voluntary; I can't control it. As hard as I try to not get angry, to feel controlled, I do. Those old feelings of torment and abuse come back. He is still making decisions in my life: when my daughter can come and go, when he can come and go, when I get to talk and when I don't. He is violating my safety in my own safe place, and I have no say in it. We usually have the pick-up at school or an exchange location to avoid bringing this energy into my home. We have a set time and place so I can prepare mentally and emotionally for the interaction. When he randomly stops by, it creates disruption that I can't possibly prepare for. What may appear to be normal to someone else is a power play by an abuser. I wonder, "Am I blowing this out of proportion? Am I just being a bitch?" It doesn't matter what anyone else thinks. I know my situation and I know him. This is a power play to continue to dominate and control my life.

From the outside looking in, it can look like an overreaction. We worry about what others think because we know that it feels crazy. You are the only one who knows your situation, what you've been through, and what he's capable of. No one else needs to understand it. You don't have to justify it. It doesn't matter how a "normal" person would respond. It doesn't even really matter what his intentions were. Just like during the abuse, actions that continue to hurt you are abuse and not okay.

> *Sometimes, I see a vehicle on the road that looks like his. My body tenses up, my heart races, and fear rushes over me. I wonder, "Is he following me?" It's a response I can't control.*

We think *"mind over matter," "I can handle this."* For less complex trauma, that might be the case. During trauma, and particularly stacked trauma, the brain actually stops working the same way. It rewires to protect itself. We feel threatened by less, see things differently, and even interpret things differently based on our experiences. We simply cannot compare our experiences or responses to the experiences and responses of others.

> *It was my husband's birthday. We were on the couch together; I was working, and he was watching TV. I noticed that he had fallen asleep. Being his birthday, I would have liked to have woken him up and ended it right. I sat there staring at him, wishing I could, but I couldn't. I was in the middle of a flashback, and my body and mind just wouldn't let me do it. Fortunately, he is very loving and understanding, but it's still hard not to feel violated due to the past. I can't imagine life without flashbacks.*

One powerful response to trauma is the occurrence of flashbacks. Although traumatic themselves, they are the mind's way of processing, and eventually healing from, trauma. The neural pathways that created that memory will continue to fire until new ones are built.[2] Although our minds blockout many memories, some are still there.

As I read an old journal entry or an event hits it just right, the memory floods back in. That's what makes them so difficult. You never know when one will come back. Flashbacks and recalling memories are so different. A flashback will just come swooping into your mind and with no warning really. It feels as if you can't control it. Whereas a memory, you can pause, rewind, and recall over and over.

At times it feels exhausting, especially after a hard, all-consuming moment. I have to remind myself of the truth, what is real and what is not, what is ok and what is not. This provides an opportunity to fix the shame, blame and unworthy pattern that has been established or it can make me hide away even more. Those are my options.

No two situations are alike. No one else needs to understand it. *You* don't even have to understand it. Just know that it's okay and completely natural to have these feelings. Over time, through intentional effort, you will begin to heal, and those feelings will begin to break down.

HEALING

The damage that abuse and trauma does to the victim's mind and body is not easily healed. It does not go away when the situation causing the trauma ends. Just as the pain of losing a close family member lingers for years, the effects of trauma do as well. Some trauma fades faster than others, and some trauma requires more work to heal.

At camp, when I was ten years old, I was dreaming that I was diving into the swimming pool. Miserably, when I dove into the pool, I was actually on the top bunk, and I broke both bones in my right wrist. Thankfully, I only broke my wrist and not my neck. I started the 5th grade with a cast and had to learn to use my left hand. I can still remember sticking pencils and nail files down into that cast because of the itching, and how tiny my arm was when they finally took that cast off after many weeks. For a long time, I could remember the pain of lying on the floor crying, trying not to wake anyone up and the fear I felt when I looked down and saw that my wrist looked like a triangle. As I type these words, I can see the two scars on my wrist, side-by-side, marking where those pins held my bones together for several months. Although I can still see them and they serve as a reminder of the pain and trauma I experienced, the outward scar and a faint memory are all I have left of that experience.

Unlike some forms of trauma, trauma caused by abuse doesn't just fade over time. Outward scars fade, but the internal scars created by persistent psychological abuse, those scars that are invisible to others and often get covered up by our own attempts to forget, still show up in our lives. They show up in the form of anxiety, inability to know and find healthy relationships, being short with our children, and wondering when the rug will be pulled out from under us. Psychological scars may not show up as physical imperfections on the skin, but they often do manifest themselves physically in the form of diseases, weight gain or loss, hair loss, anxiety attacks, inability to sleep, eye problems, and more.[1] Even after you have moved on, the scars take time to heal. There is no "normal" time table for healing just as there is not a specific path for grieving.

The healing process is similar to the grieving process we hear more about. The same tactics and tools can be effective for both. There can be much grieving in healing, because in the situations we are talking about many things and people are taken away in some form or fashion. The pain of it all can feel very overwhelming. This loss and form of grief is very personal and never shameful. If there was significance in those moments, person, career, house and more that you no longer have, or your abuser removed from your life using abuse tactics, then it is highly likely some of what you feel is grief.

So, how do you heal with that type of trauma and get to the point where it doesn't consume you in the same way it consumes your abuser? The cliche says, *time heals all wounds,* but the truth is, healing takes intense effort. Time alone may serve to diminish the response, but true healing requires more than the passing of time. As we make daily decisions based on old hurt and pain, those actions further reinforce the response. We must pause, recognize the response, seek to understand where it is coming from, and actively change it.

One great example of stacked trauma and the associated healing process can be seen in the show Hoarders. For those who haven't seen it, a crew follows the journey of a severe hoarder through the process of recognizing they need help and subsequent recovery. It's an excellent example of how stacked trauma works and the effort it takes to heal.

Now, in these shows, we aren't talking about Grandma's doll collection. These hoarders have often been collecting for decades. At times, they are carrying on the hoarding behaviors of their parents. They are often living in eight feet high piles of garbage, infested with rats, roaches, and feces. As the show progresses, a psychologist and professional organizer are brought in to help the hoarder dig through the trash and understand the deep root of the hoarding behavior. Throughout the show, we learn of intense trauma these individuals have experienced from the pain of divorce, abusive marriages, loss of children, rejection from parents, growing up in a tent, never having a home of their own, and so on. Hearing their stories, we begin to better understand why they are the way they are. The trauma some people experience is so intense and so great, it's amazing that they function as well as they do.

Through the course of the show, the hoarder begins peeling back layers of their past while peeling back layers within their home. They start with the easiest, obvious trash. Even in this phase, the hoarder generally struggles with letting go. Expired food covered in rat droppings are carefully analyzed and the hoarder begs to keep it. Just like that hurt and pain, they are holding onto it. It has become their identity, and they are terrified of how to live without it.

As trauma is slowly uncovered, the psychologist works with the hoarder to process it. Items are moved from the house into buckets to keep, donate/sell, and trash. Symbolically, those buckets represent our own processing of trauma. There are certainly things we should keep: treasured memories, lessons, joy, strength, growth, bravery, who we have become. There are also things we can give to others, such as our stories and hard-earned wisdom. Once you have been through something difficult, you are in a special place to connect with and relate to others. You have a chance to connect with and impact them in ways that no one else can. That is a rare and true gift. Recognizing that gift and using it to support others is a very powerful part of the healing process. Not everything needs to be trashed, but that doesn't mean it needs to sit in your home and continue to interfere with your life.

The biggest bucket of all is often the trash bucket. Organizers haul off many dumpsters, often thirty or more tons of trash out of these homes. It sounds absurd until you start unpacking your own brokenness and pain. We carry the hurt, self-hatred, doubt, insecurity, and blame from one room to the next until it fills every space. We close the door, thinking no one will see it, but the reality is, it's still there. In some houses, the amount of stuff in the home has actually pushed walls away from the frame. The house is crumbling from the weight of the junk that is hidden behind closed doors, stuffed under beds, and in most cases, piled up in plain sight.

We keep our doors locked and don't let anyone in, but the hoard is still there until we dig it out. We may have to start slowly, looking at every item and reliving every memory with it, but as we do that, it will become easier. We will learn to let go of entire sections or rooms without needing to look at it again. It takes time and it isn't easy. In each case, the show offers after-care for hoarders, including therapy. Just because the house has been cleaned out doesn't mean we can't begin bringing those things back in. It takes continuous effort to make sure we don't recreate the hoard that we have been living in. We must make a decision with every item we pick up, am I going to bring this into my home? Is it worth it?

Those old habits come back quickly and easily. Like a disease, intense, stacked trauma could always be a part of your life. Even at times when you are feeling better, you may feel the residual effects of painful memories or emotions, especially in response to things that remind you of the trauma. This is normal, but you must cope with the loss, similar to someone who grieves a death.

Losing my son at a young age, in some aspects, has been harder to bear than the personal suffering and hurt I have felt at the hands of others. It has also provided some of my greatest understanding. If I allow my grief, shame, guilt, worry or anxiety to engulf me, how can I ever see or remember the great things? How would that honor his life? It is possible to have amazing moments in some pretty dark times. Letting go of those things you could not control and holding onto the things you can be grateful for does help in the releasing process. Holding on and letting the pain consume you only defeats you in the end.

Healing is a very individual process. It can be lonely and exhausting. It sometimes involves bringing up old memories, experiencing old emotions, and thinking through parts of your life that you would rather forget. Even though we may think we have put the past behind us, the trauma continues to impact our lives in ways we don't even recognize.

Writing this book was difficult. I was perfectly happy leaving memories tucked deep in the past. Until I started telling these stories and doing this research, I didn't fully understand the impact that years of abuse had on me. I began to see why certain things hurt me or why I react so strongly to a behavior or phrase. It hurts to relive it, but only through digging into those experiences can we begin to recover. At times, I had to leave the house because it was too difficult to be around my family while I was reliving the past.

Sometimes, to fully process the events, emotions, and responses, we must put ourselves back in that space, mentally. At times, we both had to leave our homes and write somewhere else because it was too difficult. We didn't want to bring old hurt into our safe space. It was also hard to even get there at times, with kids laughing in the other room or seeing our new, beautiful lives around us. It can be difficult to process in certain surroundings, and may require getting into a new physical environment. Our hope, though, is that this book can start the healing process even for those who have been out of the abusive relationship for a long time.

It's easier to stuff it sometimes rather than remember, bring it up, and move on. Not all of it was bad. Not all of me was bad.

There are some good things that I was and that helped me
survive. To disregard all of that is to disregard everything I did
to survive.

We have only scratched the surface of trauma and the healing process. For many, it will take a significant amount of time, counseling, and self-discovery to get to the point where you feel that your past is no longer a significant factor in your current situation.

Please note that recovery is not a one-and-done thing. It takes continuous effort and significant mental fortitude. We often hear people say, "I just need to deal with it and move on." If the same issues come up again tomorrow, next month, or even five years from now, that's okay. Just don't shut the door and pretend like it doesn't still affect you. Pull it out and work on it then. That is the only way we can continue to heal and grow. Every step of the recovery process requires significant mental fortitude; not just the beginning but every step along the way. Although we aren't all born with it, mental toughness or fortitude can be developed. By pushing through time and time again, we continue to develop this muscle, making the process a little easier each time.

Myths regarding healing:

MYTH: The pain will go away faster if you ignore it.

FACT: Ignoring your pain or suppressing it from surfacing will only make it worse in the long run, harder to heal and cause more problems in your current and future life.

MYTH: It is important to remain and appear to "be strong" in the face of adversity and loss.

FACT: Feelings and reactions to the pain and loss are normal expressions. Crying does not make you weak and you don't need to "protect" others by putting on a brave face. Expressing feelings can not only help you but those around you. Crying is a normal response to sadness, but it is not the only one.

After the first year of being free it was clear to me that I needed to work on some things. One being that I didn't cry. It wasn't that I didn't want to or that a tear would not form and fall–I wouldn't allow myself to cry. The years of being told "Don't cry," "If I see one tear fall I will give you something to really cry about," "Please, you are not going to seriously cry now are you?" My body learned to not cry. I learned to not cry. I learned to stop the tears from falling and then I learned how to hold the watering in my eyes and pull it back. It became habitual for my body to not cry.

It took some time and intentional determination to allow my body to cry and release. I can't say that I'm to the point where it even feels natural again but I can cry whenever my body needs to let go.

MYTH: Healing should last about...

FACT: There is no specific time frame for grieving, healing, or recovery. This is an individual human process and no two are exactly the same.

MYTH: Moving forward with your life means you are fine, or nothing that bad must have happened to you..

FACT: Moving forward is a natural progression and it is very important in times of dealing with trauma and hurt. It does not mean that nothing happened or that you didn't or aren't suffering. You can move forward with your life and it doesn't mean anything other than you are doing what is necessary to live.

MYTH: You just need to do more/better self-care, such as taking a bath or treating yourself to a fancy meal.

FACT: Intentional care to yourself is more than just the occasional pedicure or using oils in a hot relaxing bath. Caring for ourselves involves resting when you need to, taking time for yourself, spending an evening watching your favorite show, exercising, eating well, educating yourself, and so many other things. Caring for yourself is part of a balanced, healthy life. It is not just an item on your to-do list or your shopping list.

Social Stigma / Societal Pressures

Related to the language we use is the social stigma around divorced women and single moms that adds significant challenges to the healing process. These societal pressures are often ingrained into our own minds, influencing the way we feel about our current situation and the choices we make to avoid ongoing stigma.

- The pressure to be married in order to be whole and accepted.

Don't worry. You will find someone else.

- The knowing glances when people hear your children's last names and then hear yours is different, as if they suddenly know everything about you.

    When I post my presentations and publications on my resume and highlight names that are different from my current name. I imagine them counting to try and figure out how many times I was married and making judgments based on it.

- The stigma of having a single-parent household coupled with terms used like *broken home, broken family, a son needs a father, or women aren't capable of raising a boy.*

The Ripple Effect

Trauma stacks, but so does positivity. Just like negative effects of even seemingly minor abuse or trauma can stack thick and dense, positive effects of encouragement, self-care and affirmations can too. Do one thing differently today, and it will have a ripple effect tomorrow and every day after that.

Have you ever thrown a rock or a pebble into a pond? Watched the ripples crescendo through the water? As children most of us have likely done this more than once. Every rock makes a different amount of ripples because there are many different factors with each rock. Size, weight, and shape are all factors in the resulting ripples. Not to mention the speed at which that exact stone hits the water. There are so many different factors, all out of our control. Like these stones, our lives consist of actions resulting in a wide range of ripples, and many of these factors are beyond our control. These factors influence the ripples, but they also *prepare* us for the many ripples in our lives.

However, the same can be said with intentional rocks or changes. If the bad, sad, and mad can ripple through your life, so can the flip side. There is a good deal to be said regarding this type of discussion within our world these days. Time after time, the ripple effect of change is proven to be a normal phenomenon and one that we as individuals can harness and use in order to better our lives and circumstances.

One simple change, one simple moment has the ability to have such a profound effect on us, and if it applies to the bad it also applies to the good.

We want to encourage you to keep intentionally finding and throwing in the good pebbles into your life because it does have a ripple effect, not just inside of you but around you. Every time we choose to do a little better, the ripple grows. Doing a little better than the day before is like grabbing for a pebble that is just a bit larger than the last one you used. It will create larger ripples, and those ripples can change your world dramatically and the lives of others around you.

Healing Through Journaling

Time does not heal ignored pieces. There are so many times when I start to write something or a caption and I still hesitate to this day even though I know I am in control now, and he is not. I question, and I hold back. Sometimes I move forward, and sometimes I hit the delete button. Lately I have chosen to move onward, and that is what I am choosing to continue to do while I count my blessings every day! But that is just it. It has been a choice I have had to make every single day and sometimes every single moment. To sit and say that everything is rainbows and butterflies, recovery has been a breeze, or that I have all the answers is nowhere near accurate. Standing firm for yourself, not only from others but from the corruption and lies that are ingrained into your mental conversations takes dedication and intention that sometimes you just don't want to put forth. I have lived when I had to choose every millisecond, and it was the hardest time of my life. There was something inside of me that told me to keep fighting, to never stop believing and to never give up.

Journaling is undoubtedly a powerfully beneficial part of the healing process. Returning to activities that were once fulfilling can also serve to begin and support the healing process. Though these may feel small, every step adds up to huge leaps over time. Just like ripples in the water, they add up.

- Return to activities that were once enjoyed and validating to you. This will serve to help you find your old self and be reacquainted with who you are as a loving and kind person.
- Being in nature
- Reading
- Listening to music or returning to your own style of music
- Playing music
- Making art
- Keeping a journal or 'morning pages'

Stop the Cycle

Silence is the abuser's most powerful weapon. When we remain silent, the abuser can continue without consequence.

Our hope throughout this book has been to create awareness around abuse and give victims and allies a new sense of understanding. At times we pushed your thinking, challenged your ideals, and took you outside of the comfort zone of your current understanding, stereotypes, and expectations. Only by pushing these limits can we start thinking differently, and only by thinking differently can we truly influence change.

Once you have this information, you can never *unknow* it. All of this knowledge, though, is useless unless we act on it. With knowledge comes great power, but also great responsibility. It may feel daunting, but if we all do our part to stop the cycle, we can change the course of history for those around us and generations after us.

Generational Abuse

Many children with abusive parents fear growing up to be abusive themselves. Whether taking on these tendencies because that's what they know or because they are predisposed to be abusive is an ongoing debate. It's the classic 'chicken or the egg' debate or 'nature versus nurture' from Introduction to Psychology.  Although children raised in abusive homes or born to one or more abusive parents may be predisposed to respond in certain ways, engaging in abusive behaviors, in itself, is not genetic.[1]

Children growing up in abusive homes or experiencing continuous and/or significant trauma often do not have an opportunity to learn healthy responses to frustration and desires. Additionally, healthy responses are often not reinforced or rewarded, while unhealthy responses are. Whether you were raised in an abusive home, or were in an abusive relationship, you can indeed stop the pattern, though it may take a great deal of effort and learning new ways to cope with difficult situations, anxiety, and frustration.

Similar to children raised in abusive homes, when a victim has been abused by a romantic partner, she can take on characteristics of her abuser. For years, you may have been absorbing abusive responses to behaviors and having to adapt to that abuse as a result. The reason is because you haven't seen healthy responses in quite some time and may not have been practicing them yourself.

It sounds odd, we know. Why would you become an abuser when you have been in an abusive relationship? Many people would think quite the opposite. In reality, living in an abusive relationship can turn you into an abuser as well; often the very behavior they suffered through themselves.

When closely engaged with your abuser daily, you enter survival mode. You do what you need to do in order to keep the peace and make it to bedtime, his shift, when he passes out from drinking too much. Whatever it is, that is your goal. Sometimes, oftentimes, doing things *his* way avoids an argument, even for just the moment. So, instead of patiently working with the children to quiet down, you yell at them, hoping to settle them more quickly and showing him that you are in control of the situation. By yelling at them first, then maybe he won't. Perhaps you discipline them with harsh punishment or hitting them the way he would just to get the desired response more quickly, therefore keeping him satisfied with your efforts. You may be trying to protect them, but now they are being abused by both parents, including the one who is supposed to be their place of safety.

Maybe you don't have children and/or your relationship isn't physically abusive. The way we address arguments between each other may be quite unhealthy and abusive as well. Instead of having a healthy discussion with your partner, you take up the practice of throwing dishes, slamming doors, yelling insults, or going silent. Whatever is required at the time for you to get through that moment is what you begin to do, this includes picking up behaviors that you may never have participated in before. It also includes taking on a reaction that is similar to a way he would respond, a see how it feels attitude. You no longer recognize yourself but are delivering messages in a manner similar to the way they are received.

Over time, these patterns of behavior become habits, and those habits become the foundation of who you are. You may begin taking them with you into other relationships. You start to wonder, "Who am I?" Struggling to understand what you have become.

Ten years after my abusive relationship ended, I still find myself responding to my new husband in ways I don't like. I fear our relationship becoming what I experienced in the past, so I go out of my way to shut down even the slightest signs of serial adolescence, being taken advantage of, or mental abuse. This list was hard to create because my husband is so far from anything that would resemble abusive, but sometimes I find my heart racing at a joke that felt a little too pointed or him sitting on the couch while I do chores around the house. Instead of handling it in a loving, mature way, I overreact by slan-

dering his character, raising my voice, or giving him the silent treatment. In an attempt to keep myself safe, I am treating him in ways no one deserves, especially someone I love. I find myself snapping at my kids, jerking their arms, or raising my voice more than I should. It is my first response, and it lingers from the past.

Fortunately I recognize this behavior and am not too proud to apologize. Actually, I find myself apologizing a lot. To my husband, to my kids, to my friends, and to my family. I want them to know that they didn't deserve the way I responded. I want them to know how very loved they are. I want them to know that it is inexcusable and that I am working to change things. Unfortunately, that change takes time. Because I am different now. I have become a different person. It was me, it is me, and it will always be me—It's part of who I am. I can't change that, but I can change who I am because of it. I can't go back to who I was before, but I can decide that this will not be me now.

When a victim leaves an abusive relationship, whether leaving abusive parents, partners, friends, or bosses, they often walk right into another one. It may not be an abusive romantic relationship, but rather an abusive friendship, a work relationship, or abuse of food, alcohol, or drugs.

Past abuse sets the stage for future abuse. Whether they have been conditioned to accept certain behaviors or possess certain characteristics, victims often *become* victims because there is something about their past or their internal makeup that make them vulnerable to being taken advantage of in this way. Characteristics like empathy, vulnerability, honesty, and a desire to be of service to others are *good* qualities that get taken advantage of by abusers.

Stopping the cycle of abuse requires vigilance and the ability to recognize when others may be preying on your past or positive qualities. We *want* to love and be loved. We *want* to keep our rose-colored glasses on. We *want* to live in a bubble or fairytale. As a result, it's often hard to accept that another person would intentionally hurt us. We are not recommending constantly looking for the negative in others, but a certain level of awareness is required to keep from walking away from one abusive relationship, right into another.

And this does not apply just to romantic, intimate relationships. Stopping the cycle of abuse means stopping it in all areas of your life. You may get out of an abusive marriage and into an abusive job. You may end an abusive relationship only to spend more time with toxic friends. This pattern perpetuates a cycle of abuse that affects every type of relationship.

> *I had just started a new job when we separated. Unfortunately, my boss was misogynistic and established a highly competitive work environment. We all worked too many hours, there was very little teamwork, and we all started to think that was normal. He was incredibly critical of my work, my personality, and my character. In the midst of a painful divorce, it was like being kicked in the ribs when I was already down. I had no more strength left to fight it and started to believe there really was something wrong with me. I would cry all the time. When I talked to my mom, she said, "You got out of one abusive relationship and walked right into another." It took me a long time to realize that is exactly what happened.*

If we want the cycle of abuse to stop, then we must all do our part. As mothers, as aunts, as grandmothers, as godmothers, as friends, as co-workers, as mentors, as women who take on the responsibility of motherhood. It's up to all of us to create healthier patterns, leading by example in our own relationships..

This means first acknowledging the role we played, the behaviors we engage in now, and the situations we avoid confronting. Every generation must do its part, its due diligence to stop it. One piece doesn't form a puzzle. It takes every piece finding their place to see the full picture.

You may be reading this book to better understand abuse. You may be reading this book to support a friend. You may be reading this book because you have experienced abuse or are currently in an abusive relationship. Whatever your reason, you play a role in the solution. What can you do to begin changing this cycle of abuse and let it stop with you?

> *The sister of my abuser decided that she wouldn't have kids for this very reason. She didn't want to pass down the abuse that she experienced growing up, and thought the only way to stop the cycle was to not have children at all. This is such a painful reality for so many. It can be a lot of work to stop the cycle, but you can do it.*

Although many victims choose not to have children to avoid passing on this cycle of abuse, many more *do* have children with or outside of their abusers. When children have experienced abuse as well, it is even more important to take the time and effort to acknowledge the abusive patterns they experienced during the abusive relationship, but also the abusive patterns they may experience from you or that they may be engaging in themselves. Either way, it is critical to have continuous conversations with your children to break the cycle. Although it is possible and often happens that children from abused homes do *not* grow up to be abusers themselves, many do, simply because it is all they know.

Recognition

Until we recognize it in ourselves, we can't recover from it, or stop the cycle.

The majority of this book is written with a wide-range of readers in mind, including those currently experiencing abuse, those who have experienced abuse in the past, and those who have never personally experienced abuse themselves. Therefore, most sections are applicable to anyone.

In this section, we are speaking specifically to those who are or have experienced abuse. It will be a short read, and we certainly recommend everyone read it to gain a better understanding of the role recognition plays in stopping the cycle of abuse.

With any type of abuse, stopping the cycle begins with recognition. We have laid out the various types of abuse and provided a number of examples to highlight the wide range of abusive behaviors and experiences victims may have. We believe it is fairly representative, but as with any human experience, the possibilities are endless. Whether or not you were able to identify with any of the previous discussion does not dictate whether or not you experienced abuse. Only you can determine that based on your unique circumstances and how certain behaviors made you feel. Once you recognize that the abuse happened, you can begin to take the next steps in stopping the cycle.

The 3 Step Recognition Process

Step 1: Recognize that it *happened to* you; it isn't who you *are*.

Step 2: Recognize that you can't change *him* or what happened

Step 3: Recognize that you *can* stop it. *You* can change.

Step 1: Recognize that it *happened to* you; it isn't who you *are*.

As victims of abuse, it is easy to begin believing that a victim is who we are and that these things happened to us because there is something wrong with us. This can be a difficult belief to overcome because it is so ingrained in the way we think. We have only begun changing the way we speak to children saying, "you are behaving badly" instead of "you are a bad boy." We recognize that the behaviors they display at a given time are simply behaviors and not who they are. Rather than damage their self-image by referring to them as "bad," we discuss the *behaviors* as bad.

When it comes to recognizing our own behaviors and actions versus who we are as human beings, it is a little more challenging. We find ourselves saying, "I am so stupid," or "I'm such an idiot" rather than recognizing that sometimes very smart, capable people do questionable things. Additionally, we often fail to take into account the circumstances in which decisions were made. When under stress and duress, the court of law does not consider the choices people make as free will and does not associate them as part of one's character.

Furthermore, this one part of your life (as significant as it may be or may have been) does not define you. You are made of so many different pieces. The abuse in your life is a piece of a much bigger picture. We discussed at the beginning the various terms available rather than "victim." We had a great deal of discussion regarding which word best described what we were trying to say.

Ultimately, we decided that "victim" was the most appropriate term for this book, but "victim" does not define you. Rather, it describes one part of your life, the part we happen to be discussing in this book.

You are a victim of abuse. You are also a survivor, thriver, mother, entrepreneur, employee, daughter, homemaker, advocate, wife, creator, dancer, artist, writer, speaker, reader, breadwinner, educator, learner, friend, co-worker, gamer, comedian, nurturer, and the list goes on and on. There isn't a single word to adequately define who you are. It is critical for you to recognize that choices you made, behaviors you engaged in, and things that happened to you in abusive situations are not the whole of who you are.

Step 2: Recognize that you can't change *him* or what happened

As we discussed previously under Language We Use: Characteristics of the Abuser, it is not our place, nor do we have the capability to change his behavior. The second step of recognition is internalizing and accepting this. Until you do, you will be focusing your mental energy and attention in the wrong place. Instead of focusing on what you can control, you will be reliving past experiences, questioning your decisions, and trying to figure out how things could have gone differently.

BUT THAT'S NOT ME.

We are no longer focused on the abuser. At this point, it is time to focus on you and change the story for future generations. To do that, you must recognize the roles you play and the ones you don't. It is not your role to change him or what happened. It can't be done. Once you recognize that, you will be ready to move on and focus on improving yourself.

Step 3: Recognize that you *can* stop it. *You* can change

The third step of recognition is recognizing that you have the power to change; to stop the cycle. It can feel daunting to begin unpacking possibly years of hurt, to change thoughts and patterns of behaviors that have very much become a part of who you are. It won't happen overnight. Change takes significant effort, but recognizing and believing that you *do* have the power to make that shift is such a critical step. Until you believe it, there will never be a reason to even try. If you don't believe that there's something better out there, and that you deserve it, it will never be worth it to take those hard steps forward. You have to believe that there is better, that you can be better, and that whatever it takes to get there is worth it.

As we have discussed throughout this book, there are times when we engage in abusive behaviors either because that's what we know or because we are responding to existing trauma. Either way, when we engage in those behaviors, particularly with our children, we are continuing this cycle. In these cases, it is more critical than ever to apologize and share how the behavior was unacceptable. This is a healthy practice to get into anyway, but particularly when the experienced behaviors are borderline abusive.

4-Step Process for Breaking the Cycle

Step 1: Acknowledge

Step 2: Apologize for what you did (how you responded, overreacted, etc.)

Step 3: Apologize for the feelings that you may have caused.

Step 4: Address how you would like to handle the situation in the future.

Example: I know that I hurt your feelings. I apologize for snapping at you, and I am sorry that I hurt your feelings when I yelled at you. I do want to hear what you have to say, I need you to wait until I am finished talking to Grandma.

You must make it a *priority* to change the pattern. It will not come automatically. In order to change a behavior, especially one that has become a habit, you can't just *stop* the abusive response, you must *replace* it with a positive, healthy one. That creates new pathways in the brain. Over time, the behavior that resulted in the abusive reaction will stop triggering the abusive response and will trigger the new one. The process of new neural pathways being formed and connections developed is called neuroplasticity and demonstrates the incredible power of the brain to heal and grow after trauma, both physical and psychological.[2] That process takes a lot of time and practice, which is why so many new behaviors never take off. It requires a continual effort to retrain new behaviors.

Give yourself (and your children) grace during this process and above all, don't give up. We promise you; it may not always feel like it, but it is working.

BECOMING AN ALLY

During summer break, I would often flip through the channels. When I would stumble on Jerry Springer, I would pause thinking I would only watch for a moment. Inevitably, I would be sucked in by the drama. Watching the fights and hair pulling made whatever struggles I was having in my own life just disappear. It never failed that there would be a story where the husband or boyfriend was cheating on his lady with someone else. Sometimes the mistress knew he was spoken for, and sometimes she didn't. Either way, the women would come out swinging at each other while the man either sat back and watched or tried to break them up. Even as a young woman, I never understood why these women were attacking each other instead of joining forces to take down the true devil in this scenario. I vowed that if I was ever in that position, I would come swinging at my man. Granted, my goals have advanced since then.

I no longer watch trashy television, but I do still see women attacking each other when we should be united. Corporate women step all over each other, fighting for the limited spots at the top. Abused women debate on whose abuse is worse. Moms

working inside and outside of the home one-upping each other
on whose life is more challenging. Why do we do this to each
other? I may not be watching Jerry Springer anymore, but
sometimes it feels like we are all stuck on that stage fighting
while the men just sit back and watch us tear each other up.

Whether or not we have personally experienced abuse in any form, we all have the opportunity to be an ally to others. Being an ally means standing in unity with someone; to be a source of connection and strength. To be an ally for victims of abuse does not require that you have ever experienced abuse yourself. It does not require that you even have a full understanding of trauma and its implications. Being an ally simply means being a safe place where a victim can share, express their fears and emotions, and receive the support they need. This support can range from helping the victim get through a single moment in time to helping them escape and heal from an abusive situation. Having a basic understanding of abuse and trauma certainly helps, but having a heart of compassion, love, and patience are what really form the foundation of a good ally.

Being an ally is not hard. Still, many people struggle with what exactly to say. Well-intending women will often try to support others by encouraging them to just keep going and fight for their marriage. In an attempt to connect and support, they often say things that serve to tear victims down or make unnecessary comparisons. We must be cautious when serving as an ally. Victims with few outward signs of weakness can be very fragile on the inside, holding on by a thread. Serving as an ally is a responsibility that shouldn't be taken lightly.

Whether we choose the role of ally or not, we may find ourselves in that situation and must be ready to take up that role. It can be difficult to know exactly how to encourage a victim. Do you encourage them to power through it, sharing that every relationship has rough patches or empower them to "leave the bastard" and offer them a place to stay?

As we have discussed, well-intending women often say the exact opposite of what the victim really needs to hear. It is impossible to outline a fail-proof plan for being an ally, but being a good ally begins with being a good listener. We have pulled together a list of tips to get you started on your journey of being a powerful and trusted resource for others.

Being a Good Ally (To Yourself and Others)

Abuse is not something you can solve with words; there are complexities and evils that our words are inadequate for.

Listen

Do not feel that you need to say something to make it better—you can't. Sit with the suffering. Your presence alone is powerful, lifting shame. Keep in mind it is good and right for the victimized to feel hurt, fearful, and angry. Do not sanitize their speech. Right now, the important thing is for them to tell their story. No matter what it sounds like, they are bringing the terrible secrets of their life into the light which is a beautiful act of trust.

Let victims know repeatedly that the abuse is not their fault. Once you discover the ways they feel responsible, work to lift shame and guilt. Never tire of making these declarations and affirming this truth. They need to hear it over and over again.

Protect their story

Do not ask too many questions about the details. Questions can cause further exposure and shame. Go at the woman's pace by asking broader questions, taking her lead as to what and when she is comfortable sharing.

Consider your role. What will it be like for her if you know the details? In some cases, it is practice to include others in the circle to provide additional support (i.e. Churches often gather around a victim to support and lift them in prayer). Before sharing, ask her who she is most comfortable with knowing and do not share outside of that request, even under that guise of confidentiality. To honor her story, ask those you tell to make an effort to connect with her. Even if it's via a note, they should acknowledge the woman's suffering. We have heard from too many victims that silence from those in church leadership who know their story is excruciating; it feels like rejection and disgust.

Share heartfelt responses

Domestic abuse is isolating, and it can feel like no one, not even God, sees or cares about what is happening. Horrible things have happened and we need to embody God's heart for them. God hates what is occurring and is grieved by it. Your heartfelt responses and tears can be healing for them.

Provide needed resources

They need to know that they are not alone. Support groups or even a single trusted companion can be powerful sources of healing. Offer to connect them with an advocate, pastor, counselor, medical care, legal support, another victim, or a trusted friend. And then follow through!

Do not make empty promises

Right now this person needs to be able to depend on something real and true. If you say you are going to do something; do it; and then follow up. Do not make offers that go unfulfilled.

Speak compassionate words of truth

Being abused, especially sexually, comes with a special sense of shame. It can penetrate so deeply that the victim begins to believe horrible lies. The woman might come to believe she is repulsive, unlovable, dirty, permanently disgraced or even worse that her story will contaminate you.

Trauma victims also tell repetitive and circular stories, and it can be hard for them to make decisions, or even consistently believe that they are victims of abuse. Keep in mind it is not always possible for them to face the trauma while they are living in it. Oftentimes, we have a greater sense of urgency about their situation than they do. To care for them well, we must live with this tension and proceed at their pace. This can be hard on us when we see the amount of pain and suffering they are enduring, but it is vital for them that we do this.

Do NOT make the common mistake of demonizing their abuser, or even labeling their partner as such. This will only serve to trigger their defensiveness and get them listing off all the positive aspects of the relationship and all the reasons they have to believe that things will improve or are improving. Don't talk about their abuser at all. Talk to the person in front of you about how wonderful and worthy of love they are. Lift them up and remind them there are people in the world who don't expect anything in return for kindness.

Provide sound and wise options

Due to the power and control dynamics fueling abuse, these women often do not have the freedom to make choices at home. Hence, they do not need one more person telling them what to do. It is important and redemptive that they make their own choices, especially considering that they are the ones who must live with the after effects. Whether they stay, leave, confront, or remain quiet, their choices will lead to more pain. Help them by providing wise options. Encourage them and let them know that they have your support, whatever they decide to do.

Involve the necessary authorities

It is not always easy to discern how and when we should interact with the legal system so here are some guidelines. Rape within a marriage is a crime, but few women wish to report it, and ultimately that is their choice. Since there are almost never witnesses, it becomes a he-said / she-said, and that's where abusers really shine, so it's no wonder few women choose to pursue legal action against their abuser. While this might leave us feeling fearful for them, we should remember that they have to endure the fall-out and be ready to take self-protective measures. Police know this, so they usually require the victim to make the complaint (not another person) unless life-threatening violence is present.

You may not have a legal obligation to report domestic violence, but we should be communicating the value and potential protection of involving the police. When a victim is ready to make a police report, help her through the process—it will be an extremely difficult experience.

A notable exception to women making their own decisions is concerning children. Anytime children witness sexual abuse (or they themselves are physically or sexually abused), it is considered child abuse and we do need to make a report. Keep in mind that this will create a dangerous situation for the mother and child. The woman needs to know that you are reporting the abuse, and a safety plan should be implemented.

Speak the new language

When unspeakable things happen, it is hard to even find the words to describe what has happened. For these women to share or ask for help, they need words. Telling their story and sharing their heart is essential to healing. Help these women find the words. We have given you language to describe abusive behaviors as well as language to understand the challenges with many of the words we currently use. By using these words we have given you, you will be giving her a voice she may not have had otherwise.

As you can see from this list, being a good ally does not require that you know everything about abuse. You don't need to know all of the resources available or have a law degree. Sometimes all it takes is listening and asking the right questions. You don't know how hard someone has had to work to even admit they need help. It may be tempting to encourage them to power through it, but we highly recommend you do not do that. Do not discourage them from considering options that they believe are best for them. Believe us when we say, it took an incredible amount of courage, sleepless nights, and self-doubt for them to even think about leaving. It is not a decision that is made easily. Trust your friends and family to know what is right for them and their family. They can always go back, but they may not always have another chance to get out. Trust them and support them.

Earlier we mentioned the show Hoarders and used it as an analogy and it is appropriate here as well. In one of the episodes of Hoarders, the mother of one of the hoarders said, "I didn't push or say anything about her hoarding because I didn't want to upset the balance." That really struck us. How often do we sweep things under the rug because we are afraid of upsetting the balance in our friendship and relationships? How often do we see patterns of abuse, but we keep our mouths shut, afraid of upsetting the person or overstepping? Instead, we let it continue, pretending that we don't see, that we don't know, that it doesn't break our hearts. Maybe we even convince ourselves that it's none of our business.

> *Throughout my relationship, other women saw and knew what was going on. Even my hairdresser frequently said he was a jerk and offered to help me hide the body. Though I know she was joking, I knew she recognized that he had a problem and was abusive toward me. She even witnessed the abuse on multiple occasions. When I asked her to testify, she wouldn't do it; she didn't want it to impact her business. When I needed her, she wasn't there for me. I used to babysit for a friend who witnessed his abusive behaviors. When I asked for her help, she said he was too dangerous and didn't want to get involved. She even put it back on me and said, "I wasn't the one who put myself in that situation."*

As women, we need to support each other. We talk a big game, but when it comes down to it, we are often afraid of repercussions against us. Of course, no one wants to put themselves in danger. But sometimes, a woman needs a little support, a little boost, a little confidence to know she isn't completely alone in this. We ask her to put her life in danger and possibly the lives of her children, yet we often aren't willing to stick our own necks out to lend a hand.

Until we risk upsetting the balance, we will never stop the cycle. Until we push the limits of comfort and press the boundaries of what we think is appropriate conversation, we will never get close enough to each other to make significant change. We must be willing to get uncomfortable, risk crossing a line, and getting in each other's space. We have the greatest influence and ability to get beyond the surface with our closest connections, but being an ally is also about standing up with complete strangers.

At the grocery store or post office, while pumping gas or at the doctor's office, I often run across women who have that same look I had for so many years. They may not be experiencing abuse, but they are experiencing something whether it is sadness, loneliness, anxiety, depression, worry, or fear. I sometimes feel compelled to just lean over and say, "You're doing a great job." It isn't much, but I know how powerful those tiny acts can be. That small moment may be the only positive thing they heard all day. It may be the only time someone has said something uplifting to them in weeks. It may just be planting a single seed, but if the next woman waters that seed, and the next woman shines some light on it, over time, that seed may take root and grow.

Finally, being a good ally starts with being a good ally to yourself. We are so hard on ourselves, aren't we? We say horrible things to ourselves that we would *never* speak to another person. We constantly bombard ourselves with negative thoughts: *that was so stupid, I am so fat, I've never been good at that, I don't fit in here.* Our minds are constantly tearing us down. We get enough of that from the outside world. When we feel down, the safe place we should have to turn to should be within. Sadly, it rarely is. There are entire books on positive self-talk, and the most popular motivational speeches are on empowerment. We need to be taught how to speak kindly to ourselves and lift ourselves up.

Victims of abuse are among the most vulnerable when it comes to negative self-image and low self-esteem. Before we can even begin the conversation of healing, we must learn to be kind and supportive to ourselves. We must be our own best friend and supporter. We must be our own cheerleader. As smart as the brain is, it is easily influenced. It will believe what it continues to hear. In the case of abuse victims, and sadly, the majority of women across the globe, it most often hears the negatives. We beat ourselves up more than anyone else. It doesn't take long before we begin to believe it.

Fortunately, this belief cycle can be reversed. The Losada ratio states that we need to hear seven or more positive things to every one negative to have a positive impact.[1] It takes time and persistence to change the way we view ourselves, but it is possible. And the best way to get started is to change the way we speak to ourselves.

We can no longer turn a blind eye, pretending that evil doesn't exist and that the lives of others are none of our business. It is our business. What happens to one of us affects all of us. If we are going to lift ourselves up, we must start by lifting up each other. Instead of worrying so much about upsetting the balance, let's change the rules; change the counter-balance. The more we recognize and talk about these things, the less acceptable they will become. By opening the lines of communication we are gaining the power that was given to us at creation, yet has rarely been upheld to the most basic of standards.

PIECES OF ME

There is something so relaxing about a puzzle. Dumping out a box of pieces, propping up the box, and slowly flipping all of the pieces right-side up. There is something peaceful and satisfying about slowly organizing a box of jumbled, mixed up pieces and making something beautiful. First, organizing all of the edge pieces to build the frame, we then work to build from the outside in. Sorting like pieces then testing out each one that looks like it might fit until one finely slides easily into place.

Occasionally, we stumble across a space that we just can't fill. After searching through every piece, we finally find one that looks perfect. The lines line up and even the colors match, but it takes way too much effort to fit in. We justify that the piece is simply swollen or just fits tighter than the rest. We want so badly for it to fit that we overlook the fact that it just isn't the right piece. After struggling to complete the rest of the puzzle, we finally and reluctantly admit that it just doesn't go there. How could a piece that looked so right be so wrong?

Once we pull that piece out, the puzzle does indeed come together, and the correct piece is eventually found. Sometimes it just takes trust that the right piece is out there.

There are always a few pieces that are so representative of a specific section that you set them aside, knowing you will want to remember exactly where you put it when the time comes.

As the puzzle slowly takes form, some pieces become easier to spot while other slots become nearly impossible to fill. After searching through every piece, you are certain the matching one is missing. Inevitably, that slot is eventually filled, and the picture takes form. Without the picture on the front of the box, without knowing what you're looking for, it's difficult to put the puzzle together at all. Yet, that is exactly what we are doing with our lives. We have a pile of experiences, and we are trying to figure out where they all go. Unfortunately, we don't always have a picture on the front of the box to go by. Pieces may feel misplaced and missing entirely.

Sometimes we wonder, *"How did this become part of my puzzle?"* Your experiences make up who you are. You can never change them; you can simply adjust how they affect you and your response to them. They will forever be a part of who you are. Even the missing pieces, the ones we have forgotten, play a part.

No, that's not me, but they're pieces of me, and will forever be part of who I am. Every experience, every event, every reaction plays a part in the bigger picture of our life. There are parts we would prefer to forget, but without them, the picture is completely different.

Puzzles have been a big part of my life. Throughout my life, I would work a puzzle when I felt lonely or scared, when I needed to work something out, or when I just needed to relax. Over the holidays, we would always put a puzzle together as a family. We would Mod Podge it, put it in a frame, and it would become part of our décor. We were surrounded by the memories of family and fun times.

I have carried that tradition into my family. Each Christmas, we put together a big puzzle. Unfortunately, we have gone several years without being able to hang the puzzle because inevitably, there is at least one piece missing. It is so representa-

tive of life. I think we might just hang the puzzle this year; missing pieces and all.

EPILOGUE

"I 'd forgotten what it felt like to lie in the arms of someone you trusted with not just your heart but your whole self. I was grateful." [1]

Those words hit me like a bucket of cold water. For so long, I didn't even know this feeling existed. I was 39 years young when I first realized what love from a man could feel like; what it was meant to be. Today, after years of self-reflection, therapy, and growth, I realize that because I was not experiencing love, I was also not expressing it in the way I was made to. Because of the abuse I endured, the privilege to love my children and those around me was severely limited. I was living in a state that prevented me from fully giving of myself the way I really desired in the depths of my being. Even loving myself correctly was a privilege I was not granted. So much of my life has been trying to close the gap.

I am so thankful not just for the love I am able to finally experience, but for the love that I can finally freely give. I feel like I have been given back a part of my nineteen-year-old self, that woman, her heart and her purpose, and I know after living a life full of the most epic lifetime movies, I have finally come to the road I was meant to walk and experience.

It has been a long journey, and it has not been easy. There are times I have wanted to turn around and times I have wanted to give up completely. I still feel raw all the time. Probably even more so since I am actively digging out the feelings and emotions rather than stuffing them with a smile. At least now I welcome the release, the tears, and I can mourn and be joyful at the same time. It's an oddly cleansing feeling. You know there's dirt there, you can feel it, but you also know the refreshing feeling of washing it away instantly. For so long I was holding onto so much dirt all the time that nothing ever felt "clean."

Despite the trials and growing pains, I am driven by the knowledge that through silence, nothing will ever change. When we lift our voices and share our stories, that is when we empower ourselves and each other. The experiences in my life have changed me, but at the core, I remain the same loving, determined fighter that I was going into these relationships so many years ago. She didn't walk away when things got tough. She didn't desert me when I stuffed her in a corner and told her to keep quiet. Regardless of how long you have been keeping her locked away, she is still in there, and she is still inside of you too. She may be bruised, bent over, or have many missing puzzle pieces, but she isn't broken. When she stands tall again, she will be stronger than you ever imagined she could be. And remember, that woman inside of you, that strong, incredible, worthy woman inside of you is YOU.

All of the women whose stories are shared throughout this book are either happily on their own or are in new, healthy relationships. Their stories were reflections of harder, more challenging times. Despite the struggles they faced during dark periods of their lives, they all found the courage and strength to leave their abusers and begin the healing process. Although they still bear internal and external scars, those scars have begun to heal. May their stories and ours be an encouragement to you in your darkest hour. There is a light, even if you can't see it just yet. We hope this book has been a light in your dark moments. Find the light, keep your eyes on it, and don't stop moving toward it.

THANK YOU ALLY!

Thank you so much for pressing forward, reading this book and equipping yourself to be the best ally for yourself and others. If you have found any benefit from the words and stories we have openly shared, please spread the word. Here are a few ways you can be an ally today:

- Write a compassionate review and post on Amazon, Goodreads, etc.

- Recommend "...but that's not me." to another woman, friend, family member or someone who needs an ally. Everyone deserves to be fully equipped in this world.

- Post about the book, it's impact and any take-aways or just a simple picture of you reading it. Be sure to use the hashtag #butthatsnotmebook and tag the authors, @erika.shalene and @the.psycho.mom on social media. We love sharing the strength we have when we do this work together!

We would also love to hear from you! Share your stories of struggle and triumph at: www.butthatsnotme.com.

If you enjoyed this book, please leave a review on Goodreads.com or on Amazon at amzn.to/3DXbdvX.

ADDITIONAL
RESOURCES

Creating a static resource for a topic as dynamic as modern-day abuse with its continuously evolving body of knowledge and resources can be quite a challenge. There is so much more we would like to share, but capturing all of this in a single book would be overwhelming and practically useless as information would become virtually impossible to apply and reference when you need it.

We are thrilled that you have invested in yourself and your community by learning more about the topic of interpersonal abuse. We invite you to continue your journey of growth by joining us on our website: www.TheCornHerOffice.com. Here, you will find updated resources, discussions, interviews, and tools to help you become a better ally to yourself and others.

As noted throughout the book, several content areas were a little too deep.. For that reason, we pulled out the material and created separate eBooks that you may access for free with purchase of this book. Visit our website at www.butthatsnotme.com to access these free eBooks and more resources.

The Pervasive Cultural Influences of Oppressive Sexism eBook dives into the history of various cultures across the globe and how women have historically been treated as second class. Through deeper examination, we explore how the treatment of women in even the most "advanced" societies have roots in some of the most extreme cultures with reference to the treatment of women.

Narcissism and Gaslighting are topics receiving increasing attention. In our eBook **Breaking Down Narcissism vs. Gaslighters**, we dive into the differences between the two and discuss the realities of narcissistic personality disorder and self-centered behavior. Language is critical to better understanding our reality. When describing abusive behaviors, it is necessary to use proper language and avoid getting wrapped up in popular but inaccurate terminology. Visit our website at www.butthatsnotme.com to download your copy.

ACKNOWLEDGMENTS

This book is the compilation of the experiences of many women who shared their hearts and their stories with us. Thank you for trusting us with those stories, trusting us to tell them in a way that allows them to impact the lives of women around the world. Thank you for your strength and courage. We recognize, more than most, exactly how difficult that can be.

As anyone who has worked on a prolonged project can attest, after several months, and now years, the initial excitement can wear off. Thank you to the team of women who supported and encouraged us to push forward. To our early reviewers and supporters who have followed this journey from the very beginning, thank you for your dedication, encouragement, and thoughtful feedback. Above all, thank you for sharing your stories with us, reminding us why we were writing this book.

To our team, thank you for your perseverance and deep commitment to this mission. It is rare to find someone as passionate about your topic as you. Through the late nights, long sessions, and endless lines of edits, you were by our side sharing ideas and pushing to make this manuscript a resource that will stand the test of time.

To our families who loved us and supported us through hours of writing, editing, crying, and listening to endless phone calls where you wondered if we were writing a book or organizing a movement. Turns out we were doing both! Thank you for showing us what strong, healthy relationships should feel like. It is your love that reminds us of the good in this world and inspires us to continue on. We want all women to experience the love they deserve; the freedom and space to love themselves.

We were driven to write this book by our combined eight children; to make this world a better place for your future and the world we wish you would have been able to experience. We want you to grow up to be strong women and men, recognizing your worthiness and standing up to the injustices of this world. It is a tall order, but we are blessed to have been granted the opportunity to hold your hands through this life.

To my co-author, Erika. You inspire me daily to be stronger, braver, and kinder to myself. You reminded me of the strength I had buried deep inside and lit a spark that I thought I had lost long ago. I had no idea where this journey would take us or the amazing story we would tell together. Thank you for reminding me who I am and helping bring to life the dreams I thought would stay dreams forever. I could never adequately express how honored I am that you trusted me to help you tell this powerful story. I am proud to call you my co-author and business partner, but most of all, I am blessed to call you my friend.

To my co-author, Cheryl. Without a doubt I am eternally grateful for your belief in me. The way this all came about will be a story to share for the rest of our lives. Who would have thought my emotional plea, "I know this sounds crazy, but I think we are meant to write a book together," would bring us together in so many ways. Thank you for joining me in this process, for listening to all the talks as we worked through so many things that needed to be processed. Thank you for being a huge part of my healing and for encouraging me to keep being the woman I was made to be, Strong, Brave, Powerful, it will always be one of the puzzle pieces. Thank you for joining your puzzle to mine.

ABOUT THE AUTHORS

Erika Shalene Hull is a Life Management Consultant, Author and Co-Founder of The CornHer Office. After spending over 10 years, primarily as a Financial Development Director for a world-wide non-profit organization, Erika sought to lessen the gap between the challenges of working and parenthood, by leaving corporate America and becoming a full-time entrepreneur. With having to overcome numerous traumas during this time, including abuse, suicide of oldest child, and the day-to-day hardship of a crippling genetic disorder, she is courageously passionate about helping others rise above their own personal obstacles. From minimizing daily burdens, creating manageability and building confidence, through The CornHer Office, Erika provides methods, tools and resources delivering the life fulfillment clients seek, intending to impact women's lives for the BETTER. When she's not taking on life's challenges, she's vlogging, road trippin' or drinking a cup of coffee with her husband and five children in Ohio. You can connect with her socially @erka.shalene on most platforms or at www.thecorn heroffice.com.

Dr. Cheryl LeJewell Jackson, author of *Strong. Brave. Powerful.* and *Family Business*, lives in Texas where she is raising two boys with her husband. After spending 20 years traveling the country, living in one state after the next, she is enjoying being back in her hometown surrounded by family. Cheryl earned her Doctorate in Industrial-Organizational Psychology and spent her career helping Fortune 100 organizations and their employees thrive through the design of workforce solutions focused on organizational effectiveness and employee engagement. As a continuous learner, Cheryl keeps active by serving as a lecturer at Texas A&M University, professional speaker, business consultant, guest blogger, and volunteer in her community. Of all the hobbies, activities, and dreams, sitting in front of the window on a rainy day with a hot cup of creamy coffee, a burning candle, and a worn mystery novel is the one she loves the most.

Together, Cheryl and Erika also founded The CornHer Office, a physical and virtual community with a mission of leveling the playing field for women in business. By changing the language, we are changing the conversation, which changes our reality. Learn more at www.TheCorn HerOffice.com and join in this incredible movement of women helping women. We would also love to hear from you! Share your stories of struggle and triumph at: www.butthatsnotme.com.

UPCOMING PUBLICATIONS AND RE-RELEASES:

The BETTER Self Formula

Strong, Brave, Powerful

and more!

About the Publisher

Red Thread Publishing Group

Red Thread Publishing is an all-female publishing company on a mission to support 10,000 women to become successful published authors and thought leaders. Through the transformative work of writing & telling our stories we are not only changed as individuals, but we are also changing the global narrative & thus the world.

See our growing catalog of books:

https://redthreadbooks.mykajabi.com/books

Visit us at:

www.redthreadbooks.com

facebook.com/redthreadpublishing

instagram.com/redthreadbooks

Notes

5. Defining The Language We Use

1. Department of Justice website: https://www.justice.gov/ovw/domestic-violence
2. Merriam-Webster online dictionary:
      https://www.merriam-webster.com/dictionary/victim
3. Anglofon Studio: https://anglofon.com/blog-difference-between-agree-and-consent
4. Bohns, V.K. (2020). Weinstein jurors must differentiate between consent and compliance – which research shows isn't easy. The Conversation. https://theconversation.com/weinstein-jurors-mustdifferentiate-between-consent-and-compliance-which-research-shows-isnt-easy-129681

6. How We Got Here: Oppressive Sexism

1. Baumeister, Roy F.; Smart, L.; Boden, J. (1996). "Relation of threatened egotism to violence and aggression: The dark side of self-esteem". Psychological Review. 103 (1): 5–33.

7. How did this happen? A Breakdown of Reality

1. Portnow, Kathryn. Dialogues of Doubt: The Psychology of Self-Doubt and Emotional Gaslighting in Adult Women and Men. Harvard Graduate School of Education. (1996)
2. Brown, B. (2012). Daring greatly: How the courage to be vulnerable transforms the way we live, love, parent, and lead. New York: Avery.
3. Brown, B (2010). The Gift of Imperfection. New York. Hazelden Publishing
4. Papadakaki, M., Tzamalouka, G.S., Chatzifotiou, S., & Chilaoutakis, J. (2009). Seeking for risk factors of intimate partner violence in a Greek national sample. Journal of Interpersonal Violence, 24(5), 732-750.
5. Papadakaki, M., Tzamalouka, G.S., Chatzifotiou, S., & Chilaoutakis, J. (2009). Seeking for risk factors of intimate partner violence in a Greek national sample. Journal of Interpersonal Violence, 24(5), 732-750.
6. Lynch, S. M., & Graham-Bermann, S. A. (2004). Exploring the Relationship Between Positive Work Experiences and Women's Sense of Self in the Context of Partner Abuse. Psychology of Women Quarterly, 28(2), 159–167.
7. Macy, R. J., Giattina, M., Sangster, T. H., Crosby, C., & Montijo, N. J. (2009). Domestic violence and sexual assault services: Inside the black box. Aggression and Violent Behavior, 14(5), 359–373.
8. Carlson, B. E., McNutt, L.-A., Choi, D. Y., & Rose, I. M. (2002). Intimate partner abuse and mental health: The role of social support and other protective factors.

Violence Against Women, 8(6), 720–745.

8. Language We Use

1. Csikszentmihalyi, M. (2020, April 3). Adolescence. Encyclopedia Britannica. https://www.britannica.com/science/adolescence
2. Merriam-Webster online dictionary.
    https://www.merriam-webster.com/dictionary/normal
3. Seven signs of an enabler. (2020, September 17). Addiction Center. https://www.addictioncenter.com/treatment/stage-intervention/what-is-an-enabler/
4. Abuse, Trauma, and Mental Health. (2018, August 28) Office on Women's Health. https://www.womenshealth.gov/mental-health/abuse-trauma-and-mental-health
5. Jojoarth, M. (2016). It's Not Nagging: Repetition is Effective Communication. LinkedIn. https://www.linkedin.com/pulse/its-nagging-repetition-effective-communication-martonjojarth
6. Jones, E. E., & Harris, V. A. (1967). The attribution of attitudes. Journal of Experimental Social Psychology,3(1), 1-24.
7. Violence Is Learned... But It Can Also Be Unlearned. (2018). Psychology Today. https://exploringyourmind.com/violence-learned-unlearned/
8. Haire, Meaghan. Time
    http://content.time.com/time/arts/article/0,8599,1904885,00.html
9. Jacobson, L. (2019, May, 31). Study: School socioeconomics affect special education placement. Education Dive. https://www.educationdive.com/news/study-school-socioeconomics-affect-specialeducation-placement/555800/
10. Mayo Clinic Staff (2017, November, 18) Narcissistic Personality Disorder. Mayo Clinic. https://www.mayoclinic.org/diseases-conditions/narcissistic-personality-disorder/symptoms-causes/syc-20366662
11. Smith, M. & Robinson, L. (2020, July). Narcissistic Personality Disorder (NPD). Help Guide. https://www.helpguide.org/articles/mental-disorders/narcissistic-personality-disorder
12. Johnson, S. (1987). Humanizing the Narcissistic Style. Norton Professional Book.
13. The 3 C's to Addiction Recovery (2014, February 10). Elements Behavioral Health. https://www.recoveryplace.com/blog/the-3-cs-to-addiction-recovery/

2. Verbal Abuse

1. Office of Women's Health (2018). Emotional and verbal abuse. https://www.womenshealth.gov/relationships-and-safety/other-types/emotional-and-verbal-abuse
2. Office of Women's Health (2018). Emotional and verbal abuse. https://www.womenshealth.gov/relationships-and-safety/other-types/emotional-and-verbal-abuse
3. Evans, P. (2010). The verbally abusive relationship: How to recognize it and how to respond. Avon, MA:Adams Media.
4. Evans, P. (2010). The verbally abusive relationship: How to recognize it and how to respond. Avon, MA:Adams Media.
5. Chopra, D. (2015) Quantum Healing. Bantum.

3. ECONOMIC ABUSE

1. What is Economic Abuse? (2017 April 12). NCADV. https://ncad-v.org/blog/posts/quick-guideeconomic-and-financialabuse#:
2. National Center for Injury Prevention and Control. Costs of Intimate Partner Violence Against Women in the United States. Atlanta (GA): Centers for Disease Control and Prevention, 2003.
3. National Center for Injury Prevention and Control. Costs of Intimate Partner Violence Against Women in the United States. Atlanta (GA): Centers for Disease Control and Prevention, 2003.
4. National Center for Injury Prevention and Control. Costs of Intimate Partner Violence Against Women in the United States. Atlanta (GA): Centers for Disease Control and Prevention, 2003.
5. Gender pay gap (2020). Payscale. https://www.payscale.com/data/gender-pay-gap

4. SEXUAL ABUSE

1. Sexual Assault (2020). RAINN.org. https://www.rainn.org/articles/sexual-assault
2. Mcclain, Adrienne. *Enough: Breaking the cycle of Emotional Abuse in Romantic Relationships* (2020)
3. Strickland, D. (2018, June 6). Sexual Abuse in Marriage. CCEF. https://www.ccef.org/sexual-abuse-inmarriage/
4. Strickland, D. (2018, June 6). Sexual Abuse in Marriage. CCEF. https://www.ccef.org/sexual-abuse-inmarriage/
5. Strickland, D. (2018, June 6). Sexual Abuse in Marriage. CCEF. https://www.ccef.org/sexual-abuse-inmarriage/
6. Strickland, D. (2018, June 6). Sexual Abuse in Marriage. CCEF. https://www.ccef.org/sexual-abuse-inmarriage/
7. Mouradian, V.E. (2020). National Violence Against Women Prevention Research Center. Abuse in Intimate Relationships: Defining the Multiple Dimensions and Terms. https://mainweb-v.musc.edu/vawprevention/research/defining.shtml
8. Mouradian, V.E. (2020). National Violence Against Women Prevention Research Center. Abuse in Intimate Relationships: Defining the Multiple Dimensions and Terms. https://mainweb-v.musc.edu/vawprevention/research/defining.shtml
9. Strickland, D. (2018, June 6). Sexual Abuse in Marriage. CCEF. https://www.ccef.org/sexual-abuse-inmarriage/

5. PHYSICAL ABUSE

1. Lindsey, M., McBride, R.W., & Platt, C.M. (1993). AMEND: Workbook for Ending Violent Behavior. Gylantic Pub. Company.
2. Penal Code. Title 5. Offenses Against The Person. Chapter 20. Kidnapping, unlawful restraint, and smuggling of persons.
   https://statutes.capitol.texas.gov/Docs/PE/htm/PE.20.html

6. SOCIAL ABUSE

1. Stark, Evan. 2007. Coercive Control: How Men Entrap Women in Personal Life. New York, NY: Oxford University Press.
2. Stark, Evan. 2007. Coercive Control: How Men Entrap Women in Personal Life. New York, NY: Oxford University Press.

7. PSYCHOLOGICAL ABUSE

1. Lindsey, M., McBride, R.W., & Platt, C.M. (1993). AMEND: Workbook for Ending Violent Behavior. Gylantic Pub. Company
2. Lindsey, M., McBride, R.W., & Platt, C.M. (1993). AMEND: Workbook for Ending Violent Behavior. Gylantic Pub. Company.
3. Stalking. (2018, September 14) Office on Women's Health. https://www.women-shealth.gov/relationships-and-safety/other-types/stalking
4. Asian, F.R., Weber, C.V., Thompson, T.M., Health, J., Maruyama, M., Hayashi, K. (2007). Battered Pets and Domestic Violence: Animal Abuse Reported by Women Experiencing Intimate Violence and by Nonabused Women. Violence Against Women, 12(4), 354-373.
5. Vivek U. (2014). The Abuse of Animals as a Method of Domestic Violence: The Need for Criminalization. Emory Law Journal. Available at: https://scholarlycommons.law.emory.edu/elj/vol63/iss5/3.
6. Sreenivasan, S. & Weinberger, L.E. (2016, Dec. 14). Why We Need Each Other. Psychology Today.https://www.psychologytoday.com/us/blog/emotional-nourishment/201612/why-we-need-each-other
7. Peterson, C., & Park, C. (1998) Learned helplessness and explanatory style. In D. F. Barone, M. Hersen, and V. B. VanHasselt (Eds.), Advanced Personality, 287–308. New York: Plenum Press.

2. THE AFTERMATH

1. Ozubko, Macleod. "The production effect in memory: evidence that distinctiveness underlies the benefit." Journal of Experimental Psychology: Learning, Memory, and Cognition, 2010 Nov;36(6):1543-7. doi: 10.1037/a0020604

3. THE POWER OF TRAUMA

1. Bremner J. D. (2006). Traumatic stress: effects on the brain. Dialogues in clinical neuroscience, 8(4), 445–461.
2. The neuroscience of behavior change (2017). Startup+Health. https://healthtransformer.co/theneuroscience-of-behavior-change-bcb567fa83c1

4. Healing

1. The neuroscience of behavior change (2017). Startup+Health. https://healthtrans-former.co/theneuroscience-of-behavior-change-bcb567fa83c1

5. Stop the Cycle

1. Porges, S. W. (2007). The polyvagal perspective. Biological Psychology, 74(2), 116-143.
2. Fuchs, Eberhard; Flügge, Gabriele (2014). "Adult Neuroplasticity: More Than 40 Years of Research". Neural Plasticity. 2014: 1–10.

6. Becoming an Ally

1. Losada M, Heaphy E. The Role of Positivity and Connectivity in the Performance of Business Teams:A Nonlinear Dynamics Model. American Behavioral Scientist. 2004;47(6):740-765.

Epilogue

1. Salmon, L. (2019). What's better than this? Glasco On Hudson Publishing LLC.

Made in the USA
Middletown, DE
18 October 2022

13003560R00222